The governance of science

ISSUES IN SOCIETY
Series Editor: Tim May

Current and forthcoming titles

The governance of science: ideology and the future of the open society

STEVE FULLER

OPEN UNIVERSITY PRESS
Buckingham • Philadelphia

Open University Press
Celtic Court
22 Ballmoor
Buckingham
MK18 1XW

email: enquiries@openup.co.uk
world wide web: http://www.openup.co.uk

and
325 Chestnut Street
Philadelphia, PA 19106, USA

First Published 2000

A catalogue record of this book is available from the British Library

ISBN 0 335 20234 9 (pbk)   0 335 20235 7 (hbk)

Library of Congress Cataloging-in-Publication Data
Fuller, Steve, 1959–
    The governance of science : ideology and the future of the open
society / Steve Fuller.
        p.   cm. — (Issues in society)
    Includes bibliographical references and index.
    ISBN 0–335–20235–7 (hbk)   ISBN 0–335–20234–9 (pbk)
    1. Science—Social aspects.   2. Science and state.   3. Science—
Philosophy.   I. Title.   II. Series.
Q175.5.F845   2000
303.48′3—dc21   99–39402
                                                                            CIP

Typeset by Graphicraft Limited, Hong Kong
Printed in Great Britain by Biddles Limited, Guildford and Kings Lynn

Contents

Series editor's foreword

The social sciences contribute to a greater understanding of the dynamics of social life and to explanations for the workings of societies in general. They are often not given due credit for this role and much writing has been devoted to why this should be the case. At the same time, we are living in an age in which the role of science in society is being re-evaluated. This has led to both a defence of science as the disinterested pursuit of knowledge and an attack on science as nothing more than an institutionalized assertion of faith, with no greater claim to validity than mythology and folklore. These debates tend to generate more heat than light.

In the meantime, the social sciences, in order to remain vibrant and relevant, will reflect the changing nature of these public debates. In so doing, they provide mirrors upon which we can gaze in order to understand not only what we have been and what we are now, but also in order to inform ideas about what we might become. This is not simply about understanding the reasons people give for their actions in terms of the contexts in which they act, as well as analysing the relations of cause and effect in the social, political and economic spheres, but also concerns the hopes, wishes and aspirations that people, in their different cultural ways, hold.

In any society that claims to have democratic aspirations, these hopes and wishes are not for the social scientist to prescribe. For this to happen it would mean that the social sciences were able to predict human behaviour with certainty. One theory and one method, applicable to all times and places, would be required for this purpose. The physical sciences do not live up to such stringent criteria, while the conditions in societies which provided for this outcome, were it even possible, would be intolerable. Why? Because a necessary condition of human freedom is the ability to have acted otherwise and thus to imagine and practise different ways of organizing societies and living together.

es not follow from the above that social scientists do not have a
role to play, as is often assumed in ideological attacks upon their
place and function within society. After all, in focusing upon what we have
been and what we are now, what we might become is inevitably illumin-
ated. Therefore, while it may not be the province of social scientists to
predict our futures, they are, given not only their understandings and
explanations, but equal positions as citizens, entitled to engage in public
debates concerning future prospects.

This new international series was devised with this general ethos in mind.
It seeks to offer students of the sciences, at all levels, a forum in which ideas
and topics of interest are interrogated in terms of their importance for
understanding key social issues. This is achieved through a connection
between style, structure and context that aims to be both illuminating and
challenging in terms of its evaluation of those issues, as well as representing
an original contribution to the subject under discussion.

Given this underlying philosophy, the series will contain books on topics
which are driven by substantive interests. This is not simply a reactive
endeavour in terms of reflecting dominant social and political preoccupa-
tions, it is also proactive in terms of an examination of issues which relate
to and inform the dynamics of social life and the structures of society that
are often not part of public discourse. Thus, what is distinctive about this
series is an interrogation of the assumed characteristics of our current epoch
in relation to its consequences for the organization of society and social life,
as well as its appropriate mode of study.

Each contribution will contain, for the purposes of general orientation,
as opposed to rigid structure, three parts. First, an interrogation of the
topic which is conducted in a manner that renders explicit core assumptions surrounding the issues and/or an examination of the consequences of
historical trends for contemporary social practices. Second, a section which
aims to 'bring alive' ideas and practices by considering the ways in which
they directly inform the dynamics of social relations. A third section will
then move on to make an original contribution to the topic. This will
encompass possible future forms and content, likely directions for the study
of the phenomena in question, or an original analysis of the topic itself. Of
course, it might be a combination of all three.

In *The Governance of Science*, Steve Fuller steers a course between the two
views on science that I alluded to in the first paragraph of this Foreword.
He is neither 'pro' nor 'anti' science. At the same time he asks a simple,
frequently neglected, but fundamental question: given that science seeks
universal knowledge, how is it that so few 'unelected' practitioners may
claim to speak in the name of all? While defining science as the systematic
pursuit of such knowledge and so encompassing the social sciences, he
takes the experimental sciences as the ideal to which all aspire. Yet in his
interrogations, influenced by Karl Popper, science is not found to live up to
such canons. However, this conclusion leads him to celebrate neither artificial
negativity nor positivity.

Artificial negativity represents the type of thinking associated wit Frankfurt School of Social Research and elements of postmodernism that leads to a high level of abstract theorizing without engagement with the object of its attention. Artificial positivity, on the other hand, is representative of the work of those such as Thomas Kuhn, for whom the ideal of the open society is already present within scientific practices. Indeed, it may be argued that Kuhn's work was a catalyst for the earlier social studies of science in terms of being a means of reconciling the differences between C.P. Snow's now famous 'two cultures'. Nevertheless, the result of Kuhn's approach is to endorse the status quo *as if* that were representative of the open society. Therefore, these approaches, albeit in different ways, fail to engage with science policy and the mediation of scientific activities through prevailing economic conditions. The material basis for the realization of the republican ideal is thus left unexplicated.

The author then moves on to argue that the conception and application of science should be open to democratic accountability for the purpose of enabling a greater understanding of the implications of scientific endeavours within the public domain. This necessitates a resort to normative arguments about the governance of science by way of an interrogation of liberal and communitarian ideas. Finding both wanting, in the sense that they deny the 'right to be wrong', he argues for republicanism as representative of the ideal of the open society.

One of the central sites of the knowledge production process is the university. It is for this reason that Steve Fuller turns his attention to this institution in the second part of the book. Returning to the question of science claiming to speak for all in the pursuit of universal knowledge, it may be the bureaucratic status quo within universities that enables this endeavour. From this point of view multiculturalism represents a challenge as does what he terms the 'military-industrial metaphor'. This may be witnessed, for example, in terms of a tension between the instrumental and goal-orientated nature of knowledge production and that approach which regards knowledge production as a never-ending quest. Here, new recruits undertake apprenticeships in order to acquire the tools to produce yet more knowledge.

The university is thus a site of ambivalence exemplified in the divide that they seek to bridge between their research and teaching activities, as well as between ways of knowing and the claims of particular academics to epistemic superiority based upon the status of the group to which they belong in general. This ambivalence is also manifest in the ways in which publishers increasingly dictate what can reach the public domain and between the pursuit of academic credibility via citation indices and the curiosity that must inform the scientific ethos in which, to paraphrase Bertrand Russell, one comes to recognize that the more one learns, the more one realizes how little one knows. Steve Fuller considers these issues with much insight and never hesitates to furnish the reader with a clear perspective on these important matters.

With the above in mind, Part 3 of this book is devoted to the secularization of science: that is, the deconsecration of state funding, along with the promotion of alternative programmes of research as contributions to the public understanding of science. In this discussion the author remains spirited in his defence of an ideal, while never failing to engage with material reality. This is exemplified by the justification of a discovery being a consideration of the diversity of its applications. The claim to speak in the name of all is thereby tempered by how applications may be of benefit to different peoples. It is by virtue of such arguments that this book deserves a wide readership not only among scientists, but administrators, policymakers and the general public.

Tim May

Introduction

This book is my attempt to make science policy interesting and important to not only students of science but also students of democratic social and political theory. To be sure, there has been a long tradition critical of abuses of science, as defined by its technological applications. However, it has been much rarer to question the very constitution of 'science' as a polity. This is an issue that should be of interest to humanists, social scientists and natural scientists alike. Few doubt that the character of knowledge production has radically changed since the advent of the atomic bomb. Not only have physics and biology acquired a scaled-up industrial presence previously reserved for chemistry, but even certain lines of social science research now sport the forbidding technicality, spiralling research costs and cutthroat competition of 'Big Science'. Moreover, and most importantly, these developments are routinely seen – even by sociologists of science – as signs of *health* in the knowledge enterprise, perhaps even worthy of emulation throughout academia.

When I speak critically of 'science', I am generally referring to this normative orientation, which takes Big Science as the standard against which other forms of inquiry are judged and to which they are supposed to aspire. Invariably, institutional and intellectual aspects of 'science' are intertwined in this definition. The historic success of the natural sciences in explaining and legitimating socially significant phenomena is often taken to mean that research conducted under their rubric can do no wrong. In this book I aim to reverse this tendency by disentangling the intellectual core of science as organized inquiry from the other institutional roles it has added. However, I do this not to preserve an impossibly idealized version of inquiry, but rather to articulate the material conditions under which the admirable features of science – especially those relating to its critical vision – have been both realized and perverted. In short, to adapt Harold Lasswell's famous

on of politics: in the republic of science, who should be doing what,
hat means and to what ends? These are the questions that the book
before you addresses.

Many of the ideas that went into composing this book were conceived in
the early 1990s, often as a follow-up to my 'Social epistemology and the
research agenda of science studies' (in Pickering 1992). Presupposed in much
of the discussion is the importance of rhetoric in breaking down disciplinary and other social barriers that prevent full participation in the science
policy process. This point is explicitly developed in my earlier book, *Philosophy, Rhetoric and the End of Knowledge* (Fuller 1993a). Two other books
written in roughly the same period should be consulted for the larger
historical and philosophical vision that informs my general orientation:
Science (Fuller 1997) and *Thomas Kuhn: A Philosophical History for Our Times*
(Fuller forthcoming).

The event that galvanized my interest in treating the governance of science
in some depth was the termination of public funding for the Superconducting Supercollider, which, if built, would have been the world's largest
particle accelerator. According to its proponents, this machine would have
been capable of revealing the ultimate nature of matter and motion, thereby
providing the key for unlocking the great mysteries of the physical universe. In its 1992–3 session, the US Congress deemed that the project failed
to meet the benefit-to-cost challenge in a tight budgetary regime. The pro-
tracted and highly publicized debate over the Supercollider drew attention
to factional divisions within the physics community, the historical shallow-
ness of 'cultural' arguments for science funding and the diminished political
significance assigned to basic research in the post-cold war era.

The demise of the Supercollider also marked the first time that scientists
openly declared that science and technology studies (STS) – the interdisciplinary field that studies the social production of scientific knowledge
– was instrumental in promoting public disaffection with science. Noteworthy in this vein was Steven Weinberg's *Dreams of a Final Theory* (1992),
which is also fairly regarded as one of the opening salvos in the ongoing
'science wars'. Readers may judge for themselves the justice of the charge
against STS in the pages that follow, as I have been actively promoting the
field for over ten years, in connection with my own research programme
of 'social epistemology'. All I would say at this point is that one person's
'funding cut' is another's 'resource reallocation': in normative disputes,
point of view is almost everything.

In keeping with the format of books in the 'Issues in Society' series, this
one is divided into three parts. Part 1 presents the conceptual framework,
which is drawn mostly from normative political theory. Here I explain the
republican ideal of science as the 'open society' and science's failure to live
up to this ideal as its scale and scope have expanded. However, in this
respect, the problems of 'Big Science' are not much different from those
facing 'Big Democracy'. In Part 2, I focus the discussion on the most
concrete site for the governance of science, the university. The coherence

of this institution is increasingly challenged by multiculturalism and capitalism, which can be seen as representing the opposing pulls of communitarian and liberal ideologies introduced in Part 1. Part 3 presents the prospects for the future governance of science, which I see in terms of a continuation of the process of 'secularization' that decouples state power from the authorization of knowledge claims. I consider both historical precedents and experimental proposals for this process, which together offer the elements for renegotiating science's social contract.

Readers will find the references wide ranging. However, those wishing a broader overview of the 'essential tension' between science and democracy in American political thought should consult *Social Epistemology*, 7(1) (1993), which is a symposium around a piece by David Guston. On the tensions surrounding the contemporary university as a site of knowledge production, readers are directed to *Social Epistemology*, 12(1) (1998), which centres on an article by Gerard Delanty. Finally, readers should note that despite periodic allusions to the commodification of expertise, information technology and intellectual property, I have *not* used this occasion to collect together my ten years' worth of writings in what I now call 'the sociology of virtual knowledge'. Fuller (1998) represents my most recent thinking on this topic and includes a bibliography that will form the basis of a book in the near future.

There have been many occasions for presenting the material contained in these pages, including my inaugural lecture as Professor of Sociology at Durham University (30 November 1995), where I introduced the idea of 'secularizing' science discussed in Part 3 and in Fuller (1997: Ch. 4). Among those who made these occasions possible were J. Anthony Blair, Roy Boyne, Richard Harvey Brown, Jim Collier, Bill Dunn, Joan Leach, Jan Nederveen Pieterse, Zia Sardar and Ullica Segerstrale. I would also like to thank Amitai Etzioni and Alf Lawrie who helped clarify my ideas about republicanism and 'the right to be wrong'. Tim May deserves the credit for persuading me to write this book and for reading through the entire manuscript with a sharp editorial eye. Many of the ideas discussed in these pages were born of discussions with Sujatha Raman. However, my biggest debt during the difficult period this book was written is to Stephanie Lawler, who was an unflagging source of emotional support.

PART ONE

The political and material conditions of scientific inquiry

The pursuit of knowledge, 'science' for short, has undergone significant material changes over the past century, probably more so than at any other point in its history. Yet, the political rhetoric surrounding science – especially the ideology of the open society – remains largely unchanged. In the first two chapters of this book, we uncover what is masked by the continued use of this rhetoric. The discussion in Chapter 1 is framed by three political theories of science: liberalism, communitarianism and republicanism. The open society is possible only in a republican regime, where, unlike liberal or communitarian regimes, a clear distinction is drawn between staking an idea and staking a life. This distinction underwrites the fundamental principle of the open society: the right to be wrong. Chapter 2 moves from defining this ground to showing how it has come to be eroded with the scaling-up of the scientific enterprise into what is nowadays routinely called 'Big Science'. Today too many other things seem to be bound up with the organized pursuit of inquiry to enable it to function in the critical capacity demanded by the ideal of the open society. Part 1 ends with a rejection of 'science literacy' as a strategy for opening up science to the public: at best, it secures a receptive attitude without provision for greater public participation. However, the current popularity of science literacy campaigns reveals the extent to which the central political issues facing science are treated as a matter of remedying certain 'cognitive' deficits suffered by the public.

Science as the open society and its ideological deformations

Introduction: the artifice of science as the open society

Most of the debilitating effects of political regimes come from people feeling they cannot either admit their own errors or reveal the errors of others – that is, unless the errors are minor ones. (Postmodernists who balk at talk of 'error' should ask instead about the capacity to change one's own and others' minds in public.) Of course, those who propose claims about the errors of others may themselves be in error. However, for most of history (including the present), people have been afraid even to speak in terms of their own or others' 'errors' because of what they fear to be the consequences of such talk. The result is that a self-imposed authoritarianism can remain in force even in avowedly liberal and communitarian societies – the two major philosophies in the western political tradition. The former finds the prospect of errors too risky to bear individually, whereas the latter portrays the admission of error as the betrayal of duty to the collective. In both cases, people lose their 'right to be wrong', which is the essence of the open society, the ideal projected by the elusive middle ground of political theory known as *republicanism* (Pettitt 1997).

   In the pages that follow, I treat the governance of science as a branch of normative political theory, so that all of the above terms and issues are made central to an understanding of the people, processes and products associated with 'science'. By 'science' I normally mean the systematic pursuit of knowledge, in the German sense of *Wissenschaft*, which includes all the academic disciplines, not just the natural sciences. The famous precedent for this usage is Max Weber's (1958) address to new sociology graduate students, 'Science as a vocation', which I shall revisit in Chapter 5. However, in the twentieth century, the experimental natural sciences have increasingly become the paradigm case of 'science', the standard against which other academic disciplines and even non-academic social practices are evaluated (Fuller 1997: Ch. 3). We shall see that often this standard is regarded so uncritically that less than ideal knowledge practices in the natural sciences are simply assumed to be normatively acceptable. For that reason, we need at the outset a clear normative vision that can be specified independently of its alleged exemplifications; hence, the appeal to political theory, and more specifically republicanism.

Why call this topic the 'governance of science' rather than, say, the 'politics of science'? Often the latter expression refers to science's entanglement with the larger – invariably conflicted – interests in society, typically in matters of technology that have serious impacts on individuals' lives, the environment and/or the economy. In those contexts, science is treated as an instrument that can be used for good or ill, but little attention is paid to the constitution of scientific knowledge itself or the people who produce it. The 'governance of science' is meant to cover this relatively neglected set of concerns. I say 'governance' instead of 'government' because, seen from a political standpoint, the accountability relations in science – the analogues of elections, referenda, trials and audits – are remarkably informal. (For more on the theory of governance, see Power 1997.) Strictly speaking, science is a representative body in which a few speak for the many. Were this not literally true, then science's claim to 'universal knowledge' would lose its meaning, given that not everyone can be involved in scientific inquiry at any given moment. Yet there is no parliament of scientists, and the days are long gone when academics were granted special voting privileges in national assemblies.

More to the point, scientists are not elected by the populace, or even a representative sample of the populace. Rather, they are 'self-selected', which means that people who are already scientists – and relatively few of those – decide who is fit to hold the title of 'scientist', through examination and publication policies that proceed with little external scrutiny. Therefore, the mystery surrounding science as a political concept lies less in its day-to-day business (i.e. 'research') than in its capacity to speak on behalf of the whole of humanity in a way that transcends national differences as well as other cultural and economic barriers. In that sense, science is a vehicle of global governance. This point is most readily seen in the efforts taken to standardize the public provision of education and health around the world. That science both governs and is governed without being formally constituted as a government implies a paradox. Scientific authority is currently founded on a principle of 'mutually tolerable ignorance': while the public understands little of the science it believes, scientists often have no first-hand knowledge of the experiences over which they pronounce.

On the one hand, the public trusts, or at least defers to, scientists, though few non-scientists have ever witnessed how scientists come up with the knowledge on which their judgements and explanations are based, and not many more can recite the catechism presented in science textbooks (Durant *et al.* 1989). People seem to live quite comfortably believing in Newton's theory of gravity or Darwin's theory of evolution, even though they are incapable of saying what the theory is or even what does and does not follow from it. Indeed, many philosophers nowadays regard this attitude as a sound epistemic strategy (Goldman 1999). On the other hand, the phenomena that scientists are authorized to judge and explain on the public's behalf typically have been experienced more directly by ordinary members of the public than by the scientists themselves. Thus, we find white, male medical scientists authorized to speak on biological topics ranging from childbirth practices to 'genetic planning', not to mention straight middle-class biochemists and psychiatrists explaining drug-taking and homosexuality. Very few, if any, religions have commanded such blind loyalty on the basis of such little mutual personal understanding between the speakers and the spoken for and about. The reason, of course, is that most religions include a pastoral mission that involves the flock in mastering a watered-down mythical version of orthodox theology and the ministry in regular contact with the spiritual and sometimes even physical needs of its flock. The constitution of science is remarkable in lacking any sense of pastoral mission or, in more secular terms, party politics.

It is also worth recalling a more conventional sense in which the constitution of science has political implications. Consider *The End of History and the Last Man*, where Francis Fukuyama (1992) declared that a liberal democratic future awaited all the world's peoples, courtesy of capitalism's systemic beneficence. Fukuyama was one with his Marxist opponents in pointing to the 'logic of natural science' as plotting an inevitable course that both transcends and transforms even the most historically entrenched of cultural differences. In that sense, science puts an end to history: once the natural trajectory of science is appropriately harnessed to the future of one society, history then simply consists of the rest of the world catching up by repeating the steps originally taken by that society. Until quite recently, this was how both capitalists *and* socialists in the first two 'Worlds' thought that the Third World would be 'modernized'. Socialists pointed to science's role in the creation of labour-saving technologies that eventually undermine the basis for any sharp distinction between the workers and their bosses. For their part, capitalists emphasized the role of science in enhancing people's innovative capacities and hence their ability to compete more effectively in the market-place. The roles assigned to science in the two political economies were different, but both were meant to have globally liberating consequences. Indeed, sometimes it seemed that 'science' was little more than the name given to the putative source of whatever progress the history of politics or economics was said to display.

Thomas Kuhn had a characteristically equivocal way of capturing accounts of science that straddle a description of its actual conduct and the standard it sets for the rest of society. Kuhn professed an interest in accounting for science 'when it functions as it should' (cf. Kuhn 1970: 237). Tactfully omitted from this aspiration was any judgement about how often, if ever, science lives up to its own standards of rationality and objectivity, the standards that then provide the normative basis for the 'knowledge-based societies' in which we allegedly live today (Stehr 1994). Consequently, Kuhn, like so many other social theorists of science, suspended his account of science in what may be called a state of 'artificial positivity', i.e. the (dubious) assumption that the clarity with which 'science' can be articulated as a normative ideal is indicative of the ideal's realizability in today's world. Let me briefly explain this concept, as it will suggest the distance between most current thinking about science and the mindset needed to address the governance of science properly.

The concept of artificial positivity is modelled on 'artificial negativity', an expression associated with the arch scepticism of the Frankfurt School's version of critical theory, which saw capitalist complicity in every form of cultural production. Such conspiracy theorizing, albeit conducted at a very high level of abstraction, ends up winning intellectual battles while losing the political war, since it induces the critic's withdrawal from the public sphere, lest the critic be sullied by capitalist conspirators by prematurely endorsing reformist measures (Geuss 1999: Ch. 4). In my usage, 'artifical positivity' represents the complementary attitude that there is nothing for the critic to do because the ideal is already presupposed in everyday practice. In that case, any perceived discrepancies between the ideal and the real are treated as localized incidents, the remediation of which will occur in the long run, either because the system naturally corrects itself or people come to see the discrepancies as systemic virtues in disguise. Sometimes this attitude is cloaked in philosophical high-mindedness. Ironically, the man who has done the most to debunk the wishful thinking that normally passes for such high-mindedness, Theodor Adorno, passed down the Frankfurt School's legacy to someone who has increasingly displayed just that attitude, Juergen Habermas (Fusfield 1997).

Normative visions of science as the 'open society' are typically subject to artificial positivity in this sense, the result being a bland endorsement of the status quo. For example, the fact that many cases of research fraud are eventually caught by the scientific community is taken to vindicate the self-critical function of science, not to signify a deeper, more systemic problem with the conduct of scientific research. Also, the fact that science displays a pecking order of researchers, institutions and even subject areas that rivals that of any class-based society is presumed to be the desired outcome of processes involving the free and open participation of all members of the scientific community. The fact that these processes cannot be easily specified and that many scientists are clearly dissatisfied with their place in the pecking order are treated as areas 'in need of further empirical investigation', not indirect proof of the artificially positive assumptions made about the realizability of the open society in science today.

Perhaps the most thorough recent defence of a vision of science in this artificially positive mode is Cole (1992), who may be uncharitably read as arguing that everyone who deserves recognition in science eventually gets it – including women and minorities. However, characteristic of this kind of research, Cole considered only scientists who actually managed to place publications in the leading journals of their fields. He might have told a different story had he considered the number of inquirers who dropped out even before reaching that stage of minimal scientific recognition. Nevertheless, over the past quarter-century, Cole has been one of the most widely consulted sociologists by the US National Science Foundation on science policy decision making.

In light of the above, it is no surprise that the arch sceptics of our own time, the postmodernists, have rejected the open society ideal of science as just so much wish-fulfilment. Nevertheless, the ideal remains sufficiently alive in policy circles and is sufficiently admirable on its own terms to deserve a rearticulation, one that deals squarely with the political and economic conditions that are necessary for its realization. This project goes very much to the heart of my own programme of social epistemology. When I began this programme, just over a decade ago, I wanted to lay the foundations of a sort of welfare economics of science, or 'knowledge policy' (Fuller 1988: 289, 1993b, 1997). While this still captures my general normative sensibility, it has become increasingly clear that the political implications of my work vacillate between liberalism and socialism, roughly depending on whether I have drawn my disciplinary resources from the humanities or the social sciences, respectively. However, implicit throughout has been a commitment to the republican values associated with Karl Popper's (1945) original popularization of the open society.

Republicanism as the political philosophy of an open science

The history of science can be told as a narrative of successive reconstitutions of the scientific polity: i.e. changing definitions of the rights and obligations of both scientific inquirers and the societies housing them. Republicanism represents the ideal state, in that it allows people to speak their mind with impunity. However, this is possible only under specific social and material conditions. When Michael Polanyi (1962) famously articulated the 'republic of science' as an ideal in the 1950s, he crucially failed to specify the relevant background conditions needed to realize this ideal. Specifically, there are communitarian and liberal 'excesses' between which a republican science would need to navigate. However, as we shall see, both are mediated by economic conditions.

Communitarian excess

If scientific utterances carry too much prima facie authority in the larger society, then it is easy to see how 'political correctness' might emerge as a countervailing response, especially in communitarian societies where matters of group identity are paramount. For example, because scientific studies that purport to prove the cognitive inferiority of blacks can all too easily translate into anti-welfarist and even racist policies, communitarians are tempted simply to prevent the conduct of such studies at the outset; that is, to impose 'ideological censorship'. However, a republican science would take a different tack: to allow the research but sever any straightforward connection between research and policy. This may be done by requiring an alternative scientific analysis of the same data or public interrogation of the research from various interpretive perspectives. Because the republican privileges the expression of alternative and even unpopular views, either option would be preferable to simply preventing the conduct of the research because of its potential for anti-group policies. Moreover, in the particular example, a republican science policy would make it clear that the mere identification of persistent group deficiencies by no means licenses a policy of neglect, or worse, subjugation. After all, most affirmative action legislation was enacted in the USA because a century of formal political and economic freedom had not sufficiently improved the conditions of black people. Here too we have an admission to persistent group deficiencies, but a more positive policy orientation. I shall return to this point at the end of this chapter with the discussion of a 'social inheritance tax'. Of course, there are now budgetary pressures on the state to divest its welfare functions, and so 'scientific' arguments relating to IQ are often made to do the work of economic expediency (e.g. Herrnstein and Murray 1994). This would seem to strengthen the case of the communitarian, who could then turn to the republican and ask: How do you prevent the existence of, say, 'racial science' from turning into a springboard for a political movement like Nazism, which is then democratically brought into power on a wave of pseudo-scientific rhetoric? I shall return to this question at the very end of this book.

Liberal excess

This excess poses a larger and more insidious threat to republican science. It represents the incursion of market values into the sphere of free inquiry, to the point that 'free market' and 'free inquiry' are seen as one and the same. It is epitomized in the idea that you can pursue any research you want, as long as you can find someone willing to pay for it. Before the start-up costs of research became so enormous (especially in the natural sciences), money was something that typically entered the consciousness of scientists only after some research had been completed and its various material rewards were reaped. However, because money is an issue at the outset of research, only research that is likely to succeed (because it fits with a discipline's expectations or it fills a clear niche in the market for new technologies) is likely to be supported. This mentality undercuts the incentive for providing substantial criticism to the fundamental presuppositions of existing research: who is motivated to accept serious criticism of high-energy physics, if its implications include rendering billion-dollar particle accelerators obsolete and forcing thousands of physicists out of work? This question highlights the emergence of 'financial censorship' of inquiry. Ironically, researchers wishing to pursue lines of inquiry that go against the grain of the status quo are increasingly forced to seek private investment, which only accelerates the flight of science from the realm of public to private knowledge.

In today's increasingly 'liberal' society, the biggest incentive for the support of independent lines of research is the prospect of intellectual property rights. From a republican standpoint, this situation is akin to plundering the commons for personal gain, the ultimate environmental nightmare (Hardin 1968). The tough questions that the republican must face from the liberal are: Is this privatization reversible? How else does one provide an incentive to do innovative research if personal gain is *not* involved? The answer to these questions would clearly involve regulating the financial side of research. In Chapter 8, I speak of 'epistemic fungibility' as an important part of the solution to this problem.

A list of republican regimes typically includes the West's iconic political settings: classical Athens, pre-imperial Rome, the city-states of Renaissance northern Italy, Whig Britain, and the US Constitution's rule by 'division of powers' and 'checks and balances'. Why has it been so difficult to establish republicanism on a long term and worldwide basis? These difficulties revolve around the need for societies to provide the economic security and cultural resources needed to protect their members' right to be wrong, which at a more abstract and collective level amounts to a policy of preventing the past from overdetermining the future. (We shall return to this point at the end of this chapter, when considering the role of social inheritance in science's claims to progress.)

Republicanism's underlying idea is that true freedom requires the expression, not merely the toleration, of different opinions. In that sense, the right to be wrong is not really a right at all but an obligation, much as the 'right to vote' is interpreted in countries where failure to vote is penalized. Thucydides' account of Periclean democracy in fourth-century BC Athens, Kant's definition of the Enlightenment's 'public use of reason' and John Stuart Mill's defence of free speech all share this obligatory character – and here we might add Popper's exhortation that scientists falsify their hypotheses (Haworth 1998: 217 ff.). In all these cases, the idea seems to be that in the performance of the very same speech act – an open critical engagement with peers – individuals simultaneously demonstrate their autonomy and help improve the collective body of knowledge.

If it seems counterintuitive to hold that one is not merely permitted but obliged to speak one's mind, then that is only because we have a polarized image of liberty that occludes the republican alternative. 'Negative liberty', associated with liberalism, is simply the absence of individual enslavement, whereas 'positive liberty', associated with communitarianism, is the realization of one's social station (Berlin 1958). Missing from this dualism is the prospect that the recognition of individual distinction might define one's social position – as in a society that compels its members to take risks, say, by participation in such competitive arenas as games, warfare, the market, or for that matter, science. I suspect that this social vision is omitted because

Figure 1.1   A matrix of socially sanctioned risks

	High separability	Low separability
High closure	Sport	War
Low closure	Science	Business

High v. Low separability: how separable are the activity's goals from the goals of other activities?
High v. Low closure: does the activity have a natural sense of closure?

of the communitarian ideology that underwrites contemporary welfare-state thought, which assumes that the collective absorption of individual risk is a desirable if not an ultimate goal of state policy. However, as we shall see below, this overriding sense of risk aversion – which pervades science policy just as much as state policy – has debilitating consequences for the pursuit of free inquiry.

In Figure 1.1 I have represented the domain of socially sanctioned risk-taking in terms of two dimensions that enable us to see how scientific practice shades off into other activities. The element 'science' in the figure approximates the republican ideal. Here 'science' means inquiry conducted in artificial settings, such as laboratories, by which the inquirer directly studies one thing that is regarded as an indirect indicator of something of greater import. For example, an isolated laboratory experiment may be seen as a kind of match one wins by correctly second-guessing the outcome. Only once it is made clear how the outcome can be used to make inferences about the 'real world' does the experiment become an episode in scientific inquiry. But at that point the import of the particular experiment loses much of its initial sense of closure, since its outcome may be interpreted in various ways, depending on the theoretical context of inquiry and/or the other experimental findings within which it must be situated. In this way, science loses its gamelike character.

However, while an experiment does not become science unless placed in a larger context, that context must always be defined by science itself and not by other activities with which it may become materially involved. This is increasingly difficult, as science requires more human and material resources for its pursuit. Under those circumstances, it is tempting to judge a line of inquiry exclusively as a long-term investment strategy, such that the critical spirit comes to be diverted by the research manager's need to keep a balanced ledger and a full employment record. Thus, science turns into a business, and both share a certain open-endedness whereby no amount of knowledge or money ever seems to be enough. (We shall explore this transformation in the next chapter.) Moreover, one can easily imagine this business mentality acquiring a more focused goal orientation, as in the race to build the atomic bomb or cure cancer, in which all other activities and resources are swept up. At that point, the conduct of science has mutated into a state of war.

The elusive material basis of republicanism

The realization of the republican ideal presupposes certain material conditions:

- that people's opinions might change for the better as a result of hearing opposing opinions;
- that people need not fear the consequences of their expressed opinions on their material well-being;
- that there is a 'public good' or 'civic ideal' to which people may appeal in deliberation which transcends specific individual and group interests.

Republican policies aim to ensure that all citizens are sufficiently secure in their material circumstances that they are not inhibited from speaking their minds. If you can express your mind with impunity then your ideas can die in your stead, to recall a phrase of Goethe's that Popper liked to use to epitomize the open society. The significance of this capacity should not be underestimated. A frequently remarked obstacle to instituting 'deliberative democracy' schemes (e.g. citizens juries, electronic town meetings) is the tendency for people to reinvent patterns of deference even in arrangements that have been designed as much as possible to be egalitarian (Fishkin 1991; Bohman 1996). While some trace this tendency to the inherently hierarchical nature of human beings (especially when large populations make it 'efficient' to sharply distinguish between leaders and followers), more likely it has to do with the fear of humiliation that comes from making one's mistakes in public (Elster 1993).

The political psychology surrounding the inhibition of republican sentiments is complex. While a measure of economic security is required for the realization of the republican ideal, it should not be assumed that the poorest members of society are the most easily inhibited from expressing dissent. On the contrary, it may be argued that the inveterate poor have little to lose and hence are more willing to speak their minds than those who regard the middle class within striking distance. For example, academia is one social environment that perpetuates a sense of bourgeois self-containment. Despite the clarity with which its 'haves' and 'have nots' are marked in terms of funding, publications and institutional location, very few academics stuck at the bottom of the pecking order ever believe that they are consigned to the dustbin of history (Fuller 1997: Ch. 4). Consequently, even the lowliest contract researchers believe that they are still contenders for tenured posts and hence think they potentially have something to gain by biting their tongues in deliberative settings. In this case, continued faith in an ideology of meritocracy is sustained by the vagueness of criteria for success and failure, combined with the smattering of success stories that compare slightly favourably with winners of the national lottery. If one wanted to make a case for the irrationality of individuals who opt for the pure pursuit of knowledge in our times, then this would be the place to begin.

The historic virtue of republicanism is its concerted efforts to mitigate, if not outright eliminate, most of the hereditary bases for wealth and power that have all too frequently overdetermined any given generation's level of achievement (Unger 1996). In past republican regimes, people who simply lived off their inheritance were despised and, when possible, dispossessed of their holdings through the levy of a heavy inheritance tax. The beneficiaries of this redistributed wealth were those who were likely to increase the wealth of all in the future (e.g. entrepreneurs) or those who had already prevented it from decline in the past (e.g. military and civil service pensioners). Property ownership, typically a requirement for full citizenship, reflected less a deference to wealth as such than a basic political competency test: how can people be trusted to exercise independent judgement in the forum, and potentially offer their leadership to the entire polis, if they cannot even manage their own affairs? At the same time, the dispossession of inherited wealth was never total, since the market had yet to govern all forms of social interaction. The classical Greek sense of economy as *oikonomikos* still ruled, and so even the most inefficient and unproductive among the wealthy were left enough to maintain a household with some dignity. In that important sense, republicanism was 'pre-liberal' (Polanyi 1944).

A contemporary proposal in the same spirit is the 'guaranteed minimum citizen's income', which reflects that now, after 200 years of liberalism, there is a greater need to protect the poor than the rich from indignity. Moreover, wage labour has gone the way of land ownership in failing to capture the economic preconditions for making a meaningful contribution to society. In general, the value that republican regimes have invested in powers of self-maintenance has related to the source of such regimes' leaders, who may well be chosen by lot, as in the case of classical Athens. No doubt, citizens of our own 'democratic' societies would be gladly taxed much more heavily for improving education if their leaders were selected in this manner. To his credit, John Stuart Mill had figured this out, when he originally called for publicly funded mass education coupled with the use of education as the main criterion for political participation.

Reproducing republicanism has proven elusive, mainly because its identity is so closely tied to its catalytic role in the West's acceptance of the capitalist way of life. Philosophical histories of European politics present republicanism as a transitional phase between the close-knit communitarianism of agricultural societies and the dispersed liberalism of commercial societies (Pocock 1985). There is a comparable philosophical history of science, whereby the ideal of the open society appears briefly realized in the Enlightenment's 'republic of letters' between the clerical authoritarianism of the feudal era and the privatization of intellectual property rights that began in the eighteenth century with the institution of copyright, and accelerated in the nineteenth and twentieth centuries with the expansion of

Figure 1.2   The scientific matrix

Is risk-seeking encouraged?	Is there a public good?	
	Yes	No
Yes	Popperian bold conjecturer	Schumpeterian entrepreneur
No	Kuhnian normal scientist	Cartesian cogito

Figure 1.3   The political matrix

Is risk-seeking encouraged?	Is there a civic ideal?	
	Yes	No
Yes	Republican	Liberal
No	Communitarian	Robinson Crusoe

patent law. According to the tacit conventions by which history is reified as 'theory', communitarianism and liberalism – or normal science and technological innovation, respectively – are regarded as 'pure types' of governance, while republicanism is taken to be an unstable 'hybrid' (especially in the biological sense that hybrids are infertile). For, no sooner had republican regimes eradicated the privileges enjoyed by the Church and the landed aristocracy, than social instability dissolved republicanism's own civic ideal. In its place emerged, over a couple of generations in the nineteenth century, a new industrial élite nurtured by laws permitting the transmission of acquired wealth to offspring, as justified by a liberal's new-found sense of individualism – i.e. 'I am entitled to dispose of my hard-earned wealth as I please'. These legal arrangements begat the great dynasties and monopolies, perhaps most notoriously symbolized by the Rockefellers and Standard Oil. In response, governments had to invent new regulatory powers for themselves that either assimilated industry into the state apparatus (the continental European route) or cast the state in the role of 'trust-buster' (the American route). Both routes were designed to recapture, however artificially, the lost world of republicanism's civic ideal.

My argument so far is summarized in Figures 1.2 and 1.3, which pursue the analogy between the organization of scientific and political life. To conclude this section it will be useful to elaborate upon the two dimensions that define the terms of the analogy: the presence of a civic ideal/public good and the degree of risk seeking.

The presence of a civic ideal/public good

Is there a commonly recognized 'court of appeal' that cannot be reduced to special interests? Both special interests and private property presuppose the inviolability of a civic ideal/public good whose subversion would be self-defeating. Special interests are never favoured in a large polity for their own sake, but only to the extent that they can serve the interests of others. Private property is not sui generis but the product of a transformed commons. Intellectual property may be regarded in similar terms, namely as the application of universally available principles, or the economist's sense of 'public good' – that is, a good to which access would cost more to restrict than to keep freely available. In this way, the epistemologist's distinction between 'pure' and 'applied' knowledge is transformed, in the economist's hands, into 'public goods' versus 'intellectual property'. Another example of the presupposition of a commons in science is that you cannot oppose a scientific theory without abiding by the same rules of evidence and method that are allowed to your opponent; to do otherwise would be to opt out of the scientific field altogether (Bourdieu 1975). If you want to alter these rules, you must propose the changes openly, which then makes them subject to public scrutiny. The presence of a civic ideal/public good provides an external boundary (or 'demarcation') to the political/scientific enterprise (say, by nation or discipline) which enables its internal changes to be clearly tracked and reckoned. At any given point, they constitute what Popper called 'conventions' and Kuhn a 'paradigm', which are recognized by the republican as necessary evils. (The mistake made by communitarians like Kuhn is to regard the evil as a good, whereas the mistake by liberals is to suppose that this 'evil' can be eliminated without negative consequences.)

The degree of risk-seeking

Once the boundary of the polity/science has been set, are there incentives to change its internal constitution? Where no such boundary exists – i.e. societies governed merely by the dictates of individual self-interest – one gets radically polarized responses. Those inclined to risk their lives for their ideas appear as heroic figures, whereas those who do not are seen as self-sufficient, not a burden on anyone else: Schumpeter's intrepid entrepreneur versus Descartes' isolated thinker. For their part, republican societies have tended to use military conscription as the link between defending the polity from external threat and enabling citizens to fortify themselves in case their own lives become imperiled by the claims they express in public. This Italian innovation is captured by the second amendment to the US Constitution: the individual's right to bear arms (Pocock 1975). Without endorsing vigilantism, one can see merit in the idea that tools honed to defend the polity can then be used to encourage the contestation of issues within the polity. Of course, one would like a less violent means of transmitting the relevant skills and attendant attitudes. Indeed, compulsory citizen education of the sort advocated by John Stuart Mill in the UK and John Dewey in the USA may be seen as sublimating the republican society's interest in cultivating the martial arts. This is perhaps most evident in the rhetoric surrounding science education, which suggests that students are training to enable the nation to be more competitive in the global economic arena, while enhancing their own employment prospects at home.

The slippery slope from republicanism to liberalism

The most obvious difference between republicanism and liberalism is that the liberal does not recognize any sense of collective interest beyond aggregated self-interest; hence, liberalism has found the idea of a 'civic ideal' elusive, if not a complete fantasy. This is because societies dominated by the market mentality – as liberalism invariably is – make it rational for individuals to measure what they say against its likely consequences for their own well-being, assuming no social buffer from the repercussions of having made claims that are ultimately deemed mistaken. Thus, sometimes the distinction between 'liberal' and 'republican' regimes is drawn in terms of the types of freedom their citizens enjoy. In liberal regimes, it is supposed that sheer lack of physical interference constitutes freedom. In other words, if I am not enslaved, I must therefore be free to do what I want, there is no other alternative. However, republican regimes do not accept the premise as sufficient to warrant the conclusion. In addition, republicans hold that people need to act in an environment where there is a good chance that what they say and do will be taken seriously by others, and not simply ignored or become the grounds for the curtailment of their speech and action in the future.

Some aspects of the historical difference between liberalism and republicanism are worth recalling. Here the master is Quentin Skinner (1997), the leading historian of political thought in our time. Skinner regards the seventeenth-century philosopher Thomas Hobbes as an originator of the liberal mentality. Hobbes periodically spoke of people's 'freedom to obey' once the social contract was in place. For Hobbes, the social contract was an artificially enforced situation, in which peace was achieved in a combative 'state of nature' by all parties agreeing to abide by the dictates of some third party, designated as the 'sovereign'. The sovereign was traditionally imagined to be an absolute monarch but could equally be a legislature. In either case, the sovereign enjoys a monopoly on force in the society. Of course, one would technically remain free to violate the sovereign's dictates, but given the low chances of success in Hobbes' ideal polity, such a person would normally be seen as irrational. On the contrary, in a Hobbesian polity, it is more rational to shape one's goals so they have a reasonable chance of being achieved within the constraints laid down by the sovereign. Hobbes' republican opponents objected to the self-debasement bred by this situation, namely, second-guessing and pandering to the whims of the sovereign: free agents would be reduced to mere courtiers.

In the late eighteenth century, the Hobbesian polity metamorphosed into the 'constrained optimization' model of rational action characteristic of classical and neoclassical economics. This change depersonalized the sovereign and devolved its powers, resulting in an 'invisible hand' governance of dispersed markets. The objectionable second-guessing and pandering of the Hobbesian regime came to be sublimated into the skills needed for speculating in the stock market and marketing goods at a mass level. In the second half of the twentieth century, this model was enhanced in two respects. The first, due to Herbert Simon (1945), internalized the constraints so that awareness of one's own finite cognitive capacities in the face of overwhelming tasks set the parameters within which 'bounded rational' action could occur. The second is associated with Leon Festinger's cognitive dissonance theory. It turned the adaptation of ends to fit the available means into an elaborate but unconsciously adopted survival strategy in a hostile world (Elster 1984). Thus, in keeping with the therapeutically oriented welfare state culture, the courtier and the trader yielded to the bureaucrat with an overflowing 'in box' in search of mental stability as he or she offered excuses as to why nothing ever seemed to go to plan.

Each stage in this potted history of the liberal mentality shares the assumption that 'rationality' – the all-embracing term for normatively adequate human action – can be relativized to virtually any set of constraints. From a republican standpoint, this implies an unwholesome intimacy between the selection of a course of action and the environment in which one is forced to act. For example, a constrained optimization model of rationality can countenance situations in which it would be 'rational' to disclose the identity of Jews to the Nazis (if one's own life were threatened, etc.). In contrast, a republican would say that, in such situations, what one says and does is inappropriately influenced by the anticipated consequences for one's own well-being. Simply put, it becomes impossible to propose an idea without staking one's life, a situation which is *intrinsically* irrational. In this respect, republicanism is exceptionally sensitive to the social and economic conditions required for institutionalizing the metaphysical distinction between reality and its representations: I should be able to oppose your ideas without threatening your life. In both liberal and communitarian regimes, this distinction is collapsed, albeit with rather opposing results, as suggested by my brief survey of their 'excesses' in the previous section.

In science today, at most its élite members live in a republican regime, while the rest live in a liberal regime where their freedom is in practice severely constrained by whether they will offend a prospective employer or grant reviewer. I say 'at most' because the symbolic capital accumulated by scientists has come to be so bound up with ordinary economic capital (i.e. better = richer) that even dissenting members of the élite can have their right to be wrong seriously threatened by the 'liberalization' of inquiry.

One such élite researcher is Peter Duesberg, Professor of Cell Biology at the University of California, Berkeley. Duesberg was stripped of his outstanding researcher status at the US National Institute of Health (which had given him virtually a blank cheque for research) for having publicized his scepticism that AIDS is caused by HIV, arguing that AIDS may be a straightforward public hygiene problem related to the lifestyle of gay men that then leads to the breakdown of their immune systems. Serious consideration of his hypothesis would clearly challenge the American medical establishment's backing of a strong HIV-AIDS link, while rekindling an unwanted public debate on the ethics of homosexuality. Of course, in keeping with US First Amendment rights to 'free speech', Duesberg did not lose his job or get thrown in jail, but his research funding and book contract were withdrawn, making it difficult for him to develop and advocate his position effectively.

In contrast, consider the case of John Bockris, Professor of Chemistry at Texas A & M University, an élite dissenter who has successfully adapted to the erosion of republican science. He has steadfastly supported cold fusion as an important key to alternative energy research, even in the face of withering critiques from the physics community (Close 1991). Though widely criticized as high-tech alchemy, Bockris' lavishly and privately funded research has insulated him from calls by colleagues to divest him of his professorship. However, were Bockris to discover a commercially viable cold fusion process, it would be immediately patented as a technology and hence taken out of the domain of pure inquiry. The point here is that the motives for long-term investment in wild ideas should not be confused with the pursuit of knowledge for its own sake; hence the distinction between liberal and genuinely republican science.

Fear and anxiety infiltrates the day-to-day operations of science even when scientists are not proposing controversial hypotheses. This fact is obscured by the norm that Robert Merton (1973: 267–78) euphemistically labelled 'communism', which in practice means that scientists have no choice but to share data and credit if they expect to be supported in the future. On closer inspection, a mafia mentality turns out to be at work, itself another by-product of the liberalization of science. Thus, in good Hobbesian fashion, the supposed 'community' of science refers to little more than the fact that everyone equally suffers under the same threat.

Consider the peer review processes that govern scientific publications. They essentially provide insurance against risk: an individual scientist is allowed to say only as much as his or her peers can tolerate, and in return they absorb collective responsibility so that he or she does not have to bear the burden of proof alone. Readers can simply rely on the judgement of the journal's editors to vouch for the veracity of the author. However, this insurance is purchased at a cost: namely, that the contestation of already existing claims to knowledge is kept to a minimum and, wherever possible, pre-empted by gestures to portray one's work as cultivating a domain charted by previous researchers. After all, a print forum that publicized knowledge claims only to have them seriously challenged in subsequent issues would appear to be promoting more a clash of ideologies than the collective search for truth. In that sense, science is a society designed to suppress conflict rather than resolve it through either a peaceful consensus or open warfare.

Increasingly, the main field for containing the possibility of open dispute in science is 'research ethics' (Penslar 1995). The next section provides a brief introduction to the thinking that informs the field, which attempts to remedy the worst excesses of liberalism without addressing the background conditions that prevent the constitution of science as a republican regime.

Research ethics as the liberal ideology of scientific governance

Once upon a time, 'research ethics' were what protected the rights of subjects in the research conducted by psychologists and medical scientists. Now, it seems, the rights of the scientists themselves require protection. Reflecting the complex social environment in which science is practised these days, research ethics has expanded to become a field in its own right. In the USA and Scandinavia, one can even hold a chair in research ethics. A research ethicist is expected to be expert in disputes involving the assignment of intellectual property rights, as well as in the detection and prevention of professional misconduct. However, their academic credentials need not be in a laboratory science. Indeed, many are primarily trained in philosophy, theology or anthropology.

In 1995, the American Association for the Advancement of Science conducted a computer interactive project, 'Science Conduct Online', which lasted for two months and promoted research ethics as a component of the professional science curriculum. The project was heralded by the 23 June 1995 issue of *Science* magazine, which reported on the different contexts in which research ethics is currently practised in the USA: week-long workshops that teach scientists how to teach research ethics to their postgraduate students, high-profile lecture series in which leading scientists air their ethical quandaries, or simply informal lunchtime 'bull sessions'.

Five 'experts' (as *Science* dubbed the ethicists) were asked to present hypothetical ethical problems or 'scenarios' that can arise in the conduct of research. These were put online and publicized throughout the Internet. People were invited to propose solutions, to which the research ethicists would offer their reactions, hopefully leading to some deep and interesting insights about the research process. In the project's two months, its website was consulted over 3000 times, with over 30 people openly engaged in dialogue with the experts. Though mainly American, they represented a cross-section of the settings in which science is conducted today: academia, business and government, as well as student and unemployed scientists. Few had any trouble relating the scenarios to their own experiences. I was one of the 30 who openly engaged with the research ethicists, and perhaps the only one not professionally trained as a natural scientist. However, as a philosopher and sociologist of science, I wanted to determine the exact nature of the research ethicist's 'expertise', and its relationship to the scientists' own views about good and bad research conduct. The use of scenarios to demonstrate the need for research ethics was familiar as the method used to justify the existence of other branches of applied philosophy, such as medical ethics and business ethics.

The five scenarios had certain common features. First, they often lacked details that would probably make a difference to whether an act was deemed ethical or unethical. However, this sketchiness was partly deliberate, since the cases were meant to function like Rorschach inkblot tests that encourage the viewer to 'read in' their own perspective. Second, all the scenarios were set in large university laboratories, where ethical concerns emerged because of uncertainties over the ownership of intellectual property. A third and subtle feature was that the narratives tended to portray the ethical quandary as symptomatic of a communication breakdown. Finally, and subtlest of all, even when women were presented as authority figures, they were generally portrayed as being in the ethically most vulnerable position.

One scenario featured the plight of Jessica Banks, a recent PhD who was about to take up a tenurable appointment and wanted to take the notes she had made while working on a research project with her major professor. However, the professor refused to grant permission and chastised Banks for the mere suggestion that she take something that belonged to the laboratory. Afterwards, a colleague of Banks said that she should just copy her notebooks at night when no one was around. Was this good advice?

Most respondents thought that Banks should copy the notebooks. Disagreement arose over whether she should do it on the sly, as her colleague suggested. Few believed that the notebooks belonged to 'the laboratory', since it was easy to imagine the professor taking the notebooks were he to start up a lab at another university. While he would probably be prevented from doing so in an industrial setting, as a senior academic authority his word was basically law – that is, unless there were explicit guidelines. Here we see a potential role for the research ethicist in laying down the proprietary relationship between the knowledge produced in a laboratory and the knowledge producers.

However, there is a difference between preventing unfortunate situations like the one described in the Banks scenario and dealing with such situations once they have arisen. The online experts were generally more adept at the former than the latter task. In the Banks scenario, the resident expert suggested that Banks offer to collaborate with her major professor. While some found this strategy persuasive, others wondered whether this was a realistic option, given the power differences between Banks and her major professor. Indeed, some respondents went so far as to suggest that Banks cut her losses and move on to another project, rather than risk receiving a negative letter of evaluation from the professor.

An interesting assumption made by both the expert and the respondents was that copying the notebooks would be tantamount to taking them, at least in terms of the professor's ability to use the data to the same effect. This assumption feeds into a larger set of issues touched upon by another scenario. In this case, one scientist wanted to publish a paper that analysed and drew scientifically interesting conclusions from data originally collected by another scientist who never published his results. This situation is common whenever scientists do contract-based research for government. What government considers useful data may not strike the contracted researcher that way. Nevertheless, the researcher may be well positioned to provide the data and may need the money to supplement her grant for research that she finds scientifically interesting. But suppose, three years after the information is made generally available, another researcher decides to capitalize on it? According to the scenario, the scientist who originally collected the data wanted to stop publication of the second scientist's paper, which had already been accepted by a major professional journal. Once again, the contrast with the business world was instructive. It would seem that the original scientist's contract with government was fairly straight-forward. It required that services be rendered to the client in exchange for money – nothing more and nothing less. However, because these 'services' involved the production of knowledge, several people thought that the scientist had additional proprietary rights over his 'products' even after the terms of the agreement had been satisfied.

My own view was that the first scientist's failure to publish in a timely fashion implied that he had not seen sufficient scientific merit in his own data until his rival came along. Now, to hold up the second scientist's article would only serve to encourage scientists to start up many projects but only complete those that attract the interest of other researchers. After all, science is risky business. Still, several respondents wanted some kind of intellectual property 'insurance'. The research ethicist behind this scenario wisely argued that scientists need to learn that analysing data is just as much serious scientific work as collecting data. And given that few scientists are equally good at collecting and analysing data, the two tasks should be clearly separated in the design of grant proposals.

The most widely discussed scenario concerned a lab director who, in the course of reviewing a grant proposal, learned of a technique that could help one of her postdoctoral fellows make significant progress on an experiment. Should she tell him? The issue is complicated because a grant proposal's 'confidentiality' often allows the reviewer to seek technical advice from a colleague at her own institution. Both the resident expert and most respondents felt that confidentiality had to be protected at all costs, and many suspected that some of their best ideas had been 'stolen' in similar situations. This reaction struck me as excessive, especially once it was made clear that the technique was already public knowledge and not the grant proposer's innovation. However, it does highlight the extent to which scientists think of the products of their labours – including their literature reviews – as personal property, even if that attitude only serves to impede the collective pursuit of knowledge. Instead of questioning the social conditions that have made this proprietary mentality second nature, research ethicists seem content with sheltering scientists from its harsher consequences. Is that all we can hope for from a field that calls itself 'ethics'? Perhaps in a liberal regime, but not in a republican one.

The cardinal republican strategy: shoring up the commons by taxing social inheritance

In contrast to the fear and anxiety that is barely governed by research ethics in liberal regimes of science, republican science is inquiry in a state of 'permanent revolution', an expression that Popper (1970) originally adapted from Trotsky to distinguish his position from Kuhn's (1970) more sanguine attitude to normal science. To be sure, the expression is an oxymoron, albeit a suggestive one. If people are always encouraged to be critical of their current situation and to propose better alternatives (rather than simply wait until the status quo fails on its own accord, as Kuhn suggested), then revolution loses its violent character, mainly because people come to realize just how arbitrary the status quo really is – perhaps little more than a historically entrenched accident. In that case, they will be less inclined to superstitiously associate longevity with destiny. They will realize that there is just as much risk in continuing the status quo as in breaking with it, at which point the past comes to be treated more as a contingent resource than a necessary burden or even a legacy.

In economic terms, the permanent revolutionary is thus concerned with 'opportunity costs' – that is, how many possible futures are closed off by my own action? Under these circumstances, induction and its rhetorical twin, presumption, lose their force as principles of rational inference. At the level of economics, republicans treat initial investments into a particular line of inquiry as a 'sunk cost' whose continuation must be gauged on the likelihood of future return and not merely on the sheer irretrievability of what was initially invested. Such a strategy would immunize science policymakers against the belief in self-fulfilling prophecies and, still worse, the idea that wrongs sufficiently compounded over time add up to a right, as in the supposition that the vast majority of scientists whose work goes unrecognized have probably not contributed a great deal.

This brings us to what Robert Merton (1973: 439–59), in another of his classic euphemisms, called the 'principle of cumulative advantage'. A republican science would treat this principle as comparable to the untaxed inheritance of acquired wealth. We shall periodically revisit this principle in the course of this book, especially in Chapter 5. Merton originally had in mind the selective advantage afforded to scientists trained at élite institutions, considered in relation to their ability to accumulate grants, publications, posts and honours. Scientists who distinguish themselves early in their careers – a group that nearly coincides with those who participate in the 'old boy networks' of the prestigious research universities – tend to be the ones who distinguish themselves later on. As in capitalism, so too in science: the rich get richer, the poor get poorer. Of course, such a pattern is common to numerous large organizations. However, the difference is that in those other cases we often say that the organization suffers from a 'structural bias' that systematically underutilizes the pool of available talent. Why not the same diagnosis in the case of science? Indeed, the American policy scientist William Dunn has neatly characterized this problem as 'the tragedy of the epistemic commons', whereby the reinforcement of individual success results in overgrazing by the scientific élite.

Nevertheless, Merton's followers have raised this tendency to a kind of 'invisible hand' at work in science (not unlike the classical political economists who, in the eighteenth century, justified the conversion of pastures to industrial sites). Since the distinction between those at the cutting edge of research and the rest of the pack is usually not the result of any central planning board, it must be the result of the collective spontaneous judgements of scientists themselves: so say the Mertonians. Neglected here, of course, is the role that the sheer size of the initial investment into a line of research (in terms of both labour and capital) plays in giving it forward momentum. Thus, the quick-and-dirty indicator of scientific progress in our times – its irreversibility (i.e. the inconceivability of turning back on an inquiry once begun) – is measured more in terms of the amount that has so far been invested than in terms of the benefits that have so far been realized. This point is central to the scale and scope of the scientific enterprise, to be considered in the next chapter. However, we can already appreciate that, from a standpoint critical of the principle of cumulative advantage, the US Congress's decision in 1993 to halt the construction of what would have been the world's largest particle accelerator, the Superconducting Supercollider, struck a blow for republican science against the superstition of irreversible progress. But generally speaking, what is the antidote to this pernicious mentality?

My first piece of advice is to regard the predictability that an Ivy League or Oxbridge degree will bring scientific success in the same spirit as Marxist and institutionalist economists have regarded the stability of the major corporate dynasties or oligopolies in capitalism – that is, as symptomatic of inequities in the way science has come to be institutionalized, not a sign that science has managed to sort out the wheat from the chaff. The appeal of both 'Big Science' and 'Big Business' is grounded in a myth of continuity, be it of a research programme or a corporate track record. In the case of the former, one speaks of the regularity with which such a programme can come up with novel findings; in the latter, the corporation's experience in manufacturing or, more likely these days, marketing new products. To political economists such as Thorstein Veblen and Joseph Schumpeter who, in their different ways, placed a greater value on the spirit of enterprise – that is, the periodic destabilization of stagnant markets – than on the sheer accumulation of wealth, the illusion of a 'weight of the past' sustained by the absence of a redistribution policy appears as more millstone than milestone to the continued existence of capitalism. Basically, capitalism's competitive edge is gradually eroded, as governments take the soft option of allowing wealth to be perpetuated in ways that resemble its current form.

Here history provides a valuable lesson. In the early days of capitalism, before high productivity was realized, inheritance taxes were seen as the only equitable policy for redistributing wealth to ensure that markets remained free to all enterprising individuals. However, with the advent of high productivity came the modern welfare argument for taxation, which assumes the possibility of benefitting the poor without disadvantaging the rich. Thus, the rich would be taxed mainly for what the state regarded as surplus income that could be used more efficiently for the overall benefit of society by being given to the poor. Arguments then revolved around the relative efficiency of taxing the rich in this way *vis-à-vis* providing them with incentives to invest their surplus income.

But of course, seen in historical perspective, this debate amounts to little more than cosmetic accounting, whereby income levels are narrowed but the difference in relative advantage that the poor and rich receive from each unit of income remains unchanged. Given that on modern welfare schemes the rich do not decline in what is nowadays called 'social capital' (Coleman 1990: Ch. 12), they are able to do much more than the poor with whatever income they earn, no matter how much their surplus is then taxed. In that case, a social inheritance tax is called for, the exemplar of which today is affirmative action legislation (Cahn 1995). In the pages that follow, I periodically return to this general strategy for redressing the inequities of Big Science. But in concluding this chapter, let me focus on its implications for the distribution of academic posts.

It is not sufficient for graduates of first-rate institutions to be hired by, say, third-rate institutions and vice versa. The difference in social capital remains and, in the long term, one would expect the former group to regain much of their original advantage. Instead, redistribution must occur in terms of who is trained at those different quality institutions in the first place, with an eye toward enabling graduates to enter the employment market with roughly equivalent amounts of social capital and hence to be evaluated solely on their own merits. Here it is worth recalling that a person's social capital is marked mainly by whether their background and training enables them to connect with others so as to realize their own goals. In other words, the same knowledge content may contain different amounts of social capital, depending on the situations in which knowledge is able to bring about action. The closest that science policy has come to recognizing and treating the issues surrounding social capital occurred during the American New Deal of the 1930s, which unsurprisingly coincided with the period in which science was most organically integrated in public policy. We shall revisit its initiatives in Chapter 7. However, in what immediately follows, we consider the current situation, in which science policy and public policy appear in collusion to concentrate social capital.

2

The role of scale in the
scope of scientific governance

○————————————————————

The ideal of the experimenting society

In the first chapter we saw that contemporary science's inability to live up to the republican ideal of the open society can be traced to an inequitable distribution of social capital, which is to say that the same knowledge does not empower to the same extent everyone who possesses it. Explaining how this is possible is the principal problem in the governance of scientific inquiry. It concerns what the business historian Alfred Chandler (1990) has called the 'scale' and 'scope' of the enterprise. Very much like democracy, nearly everyone likes science in principle, often regarding it as the pinnacle of civilization. But many cannot stand it in practice. On the one hand, many of the essential virtues of science, especially those associated with criticism and openness, seem to get lost once scientific institutions reach a certain size, complexity, hierarchy and level of material investment. These are issues of scale. On the other hand, science has had a historical tendency – to be sure, encouraged by government and business – to expand its powers beyond its initial remit of pure inquiry, often dominating, contaminating or transforming other spheres of social life. Terms like 'positivism', 'scientism' and 'reductionism' capture the class of problems relating to science's scope (Fuller 1997: 30 ff.).

These problems of scale and scope are exacerbated by a variety of scarcities: research funding gets increasingly limited as more projects require higher start-up costs; access to careers, publication and advancement becomes more difficult as the number of scientists grows; and the coverage of scientific content is compressed or curtailed as the space (in textbooks) and time (in the classroom) allotted for the educational process remain largely fixed. The presence of these scarcities is often forgotten. For example, philosophers have traditionally claimed that as scientific theories extend their scope

– say, by trying to explain and/or predict larger domains of phenomena – they make themselves more vulnerable to refutation. However, this claim makes sense only if the scaled-up scientific enterprise needed to accommodate this extension of scope does not then alter the actual conduct of science and especially the attitude the knowledge producers have towards the knowledge they produce. The increased numbers of people and resources involved in extending a theory invariably intensifies commitment to the theory, much in the manner of a social movement, rendering it that much harder to let go once obstacles are encountered. This point is driven home with a vengeance in a well-meaning attempt to extend public participation in scientific inquiry, dubbed by the great social science methodologist Donald Campbell (1988: 290–314) the 'experimenting society'.

Science certainly acquires knowledge through experimentation, but it is probably the last institution to which one would turn to find the experimenting society at work. This may explain why science policy is the least developed area of public policy. In any case, the paradox helps explain public resistance to Campbell's original vision over the past 30 years. Campbell was perhaps best known for his advocacy of 'quasi-experimental' research designs in which the distinction between 'experimental' and 'control' conditions in the laboratory are simulated by features of real-life settings. In this spirit, Campbell regarded local communities as so many sites for testing the relative efficacy of welfare policies and the relative plausibility of social scientific hypotheses. On the surface, this would seem to require no less than the technocratic colonization of the everyday life, a vision that was sustainable at the height of welfare politics in the Cold War era. In Campbell's America, this corresponded to Lyndon Johnson's 'Great Society' programme. Accordingly, the public would be swept up into the scientific enterprise. However, they would do so as citizen-subjects, not themselves citizen-experimenters: the public would not initiate research but merely react or adapt to it, albeit often in quite critical and sophisticated ways. In short, science would experiment on society without the experiment being turned back on science. Characteristic of Campbell's acceptance of this asymmetry is the following admonition: 'Accepting the important role of social experimentation at once puts clarity of scientific inference into conflict with means-idealism and acceptable political processes' (Campbell 1988: 301).

While perfectly reasonable on the surface, this sentence makes two assumptions that invite even more asymmetrical relationships to develop between scientists and the public. In the rest of this chapter, I shall subject these two assumptions to critical scrutiny. The first assumption is that 'the clarity of scientific inference' is corruptible by the introduction of non-scientists or non-scientific considerations. A less contentious way of making the same point is to say that the values associated with science are distinct from those associated with other spheres of social life: what may be good for one may not be good for the other. There is much truth to this observation, if taken to be about the actual development of science up to this point in history. Whether that development has been normatively desirable is another matter. Second, Campbell's admonition assumes a paternalistic attitude on the part of the social experimenter, whose 'means-idealism' leads him or her to worry – in the presence of colleagues but not subjects – about the possible consequences of performing a particular experiment. A less asymmetrical treatment of this concern would call for the subjects to be present at the outset to negotiate the terms of the experiment with the scientists.

If nothing else, the two assumptions of the experimenting society should remind us that the so-called 'epistemological' and 'ethical' doubts that often surround scientific practice may simply be the result of the potential recipients of that practice being absent from the places where research design is conceptualized; for, if the potential recipients were present at these early deliberations, speculations about ethically and epistemically adequate treatment of the subjects would be replaced by dialogues of a more explicitly political character, revealing that the interests of the scientists (and their clients) do not spontaneously coincide with those of the public. Some give and take on both sides is bound to ensue. Indeed, a great virtue of the ideal of the experimenting society is that the policymaker is forced to confront the exact role of science in a social order that is avowedly democratic. Specifically, two challenges are posed:

1 Is there anything more to the much-vaunted 'autonomy' of science than the asymmetrical social relationships highlighted above, whereby the public must make its actions accountable to science (say, by responding openly to a treatment) but scientists need not, at least not to the same extent, make themselves accountable to the public?
2 Do concepts such as 'testing' and 'application' merely promote this asymmetry by implying that scientists decide among themselves the terms of the research, and then the public 'votes' (Campbell 1988: 305) on the preordained set of options? In short, does the experimenting society only exacerbate the tendency of modern democratic processes to devolve into plebiscites that invite voters to make choices that are unlikely to affect current policy tendencies?

Of course, many contemporary political theorists, especially those of a 'corporatist' or 'pluralist' persuasion, would neither be surprised by these questions nor see anything especially problematic about their answers (Dahl 1989). They have argued that governments in big democracies must be responsive to public needs but that the diverse and complex character of those needs precludes direct public participation in how they are addressed.

However, as Campbell himself admitted, this view of the democratic polity runs counter to the image of science as the open society, which is one of a participatory democracy, all of whose members function as peers. Yet, instructively, the original site for the image was the Athenian polis, a small homogeneous public culture sharply divided between citizens and aliens that sat atop a slave-driven economy. While comparisons between classical Athens and contemporary scientific culture may seem invidious, nevertheless they force us to consider the political and economic terms on which the experimenting society can be realized today. But before turning to the contemporary scope of this problem, let us start with some historical perspective.

Hegel's revenge on the ideal

Modern science – that is, western science since the seventeenth century – is an aberration in the social history of knowledge production. Social theorists from Plato to Durkheim have observed that the structure of knowledge corresponds to the structure of domination in a society. To speak of differential access to reality is to refer symbolically to one's distance from the seat of power: deference to cognitive authority is a subtle but real form of submission. In these terms, modern science suffers a schizoid existence.

On the one hand, modern science's ideological commitment to free exchange and mutual criticism conjures up the image of a democratically governed enterprise. All scientists participate as equals, and any of them is capable of successfully challenging whatever any of the rest says. Indeed, the most vividly drawn examples of democratic governance in the liberal tradition, as found in the writings of Mill, Dewey and Popper, are basically extended analogies from what they understood to be the normative structure of science (Merton 1973: Ch. 13). On the other hand, however, both scientists and their defenders have been loath to extend this sense of democracy beyond the borders of science itself – that is, to make scientists accountable to the larger body of concerns represented by the rest of society. The positive way of putting this point has been to say that science flourishes in a state of 'autonomy'. And, in so far as we unreflectively accept the sharpness of such distinctions as 'producers vs. users' of knowledge or 'basic vs. applied' research, we assent to this perspective. It continues the Plato-Durkheim tradition of knowledge dictating the terms of power, though this tradition is now complicated by the fact that many modern societies are themselves democratically organized, and hence include several interest groups capable of appropriating science to their advantage. Nevertheless, these groups still retain the subordinate status of mere 'users', 'appliers' and 'consumers' of knowledge.

For the first three centuries following the Scientific Revolution (say, roughly 1600 to 1900), the relationship between the organization of knowledge production and the organization of society was one of 'uneven development'. The experimental method succeeded in democratizing scientific communities much faster than it did European society as a whole. Thus, once the achievements of science were consolidated in Newtonian mechanics at the start of the eighteenth century, philosophers proclaimed a period of 'Enlightenment', the goal of which would be to liberalize, and perhaps ultimately to democratize, society by popularizing science's distinctive critical attitudes. However, the Enlightenment philosophers did not carefully distinguish between instilling a receptive but passive attitude toward the fruits of scientific labour and instilling an interest in actively participating in such work. Did Voltaire and Kant want more people to respect scientists or to become scientists? Due to the limited social mobility of the period, few people had the opportunity to become scientists, and so the answer to this question was moot. But by the beginning of the nineteenth century, Hegel could already see what was at stake in providing an answer.

Hegel portrayed world history as the extension of freedom to an ever-expanding constituency. Here 'freedom' was understood to mean the ability to exercise one's reason to determine one's life. Hegel's signature insight was to see that the character of reason depends on the number of people functioning as rational agents in a society: metaphysically speaking, the nature of the quality rests on the quantity of its expression. When only one person, the so-called Oriental Despot, was deemed rational, his will was the standard to which everyone else's actions had to conform, or else risk death. In retrospect, we would say that the Despot's rule was arbitrary, but only because it did not face any institutionalized forms of resistance, as in the checks and balances of constitutional government, which presupposes the presence of multiple rational agents. However, as reason became more widely distributed, and the source of authority increasingly diffused, absolute freedom was gradually sublimated – ultimately, so thought Hegel, into the functionally differentiated bureaucracy that characterized nineteenth century Prussia.

If we think about the evolution of academic knowledge into university departments, then there would seem to be something to Hegel's teleology. But, of course, not everyone attracted to a broadly Hegelian historiography has ended the story as Hegel himself did. Rather, it has been more common to argue that reason becomes fully actualized only once *everyone* is allowed to exercise their reason freely, a situation most closely approximated by the egalitarian ethos of the open society. Indeed, an undercurrent barely hidden in twentieth century liberal utopias, be they Dewey's 'social intelligence', Popper's 'open society' or Campbell's 'experimenting society', is that scientific institutions would finally discard their own last vestiges of cognitive authoritarianism, their disciplinary rigidities, if they encouraged all citizens to participate in critical inquiry. (What this might entail is the topic of Part 3 of this book.) The suggestion is that just as its activities have gained the respect of society at large, science, as a society 'in the small' may have started to lag behind, if not actually reverse, the democratizing tendencies now evident in the rest of society. (A good test of this hypothesis would involve comparing politics and science as vehicles of upward social mobility over time: politics may now be a better career path than science.) Thus, at some point in their careers, Dewey, Popper and Campbell have each decried the various 'isms' – professionalism, specialism, expertism – that have characterized the institutionalization of science in the twentieth century, on the grounds that such 'isms' perverted the very essence of science.

Unfortunately, to remain true Hegelians, we cannot simply say that we have already glimpsed the ideal scientific polity but are now in danger of losing it to people unwilling to see the ideal through to its complete realization. The problem with such a statement is that the ideal scientific polity may be realizable only on a certain scale, especially if this polity depends on people interacting in ways that become more difficult as more people with diverse interests are involved, and their activities become bound up with ever greater material resources (cf. Clark 1985: Ch. 4). In terms of the republican ideal of the open society, the distinction between staking an idea and staking a life was easiest to draw when only egos were on the line. However, as science has scaled-up, the distinction has become harder to maintain. Enormous resources must be pre-committed to train people from various walks of life so that they can stake their ideas in forums where they are likely to be taken seriously. The ever-lengthening incubation period for acquiring the relevant credentials typically serves to narrow the range of ideas that are ultimately put forward. The era of the learned amateur whose personal voice signalled an unconventional attitude toward the scientific orthodoxy has yielded to a more anonymous professional voice that takes great pains to position its knowledge claims in relation to those of other worthies in the field (Montgomery 1995). Moreover, ideas are put forward with an eye to their accessibility – not in terms of intelligibility to the larger society, but feasibility to the policymakers who control the research purse strings.

The importance of scale to inquiry has been generally granted to the low end, namely, the minimal conditions needed for science to flourish. The social history of the seventeenth century has revealed how a critical mass of material and intellectual resources had to be mobilized before science could take off. Among the crucial developments were the recruitment of patrons who allowed work of the scientists' own initiative to proceed uninterrupted for a significant length of time (Biagioli 1993) and the fabrication of a complex web of correspondents whose frank opinions of one another's work were subject to the civilizing mediation of editorial gatekeepers (Bazerman 1988). The Hegelian historian would argue that these two developments cannot be sustained for an indefinite number of inquirers whose backgrounds and interests are increasingly diverse. In other words, there may be more of a trade-off between science and democracy than our liberals want to admit – indeed, that there may be maximal conditions beyond which science as we know it cannot flourish. Call it 'Hegel's revenge'. Hegel's revenge is behind the public's unease with Campbell's experimenting society.

If quantitative differences can make for qualitative change, as Hegel thought, then beyond a certain point a more inclusive science may not be, strictly speaking, a better science, but a new form of social life altogether – much as water when heated beyond a certain temperature is no longer simply a very hot liquid but a new entity, steam. But is steam a perfection, an improvement or, rather, a dissolution of water? While it must seem to strange evaluate forms of physical matter, we need to pose a question of just this sort in order to understand today's Big Science in light of the normative ideal of the open society toward which science seems to have been striving. Feminists and multiculturalists have been especially sensitive to this long-term prospect as increasing numbers of women and ethnic minorities enter the scientific labour force (Harding 1993). They paint a very hopeful picture that would cut against the liabilities associated with 'bigness' that I have so far emphasized. Nevertheless, the benchmark of radical institutional reorientation through a more inclusive policy of participation remains the role played by the Protestant Reformation in the history of Christianity. We shall return to the significance of the Protestant, feminist and multiculturalist initiatives in Chapter 4, but in the rest of this chapter we consider the gloomier prognosis that science has outgrown knowledge as its aim.

What would it mean for science to have outgrown knowledge as its aim?

Nothing in the nature of society demands that it has an institution specifically devoted to the pursuit of knowledge as pure inquiry. That such institutions have existed, typically associated with 'science', is a matter of socio-historical fact. There is no guarantee that once science has flourished it will do so forever, let alone in the same form. These are cardinal principles of my research programme, social epistemology. It is important to keep them in mind for what follows, since we typically read much more ontological significance into our knowledge talk than is institutionally warranted.

In both academic and lay discourse, behaviour is frequently explained in terms of one's possession of knowledge-related things, or 'epistemic entities'. These entities include: beliefs, reasons, intelligence, cognitive processes, (access to) information, disciplinary or technical training, theoretical assumptions, world views, and lines of thought. Although it is easy to imagine contexts in which one or more of these entities might be used to account for what someone has done, it is difficult to see how all of them could be accommodated within a single conceptual framework, as each one presupposes a somewhat different theory of how the mind works (Stich 1996). That alone would seem to demonstrate the extent to which appeals to epistemic entities are typically made without much thought to their appropriateness or reliability beyond a relatively narrow context of usage. In a more systematic vein, social psychologists have begun to challenge the power of beliefs and reasons to explain people's behaviour, including one's own behaviour (cf. Nisbett and Wilson 1977; Hewstone 1989). We need to push this challenge still further, encompassing tests of the entities mentioned above, confronting the possibility that we have reached the end of knowledge (Fuller 1993a).

What is at stake here? A useful way to think about the stakes is to consider what would follow from a demonstration that all our appeals to epistemic entities commit a version of what social psychologists call the 'fundamental attribution error' (Ross 1977). In other words, suppose it were shown that human behaviour is more a function of one's situation than of whatever 'knowledge' one brings to that situation. Consider the sorts of studies that would be relevant to such a finding. For example, social psychologists may fail to find significant differences between the decision-making patterns of economists and non-economists; in fact, manipulating the decision task itself may be a more reliable way of changing the behaviour of both groups than providing additional training in economics. Would it any longer make sense to defer to someone's judgement because of the economic knowledge they possess? What would become of education in economics? What would 'credentials' and 'expertise' in economics mean under these circumstances? More generally, how can someone be held accountable for their actions if claims to knowledge do not seem to make an empirical difference to their behaviour? Indeed, if all discipline-based training is implicated by this finding, what would be the status of the very social psychological research that had established it?

These are the sorts of probes that a truly empirical study of knowledge needs to make of epistemic entities. Just as our unreflective attitudes toward nature and society need to be subject to scientific scrutiny, so too do our unreflective attitudes toward science itself. Many of these 'reflexive' probes have already been conducted by self-styled 'constructivists' or 'ethnomethodological sociologists' (e.g. Knorr-Cetina and Cicourel 1981; Coulter 1983), social psychologists (e.g. Gergen and Gergen 1982; Gergen 1985), and sociologists of science (Gilbert and Mulkay 1984; Woolgar 1988; Mulkay 1990). They have studied the situational variability of knowledge talk in ordinary and scientific settings. There is a tendency in this literature to marvel at the virtuosity of human adaptive capacities that situational variability seems to imply. However, that 'situational variability' may turn out to be a euphemism for the fact that epistemic entities explain very little without an embarrassingly large number of ad hoc background assumptions. Indeed, I suspect that once systematized, our current knowledge talk will more closely resemble Ptolemaic astronomy than Newtonian mechanics, in both its restricted utility and its ultimate dispensability (Fuller 1993a: Ch. 3).

At this point, let me confront one obvious objection. I have assumed that if epistemic entities explain anything – or, for that matter, if there are such entities at all – then they must stand in some systematic relation to a particular class of social phenomena. Yet, this assumption would seem to beg the question against the significance of our knowledge talk, the self-contained character of which is supposed to show that the sorts of pursuits alternatively deemed 'rational', 'cognitive', 'epistemic' or 'scientific' are governed by standards internally defined by such talk, standards which are sustainable under a variety of social arrangements. Thus, Karl Popper's adaptation of Clausewitz's famous saying – that modern science is Socratic dialectic continued by other means – reflects the widespread belief among philosophers and scientists that, if one is willing and able to rise to the level of critical scrutiny demanded of scientific inquiry, then it does not matter whether one is tackling problems in the lab or in the market-place. In such a view, there is no 'in principle' reason why knowledge could not be reliably produced by individuals as well as groups, by large groups as well as small, by groups whose members are concentrated or dispersed in time and space. I want to argue not only that this view is based on wishful thinking but that those who have managed to see this point have yet to come fully to grips with its implications.

Philosophers of science are, in spite of themselves, inveterate Hegelians. Like Hegel, they believe that the knowledge enterprise has only one spatio-temporal boundary – namely, an origin. Throughout the nineteenth and most of the twentieth century, this origin was commonly located (as my previous remarks about Popper suggested) in fourth-century BC Athens. In recent years, as the motor of scientific progress has become more closely identified with experiment than with theory, the origin has been moved up to seventeenth-century Europe. Some philosophers, notably Charles Sanders Peirce and Nicholas Rescher (1978, 1979, 1984), have entertained the possibility that the knowledge enterprise may come to an end, not because we solve all the mysteries of the universe, but because it is no longer worth our while to try. The rate of return on investment in scientific research simply becomes too small. There is a certain Hegelian justice in this view, too, in that the calculative rationality so characteristic of the knowledge enterprise throughout its historical career will eventually put itself out of business by performing a meta-calculation of its own utility. Yet, curiously, this view of a possible termination of scientific inquiry is often presented as externally imposed, in that it seems to turn on letting other pragmatic concerns of the human condition trump the pursuit of knowledge for its own sake. But there is another sense in which the knowledge enterprise may terminate 'from within', and indeed, may have already done so, though our ordinarily promiscuous appeal to epistemic entities continues to obscure the fact.

Again like Hegel, philosophers of science – especially those who hold onto the notion of scientific progress – take for granted that science improves with ever more participants over ever longer periods of time. In particular, it is supposed that the principles of experimental inquiry that were first instituted by a small group of English gentlemen in the seventeenth century (cf. Shapin 1988) were gradually refined as the opportunities for their deployment were expanded. However, bigger science makes for better science only if, say, experimental inquiry is not sensitive to scale. One piece of evidence that strongly suggests that science has outgrown its original principles is the difficulties that 'naturalized' epistemologists and philosophers of science have faced in trying to situate traditional cognitive norms in an empirically adequate account of today's knowledge enterprises (Faust 1984; Fuller 1992a, 1993a: Ch. 3).

In contemporary philosophical parlance, 'naturalism' is the view that normative positions must be constrained by what is empirically known about human beings. Naturalists typically abide by Kant's dictum that one cannot be obliged to do something unless one already has the capacity to do it, with the latter determined (so argue naturalists) by the empirical conditions in which agents find themselves, including their bodies and their social and physical environments. This dictum is meant to militate against supernatural criteria of knowledge and action that would judge humans in terms more appropriate to deities – for example, requiring that one consider all possible consequences or all possible evidence before deciding what to do or what to believe. However, once we get beyond this general admission of humanity's finitude, naturalism can proceed in several different directions. Some naturalists take the deliveries of the natural sciences at face value and hence have suggested that, say, sociobiology or neuroscience provide guidance for how we should conduct our affairs. Others, such as myself, regard naturalism more reflexively: the empirical conditions under which the natural sciences have been historically conducted should be factored into normative conclusions drawn from them (Fuller 1993c). I am therefore led to treat naturalism as a 'negative' or 'critical' position that diminishes the plausibility of certain philosophical norms but does not prescribe which ones *must* be adopted.

As it turns out, virtually every cognitive norm that philosophers have advanced – be it deductive, inductive or abductive – has a pedigree that reaches back at least to Newton, and often to Aristotle. In other words, the norms harken back to a time when the knowledge enterprise was conducted on a much smaller scale than it currently is. As continuing testimony to the Cartesian legacy in modern philosophy, naturalized philosophers have typically looked for these norms in the minds of individual knowers. But in the face of strong psychological evidence to the contrary, philosophers have been forced either to relocate the norms in mental realms beyond the reach of experimentation or to offer the vague hope that some training in methodology will remedy the demonstrated 'deficiencies' (cf. Cohen 1981).

Dissatisfied with these two strategies, some philosophers have pursued the Peirce-Popper route of arguing that cognitive norms really govern group processes, but little effort has been devoted to determining which sorts of norms have a chance of governing which sorts of groups. Instead, this literature tends to be populated with abstract models inspired by neoclassical economics which, whatever their specifics, presume that the knowledge enterprise is improved by increasing the number of information processing nodes in the network (cf. Kitcher 1990; Goldman and Shaked 1991). And, as if to compound the problem, still other philosophers have suggested that computers might make better nodes than humans (Thagard 1988; Slezak 1989), though it remains to be seen whether computers are welcomed into the guild of scientists or the definition of scientific reasoning is altered so as to exclude computers once again (cf. Dolby and Cherry 1989; Collins 1990). In either case, it is clear that the knowledge enterprise has been cut loose from its traditional moorings. The question before us, then, is this: has the nature of the knowledge enterprise fundamentally changed as a result of its dimensions having exceeded certain limits (cf. Price [1963] 1986)? Is 'Big Science' a contradiction in terms?

The ungovernability of Big Democracy and Big Science: of Rousseau and Feyerabend

An analogue of the above question is familiar from political theory. Rousseau's worries about the possibility of democracy in the modern world will provide a helpful departure for thinking about the question I am raising. Rousseau is famous for confronting the scale-sensitive character of democratic regimes. A true believer in the classical paradigm of democracy, the Athenian polis, Rousseau argued that a democracy lost its 'governing principle' once it reached a size that enabled the formation of conflicting interests. His point was that democracy, in the strict sense, only flourished in relatively small, homogeneous societies, whose members respected each other as equals and were thus willing to abide by a group consensus. Given the size and complexity of eighteenth-century Europe, Rousseau saw only two options for government: tyranny or democracy. Tyranny prevailed if nation-states retained their current dimensions. Democracy prevailed if nation-states were disestablished, and people divided up into small self-governing units. The self-styled epistemological anarchist Paul Feyerabend (1975, 1979) presents us with a Rousseauian alternative to the current state of the knowledge enterprise. But with due respect to both Rousseau and Feyerabend, I believe we need to explore the option that they reject.

Feyerabend is basically a scale-sensitive Popperian, one who believes that science in the spirit of 'conjectures and refutations' can only exist in social milieux where people can freely and publicly cross-examine each other's claims, and where claimants can receive prompt and reliable feedback, so that they can propose better claims in the future. Social psychologists would see what I am describing here as an instance of 'brainstorming', which typically works in small, intimate settings where people are emotionally prepared to undergo intense and immediate scrutiny. Philosophy meetings often have this character, although they are hardly occasions that inspire confidence in the idea that knowledge has 'progressed'. There is evidence that brainstorming also occurs in some research teams in the laboratory sciences, though probably more so in corporate settings than in university ones. In any case, with the exception of a few staged public events of dialectical warfare and a nostalgic view of graduate seminars, conjectures and, especially, refutations are confined to the backrooms of Big Science. This point is often obscured because the free exchange of information that characterizes scientific inquiry today is mistakenly equated with the promotion of the critical attitude that philosophers as diverse as Mill, Dewey and Popper have attributed to a fully functioning knowledge enterprise.

With the free exchange of information has come an information explosion, an important consequence of which is that scientists are more likely now to simply ignore the sort of work that in a more Popperian world would be subject to explicit refutation. As Bourdieu (1975) and Latour and Woolgar (1979) have observed, scientists work hard in the literature review sections of their articles to construct a framework within which their research will appear credible. And here, 'credibility' is measured by a scientist's ability to get other scientists interested, and ultimately engaged, in their own projects. If they succeed, they have avoided oblivion – at least for a little while.

Given the dimensions of Big Science, credibility needs to be earned at every turn, not because today's scientists are less competent than earlier ones, but because there are too many scientists of prima facie equal competence. When the scientific enterprise was smaller, it was reasonable to presume that whatever one wrote would be subject to critical scrutiny by the relevant disciplinary community, whose members would be on the lookout for new work in their area. It is no longer possible for scientists to take their audience for granted in this manner. To gain credibility, they must often embed their research in so many different technical contexts at once – theoretical, methodological, experimental – that it would be impractical for a prospective reader to approach their texts without already expecting to incorporate them in their own research. The style manuals of most science journals contribute to this effect by requiring that authors frame their discussions of 'theory', 'method' and 'data' as detachable modules, ostensibly in an effort to make their articles usable by a wide range of scientific readers, most of whom will be interested in some sections but not all (Bazerman 1988). Indeed, research articles are becoming increasingly stereotyped (cf. McCloskey 1987). Moreover, the high expense and low pay-off (in terms of publication possibilities) of redoing experiments and reanalysing data produced by other scientists are well-known. None of these developments bodes well for the future of the critical attitude in science – a point to which we shall return in Chapter 5.

Perhaps the closest that scientists nowadays come to refuting one another is by offering alternative theories for roughly the same range of phenomena. But, of course, providing another viewpoint falls far short of formal criticism, especially in terms of giving one a clear basis for changing one's behaviour. At best, it serves to signal dissent in the scientific ranks. Finally, even in the few cases in which a piece of research is formally criticized, the effectiveness of the criticism as negative feedback is often undermined by delays in publication and distribution. Given the ever-quickening pace of Big Science, even if we assume that a piece of criticism is unequivocal in its consequences for a line of research (a *big* if, given that the same evidence can support several competing theories), considerable bodies of work incorporating faulty research may be corrupted by the time the criticism comes out.

As epistemology's answer to Rousseau, Feyerabend too is enamoured of the polis, but this time as the model of critical inquiry. And, as critical inquiry gets shunted to the periphery of Big Science, he poses the following Rousseauian dilemma: either admit that the human condition has outgrown the possibility of critical inquiry or reclaim critical inquiry by scaling down Big Science. Again, tyranny or democracy. Like Rousseau, Feyerabend clearly opts for the latter, which he pursues in the spirit of showing that science as it exists today is primarily *not* a knowledge enterprise. Aside from the marginalization of criticism discussed above, the evidence for this side of Feyerabend's argument is easy to come by.

Put most generally, the production of both basic and applied research and the production of what the sociologist C. Wright Mills (1956) originally called 'the military-industrial complex' constitute increasingly larger portions of each other's activities. For example, until quite recently, the US Defense Department spent more of its money on research, and more money for research was coming from the Defense Department than from anywhere else in the government. At the very least, this symbiosis seriously altered the terms in which, and to whom, research could be held accountable (cf. Noble 1984). I do not deny that 'methodological soundness' might figure prominently in, say, military criteria for evaluating radar detection devices. But that only shows the extent to which the military regards philosophically familiar standards as instrumental to its ends. But are they right (cf. MacKenzie 1990: Ch. 7)? So much the better for science funding that the military can take cover under philosophical rubrics. But to what extent is research any longer evaluated as a product of *inquiry*? Let me offer three philosophically inspired reasons for thinking that the extent is rather small, and, indeed, were we seriously interested in evaluating research as a product of inquiry, we might need to return to Little Science. These reasons, though offered in the spirit of Feyerabend's radicalism, should be seen as motivated by 'scientific realism' – that is, a fairly traditional understanding of science as aiming to represent the structure of reality.

Pro Little Science I: theory does not entail method

Nothing in the formulation of a theory dictates the means by which it should be tested. Historians and sociologists of science have no trouble showing the conventions that have had to be instituted in order for certain theoretical practices to be related to particular data-gathering techniques and standards of evaluation (e.g. Galison 1987). Only institutional inertia and historical amnesia make these conventional connections seem, in some way, 'necessary'. In that case, why must advanced physical theories be tested on ever more expensive equipment? The only clear function that this trend serves is to reinforce a certain nexus of scientific, commercial and political interests. The interests of inquiry might, by contrast, be better served by considering alternative techniques for resolving theoretical disputes. Without endorsing any specific proposals here, one may find precedent for such considerations in the controversies surrounding the Critical Legal Studies movement in American jurisprudence, part of the agenda of which is to construct institutions of dispute resolution that destabilize, rather than reproduce, existing power structures (Unger 1986). If inquiry aims at The Truth, then different combinations of interests should stumble upon the same findings. However, if only a particular combination can make all the relevant findings, then one may reasonably ask – as has been recently asked of sociology itself (Turner and Turner 1990) – whether those findings might be an artefact of that scientific-economic-political complex.

Pro Little Science II: science need not benefit scientists

If a strong distinction can be drawn between the social processes of knowledge production and the objective products resulting from those processes, then the progress of science need not be impeded by diminishing the scale of its production, say, by eliminating scientific jobs and deterring people from entering scientific careers. After all, what may be best for science may turn out not to be so good for scientists. However, the realist should not fear that a decline in scientific employment would necessarily lead to a concentration of scientific activity in the hands of predictably élite individuals from élite institutions. What may be best for promoting intelligence in the individual may turn out not to be so good for promoting knowledge in the collective. In other words, it may be that knowledge production is optimized by maximizing the spread of competences, and perhaps even the spread of intelligence levels (Elgin 1988). The latter spread may be needed to counteract the tendency of quick-witted people to find holes in theories all too easily, and hence to reject them before they have been put to a proper empirical test, perhaps because the equipment needed for conducting the test has yet to be invented.

In this sense the natural sciences might have never progressed beyond their philosophical roots, had a surfeit of the super-intelligent been employed! Scientists regard the signature philosophical attitude – scepticism – not as a mark of sophistication but simply of impatience with the idea that a problem may require more for its solution than sheer thought. Indeed, by resisting the sceptic's impatience, scientists managed to cultivate the artisans and other masters of the experimental craft, which in turn has enabled science to cross class boundaries and enroll large segments of society in ways that philosophy's emphasis on sheer mental acuity restricted its appeal to the élites (Collins 1998: 332 ff.). Thus, the progress of science may be seen as a search for the optimal integration of what may be called the 'mental' and 'material' tendencies of the human condition, such that the former does not outstrip the latter.

Pro Little Science III: specialization might not signify progress

The plausibility of the realist position may actually be *increased* by admitting that the highly specialized, fragmentary character of knowledge in the world of Big Science constitutes an epistemic step *backward*. At least the realist would then be able to argue that their position is not parasitic on a self-vindicating Whig history of science that presumes, without argument, that today's science is the closest we have yet got to The Truth. General cultural history offers many precedents for this 'Silver Age' mentality. Typically, the period of decline is cast as one of bewildering complexity, by contrast with the unity and simplicity of the earlier 'Golden Age' (cf. Fuller and Gorman 1987).

For example, if we suppose that, at the limit of inquiry, scientific theories correspond to the structure of reality, then we might say that at a certain point in history – say, when physics became committed to searching for the ultimate constituents of matter in highly artificial laboratory settings – theoretical elaboration became more finely grained than the structure of reality itself. Scientists began to make distinctions in their language that did not make an empirical difference – that is, without the aid of the manufactured environment in the lab. If this is an apt story of the twentieth century, then there is a sense in which the dimensions of science exceeded the limits of 'natural' reality. Indeed, such was the subtext of Feyerabend's doctoral dissertation on Niels Bohr (Fuller 1988: Ch. 4).

Inadequate philosophical solutions to the problems of Big Science

Scaling down science to a size that makes it accountable to the community in which it is practised would clearly enable more people to be directly involved in the conduct of inquiry, but it would also continue to obscure the impact that even such a 'little' science has on those living outside the community. In that sense, unless special provisions are made, Little Science is no different from Big Science in holding scientists responsible only for consequences that affect those to whom they are directly accountable: that is, members of their own community. So, instead of continuing to explore Feyerabend's 'little scientism', let me focus on the negative side of his position, namely the assumption that science no longer exists. Or, to put the thesis more carefully, the markets in which scientists currently conduct their business have expanded to the point of rendering obsolete the treatment of certain artefacts and skills as knowledge-bearing. Thus, descriptions of scientific activity that make reference to epistemic entities will be unreliable predictors of that activity because the course of science has come to be determined by extra-scientific factors. If this side of Feyerabend's argument holds, then philosophers have yet again been fooled into thinking that the persistence of a certain kind of talk – in this case, epistemic talk – reflects the persistence of a certain underlying reality, namely the knowledge enterprise. But how would such a ruse have worked? Three tendencies in recent philosophical discussions about science provide some clues (on the specific philosophers implicated in this account, see Fuller 1996).

First, while epistemologists and philosophers of science now give some, usually rather abstract, attention to the social conditions of knowledge production, they still assess these conditions solely in terms of their specifically 'epistemic' consequences, rather than in terms of their more general impacts on society, which, of course, together constitute the social conditions for subsequent knowledge production. And so, while there is some talk about which social arrangements foster or retard knowledge growth, the full dimensions of Big Science – who and what ends up being enveloped in its sustained pursuit – remain obscured. This situation is largely an artefact of the subdivision between ethics and epistemology within professional philosophy in the Anglo-American world, which fosters the illusion that a clear distinction can be drawn between the morally and epistemically relevant consequences of a given course of action.

Second, philosophers employ a curious doublethink about the 'autonomy' of modern science, which leads them to assert that, say, physics has become more autonomous in its research trajectory precisely during the period that it has been most subject to government interference and direction. This tension is often managed by drawing a sharp distinction between what is 'internal' and 'external' to science, such that the latter category contains, say, funding, over which practising scientists have little direct control. Under duress, most philosophers would concede that funding decisions play a preponderant role in the direction that scientific research takes. Yet, they would continue to stress that these economic matters are not constitutive of science 'as such'.

Third, philosophers simply fail to take seriously the fact that scientists today spend an increasing amount of time on entrepreneurial, managerial and accounting tasks at the expense of 'research' in the traditional sense of doing experiments, consulting the literature, and the like (cf. Etzkowitz 1989). Moreover, this is not simply a matter of scientists being overworked, but more a matter of their coming to view the traditionally 'scientific' aspects of their work – especially reasoning with hypotheses and writing for peers – as routine, perhaps ultimately computerizable. The seat of 'real' creativity would seem to lie in the tactics one uses to sustain funding and earn credibility, especially given the growing number of competitors who are trying to do exactly the same thing. Any organizational sociologist would conclude from this that the character of scientific work has changed to the point that the scientist's primary function is now a sophisticated form of publicity-seeking and record-keeping that enables others, both scientists and non-scientists, to legitimate or delegitimate certain courses of action. In fact, not only are funding agencies fully aware of this shift in the scientist's work habits, they often actively encourage it (cf. Mukerji 1990).

If the classical search for knowledge has indeed come to an end, how did it happen, and, more importantly, what should we who believe in a critical epistemic attitude do about it? Historians interested in this question should look at the roots of two developments:

1 Fewer people have become eligible to dispute a given knowledge claim as the qualifications needed for entering the forum have increased. These qualifications include not only the training needed to read and write in the relevant journals, but also the more elusive knowledge needed for turning archival and technical resources to one's advantage.
2 At the same time, as the eligibility for disputing knowledge claims has come to be restricted, those claims have come to play a greater role in explaining and legitimating policies, actions and events – hence the increased government reliance on science to underwrite its activities (Mukerji 1990: Ch. 2).

Together, these two developments point to the long-term tendency of science to become a more acute instrument of social power as its sphere of accountability diminishes. The overarching implications of this political asymmetry are clear: science is producing proportionally fewer people (not necessarily the scientists themselves but those with *access* to science) with the capacity to exert proportionally greater impact on the lives of others. And here, 'impact' should be measured in terms of not simply the capacity for destruction and dislocation, but also the capacity for pauperization through the money that people involuntarily and unreflectively contribute to research in the form of taxes.

Once again, the philosopher may return by saying that these developments are not 'necessary' or 'essential' to science. But, as the checkered track record of naturalized epistemology suggests, the various norms that philosophers have proposed as integral to inquiry turn out to be remarkably hard to find in practice. Philosophers of a postmodernist sensibility, such as Richard Rorty (1988), conclude from this that science simply has no essence. They say that 'science' is a genre, a way of telling the story of western culture that uses terms like 'rationality', 'method' and 'truth' as elements of the plot structure. Without denying the importance of such a narrative in normalizing the transition between 'Little' and 'Big' Science, the postmodernist's complete disregard for essentialist talk makes them unable to distinguish two conceptions of the history of science that are crucial for my argument: namely, between (a) a loose collection of practices whose narrative relevance to one another – and that alone – makes them sciences and (b) a real process whereby one practice evolves or mutates into another practice that turns out to be better adapted to the new social environment. The directed and perhaps even irreversible character of this second sense of history – that the bigness of the world has forced science to outgrow traditional epistemic conceptions – encourages us to think of science as having acquired a new set of governing principles, a 'new essence', so to speak.

To cite only the most vivid case in point, the pursuit of high-energy physics has become so expensive that nation-states and large corporations are the only institutions in which capital is sufficiently concentrated to enable physicists to work in a relatively uninterrupted manner. Should these centres of capital ever become radically dispersed, physics would have a hard time continuing in its present form (cf. Kevles 1987, esp. preface). In short, science depends for its livelihood on the military-industrial complex, just as much as the latter depends on the former for its legitimation. A case of this sort is about as close as one ever gets to demonstrating that something is 'essential' for something else.

An inadequate educational solution: science literacy

Finally, I want to discourage one line of advice that philosophers in the liberal tradition have held to be sufficient to empower people in this era of Big Science – namely, 'education', especially when this term is taken to imply the elimination of epistemic privilege simply by distributing the crucial elements of the privileged class body of knowledge or set of reasoning skills to society at large: in a phrase, 'science literacy'. For all its nobility, this proposal mistakenly assumes that the locus of epistemic privilege lies in the sort of intellectual qualities that, say, scientists have but ordinary people lack, rather than in the sort of access to intellectually empowering tools that one group has but the other lacks. One of the more frustrating findings that naturalized epistemologists have had to face is that very little seems to distinguish the minds of scientists from those of non-scientists. The former are no less susceptible to bias and error than the latter, even with the 'right' training in formal logic, statistical methodology and experimental design (Fuller 1993a: Chs 3–4). However, scientists are organized in a way that enables the whole to greatly exceed the sum of the parts. This point has far-reaching consequences.

Science consists of distinctive networks of disciplinary languages, shared technologies and professional forums. However, these networks function – as a matter of consequence, if not of design – so as to produce a certain distribution of power in society. In particular, science is permeable by state agencies and corporations. They can make a strategic difference to the direction that the knowledge enterprise takes by adding or withholding support. This, in turn, serves to enhance the power of these institutions at the expense of other groups in society. By contrast, ordinary citizens, who are typically on the receiving end of a 'knowledge transfer', encounter science as a *fait accompli*, a 'black box' in Latour's (1987) sense, over which they exert control only in determining the 'applicability' of a particular scientific product to the place where they live. And even here, the degree of control can be overestimated, since often the products of science that would most benefit people in a given locale are not made available to them, while economic and political pressure may be placed on the very same people to accept other products of science that they would normally not have any use for. The fruits of cutting-edge medical research fall into the former category, while nuclear and chemical plants often seem to fall into the latter.

However, the relative power that government and business have over ordinary citizens consists less in the actual research sponsored and more in the concentration of the sponsorship. For, just as the scientist's access to intellectually empowering tools should not be confused with their having any special intellectual qualities, similarly, increased institutional control over the production and distribution of scientific research should not be taken to imply that the research itself heightens the technical capabilities of the controlling institutions (MacKenzie 1990: Ch. 8). On the contrary, technical capability may never be extensively tested, as appeals to 'corporate secrets' and 'national security' rhetorically pre-empt the usual scientific forms of scrutiny. As a result, even the CEOs (chief executive officers) and generals who deploy the rhetoric often have an unjustifiably optimistic sense of what the products of scientific research can do in 'real life' situations.

My rejection of the science literacy solution to Big Science can thus be summarized in two points:

1 it presumes a false sense of the intellectual differences separating 'scientific' from 'ordinary' people;
2 even if it presumed a correct sense of those differences, increasing the public's science literacy does not, by itself, open up any new opportunities for citizen participation in the conduct of science.

In fact, most theories of ideology would predict that programmes of science literacy that promise no new political outlets ultimately serve those who dominate the scientific enterprise by breaking down the cognitive barriers that prevent the citizenry from being completely comfortable with the 'scientific' way of thinking. After all, how does one measure the success of science literacy campaigns: perhaps high ratings for science-based television programmes, high sales for science popularizations? But why are science literacy initiatives not normally accompanied by greater enrolments in science courses or, more to the point, greater public involvement in science-based policy issues? In Part 3 I propose a set of strategies for dealing more effectively with the problems that science literacy campaigns inadequately address. But first we need to examine the institutional setting that has most exemplified the tensions associated with a scaled-up scientific enterprise. Thus, the university is the main focus of Part 2.

PART TWO

The university as a site for the governance of science

The university is the institution most closely aligned with knowledge production processes in the history of the West. Indeed, many of the West's signature epistemic contributions can be traced to the fortunes of this institution (Fuller 1997: Chs 5–6; Collins 1998: Ch. 9 ff.). In the political terms introduced in Part 1, the university has tried to steer a republican course between the Scylla of communitarianism and the Charybdis of liberalism, subject to changes in the scale and scope of academic enterprises. Chapter 3 surveys the history of this tension. Scylla appears in the guild-like character of the university taken to an extreme, as in the form of self-censorship that has passed for 'academic freedom' in German and American universities since 1870. Radical versions of this tendency are seen in contemporary debates over 'political correctness' and will be treated under the rubric of 'multiculturalism' in Chapter 4. Charybdis appears in the tendency of laboratory scientists in particular to treat the university as little more than a relatively efficient space for doing business, not as a concept constitutive of the scientists' own sense of identity. This attitude, which has now infected to varying degrees the practices of most disciplines, will be examined in Chapter 5 as part of the ongoing 'capitalization' of academic life.

3

The historical interdependence of the university and knowledge production

The elusive social value of the university: can't live with it, can't live without it

The historical durability of the university is so taken for granted that academic departments are often presumed to carry ontological import. For example, as the university's administration proliferates divisions and subdivisions, we are asked to imagine a 'functional differentiation' of the knowledge system that, in turn, reflects a reality whose complexity only becomes gradually known to us. Such imaginings should give us pause. Whenever a social function is identified with a unique institutional arrangement, our critical faculties have probably lapsed into a dogmatic slumber (Fuller 1993b: Ch. 2).

We do not normally assess, say, 'democracy' solely in terms of the strengths and weaknesses of the Athenian polis. We can easily imagine other political arrangements that might preserve, or simulate, the strengths of the polis while removing its weaknesses. Yet, one does not find the same spirit of institutional design in the arena of knowledge production. Rare is the scholar who does not presume that the products of inquiry fall under the jurisdiction of one or more modern university departments. Thus, when one wants to cast aspersions on the 'alternative' forms of knowledge defended by multiculturalists, usually the easiest route is to show how they would never pass an academic quality control test, such as the 'peer review' process of some recognized discipline. Today's multicultural challenge to the university is interesting precisely because it queries why the university cannot come up with a better test than sheer assimilation to the bureaucratic status quo – and whether that failure is symptomatic of deeper structural flaws in the constitution of the university.

The effects of identifying the work of the university with knowledge production *per se* are far reaching. It may even warp our ordinary understanding of the history of western culture. Only someone with an Orwellian sense of justice can truly appreciate the fact that the modern movements nowadays most closely associated with 'university culture' – the Renaissance, Reformation, Enlightenment and socialism – were all rooted, to varying degrees, in revolts against that very culture (Wuthnow 1989). Of course, they were all eventually co-opted by the university, which in turn made the movements its own, by channelling their dynamic energy into the university's processes of disciplinization. Humanistic scholarship is the residue of Renaissance humanism; theology as a 'free inquiry' unbeholden to the Church is a product of the Reformation; naturalistically inclined social sciences crystallized the Enlightenment legacy; and socialism of course has been the source of self-styled 'critical' movements in both the humanities and social sciences.

A somewhat more controversial claim, but probably not too far off the mark, is that the assimilation of the laboratory-based natural sciences into university culture in the second half of the last century was an attempt by prescient industrialists (the benefactors of the great universities built at that time) to absorb and resolve capitalism's intensified class divisions between verbally and manually oriented workers. As the liberal arts core of the university remained the preserve of aristocrats, advanced studies in the natural sciences, engineering and technology became an important avenue for the upward mobility of the working classes. In fact, over the course of this century, they have virtually eliminated all the other paths to self-advancement (Ringer 1979). Proponents of multiculturalism and feminism need to bear this history in mind when taking the measure of the overall effects that academic institutionalization has had on their movements.

The university's historic co-opting of anti-academic elements is complemented by the rather streamlined history that is usually told of the university as the canonical site for knowledge production in society. Instead of attending to the conflicts among the university's research, teaching and service functions, historians of science tend to treat the university exclusively as a place for promoting discipline-based research. Thus, universities appear as supportive environments for disciplinary specialization, rather than such specialization itself appearing as an artefact of university bureaucratization. Consequently, university teaching tends to arise as an object of historical study only in terms of its contribution to a distinctive style of research that comes to be recognized in the discipline as a whole. In sum, the history of science remains largely a history of scientific research, with teaching and service entering only as promoters or inhibitors of various research programmes. This may be history from the standpoint of the professional association, but not from that of the university, strictly speaking. One would never guess, for example, that the university's impact on the larger society may be more pronounced on the non-specialists who are forced to take specialist courses as part of their general education than on the specialists themselves.

Even among social historians of higher education, universities appear to enjoy a schizoid existence. In discussing the rise of the American university system, which has perhaps striven the most to be most things to most people, Laurence Veysey (1965) and Joseph Ben-David (1992: 125–254) represent two characteristically polar positions. On the one hand, a historian like Veysey is prone to portray the university as an embarrassingly makeshift and contentious entity that gives the lie to any pretences that academics might have about becoming philosopher-kings. On the other hand, a sociologist like Ben-David finds the university to be the most splendid product of the invisible hand in modern society (*especially* in the USA), the collective result of free academics adapting to their changing social and cognitive environments.

Both extremes have found a place in the recent debates about the future of the American university that have centred on 'political correctness' and 'multiculturalism'. The difference between Veysey and Ben-David does not turn out to be as great as it may first appear. The views range between, say, Gerald Graff (1992), an English professor who has written extensively on the politics surrounding the institutionalization of his field in America, and Edward Shils (1992a), the sociologist who has perhaps most endeavoured to update the 'mandarin' image of the academic as cultural protector for late twentieth-century audiences. For his part, Graff wants to get 'beyond the culture wars' by ascribing positive significance to Veysey's contentious view of the university, even to the point of reproducing some of the conflict in day-to-day classroom activities. Meanwhile, Shils exhorts university administrators to have the courage to resist multiculturalist attempts to shatter the Ben-Davidian image. Despite their differences in what they take to be the nature of the university, Graff and Shils only want change to particular practices at particular universities. This underlying satisfaction with the institution of the university is especially curious in the case of a progressive like Graff, who founded Teachers for a Democratic Culture, the leading organization for promoting critical multiculturalism in American universities.

The picture of the university as an intellectual pressure-cooker, a house designed always to be divided against itself, is certainly a familiar and attractive one to leftists, myself included. But this image is rarely accompanied by an account of how universities might trigger some larger societal change. This lack of political imagination among progressive academics casts the metaphor of the pressure-cooker in a new light, one that calls to mind the idea of the university as a safety-valve that lets off the excess steam of intellectuals who might otherwise stir up the masses, who might then disrupt the relentless drive toward capital accumulation (Schumpeter 1950: 145–55).

In what sense might the university's grip on knowledge production be slipping?

So far we have seen accounts of the university as functionally adapted to its social environment, in a way that only Voltaire's Dr Pangloss could truly appreciate: 'No matter how badly you think the university operates, any other institutional arrangement would be worse – and, in fact, if you look at the university from a long enough perspective, it does not look so bad, after all!' While leftists would ridicule such a position were it taken of any other contemporary institution, they seem to suspend their scruples when it comes to the one they call home. As a result, they often find themselves in the intellectually and politically awkward position of defending the 'status quo' against what, on the face of it, would seem to be neo-liberal and neo-conservative social engineers, who themselves cannot decide whether the confusion and infighting that characterizes today's universities are the result of self-important rent-seekers feeling a financial pinch or signs of a natural resource in danger of extinction.

For example, teaching and research are presumed to be two activities that naturally go hand in hand, and both ideally within the university. But might these activities be better performed separately and/or under some other institutional arrangements, and might not the old arrangements have outlived their usefulness? These days a common reply is that universities unify research and teaching under one roof by supporting scholarly projects that seem to be the best bets to add value to the credentials that the university will be dispensing in the future, once these projects come to fruition and trickle down into the educational process – in short, today's research in the service of tomorrow's teaching (cf. Stinchcombe 1990: 312–40). The only problem with this solution is that it is basically making the most of what has become a bad situation, since it openly admits that research and teaching are out of step with one another. When Wilhelm von Humboldt founded the modern university on the unity of teaching and research, he imagined that the two occurred in the very same act. We still have something of this Humboldtian ideal in a humanistic subject like philosophy, in which students are examined on questions that continue to exercise their teachers, and what the teacher does in the classroom is a good indicator of what he or she does outside of it, in a 'research setting'.

To focus my concern, consider a very explicit statement of that Panglossian image of the university that we all hate to love. Nearly two decades ago, the then president of Harvard University, Derek Bok, considered what it would be like if the university were disestablished and its various functions were distributed to independent agencies, such as liberal arts colleges for general education, specialized institutes for advanced research and consulting, and independently licensed professional schools for job certification:

> While the various functions of the university could be reorganized and redistributed in this fashion, something important would be lost. Neither colleges, nor consulting organizations, nor professional training schools can satisfy society's need for new knowledge and discovery. True, one could look to some sort of research institute to perform this function. But even this alternative would not wholly replace what

universities can supply. It is the special function of the university to combine education with research, and knowledgeable observers believe that this combination has distinct advantages both for teaching and for science and scholarship . . . Without the marriage of teaching and research that universities uniquely provide, the conduct of scholarly inquiry and scientific investigation, as well as the progress of graduate training, would be unlikely to continue at the level of quality achieved over the past two generations. In a society heavily dependent on advanced education and highly specialized knowledge, such a decline could be seriously detrimental to the public welfare.

(Bok 1982: 19–20)

Anyone acquainted with the changes of fortune of higher education in the twentieth century should be sceptical about Bok's dire counterfactual prognosis concerning the threat to public welfare that would follow in the wake of the university's demise. True, the chains of legitimation would be forged differently: certain people, texts and courses of study that are now required in the quest for credentials would no longer be standing in the way; perhaps others would instead, and conceivably a wider variety of ways of getting around them. Stories like this have been told by those who would like to 'open up' the university's activities to the market-place.

Interestingly, Bok's thoughts about the detrimental consequences of a devolved university were presented in the course of defending academic freedom – a 'guild right' that academics have by virtue of their place of work, the university, which focuses on the production of knowledge itself and not on the ends to which that knowledge may be put (a point elaborated in this chapter). If the university ceased to exist, say, by its functions being divested in the manner described by Bok, there would be no need for such freedom: the conduct of intellectual labour would simply be dictated by standards negotiated between its producers and consumers, as in any other market-driven activity. Conceivably, then, an academic subject such as 'biology' would lose its integrity as a body of knowledge. For example, parents concerned that their children receive a morally appropriate education might insist that the nature of life be taught so as to make the Book of Genesis appear intellectually respectable as evolutionary theory, while corporate clients interested in resilient organisms on which to test their products would ensure that genetic engineering became a pure technology. Similar scenarios can be conjured up for the other academic disciplines. (Hague 1991 subsequently canonized the early stages of this process as the emergence of 'knowledge businesses'.)

At this point we arrive at a delicate chicken-and-egg question about the relationship between the university and the autonomous pursuit of knowledge: was the university created in order to provide a secure place for free inquiry, as Bok would seem to suggest, or is 'free inquiry' itself simply the name given to whatever happens to take place in an institution enjoying the legal status of a university? If it is the latter, then 'knowledge' isn't a special sort of thing that requires the free space of the university. Rather, 'knowledge' is a reification and rationalization of the social relations that have endured in those spaces we have called 'universities' over the centuries. To sharpen the point, we might say that once the university has been fully divested of its functions, the pursuit of free inquiry disappears along with it, as such a pursuit has no clear meaning outside the institutional arrangement of the university. We would then have reached the literal end of knowledge. Pertinent to this point are my earlier remarks about 'biology' losing any clear sense of identity once it is left entirely to the interests of divergent clientele. Such a state of affairs would be characteristic of the 'post-epistemic condition' (Fuller 1993a: 281–90). As it happens, I do, indeed, believe that something that could be called the pursuit of knowledge '*per se*' or 'for its own sake' stands or falls with the fate of the university.

Academia through the ages: from cloistered philosophers to besieged administrators

Historically speaking, the emergence of knowledge as an autonomous pursuit coincides with philosophers establishing fixed places of business on the edge of Athens that required students to live on the grounds of the establishment for a period of time. The sociologist Alvin Gouldner (1965) was struck by this transition from the free-floating, market-style engagements of Socrates and his Sophistic foes to the cloistered, cult-like atmosphere that surrounded the schools of Plato and the later Greek philosophers. Gouldner offered a social psychiatric diagnosis of the transition. The previous 100 years – what we now regard as the Golden Age of Greece – had been marked by a cycle of wars, culminating in a humiliating defeat for Athens at the hands of Sparta in the Peloponnesian Wars. The Greek philosophers came to believe that this ill-fated volatility was intimately tied to an all too free and easy deployment of reason in the public sphere – the lust for contests and calculated risk-taking which most foreigners took to be emblematic of Athenian culture.

In particular, Gouldner observed that the terms used to characterize the dialectical play of the courtroom were precisely the ones used to describe military combat. Both were treated as 'rational' activities in exactly the same sense, only using different means. Both were even protected by the same god, Apollo, a point often forgotten in today's uses of the word 'Apollonian'. Perhaps the most interesting point of convergence was that one's rationality was displayed more in the artfulness of the arguments or tactics one mobilized than in their actual outcomes. In fact, it would seem that visitors to Athens found the natives peculiar in their eagerness to debunk the exploits of a victorious general if he lacked a certain 'cunning' in his *modus operandi*.

Academic philosophy, starting with Plato, has largely been a systematic rejection of these, the most distinctive features of the Athenian character.

While 'self-loathing' may put the point too strongly, I think it is fair to say that the academic philosophers did as much as they could to distance themselves from their polis identity. For example, it is now thought that Plato himself invented the word 'rhetoric' as a term of disdain for those philosophers who continued the Athenian tradition of publicly displaying the dialectic (Schiappa 1992). Moreover, the vehicle of reasoning that most easily excited passions and actions – speech – was gradually demoted and disciplined as students of philosophy were taught to write down their arguments in private before uttering them in public, and to judge what they spoke against what they had written.

Along with the cloistering of reason came a new sense of the spacing and timing of knowledge, one which identified autonomous inquiry with speech that was not tied down to a particular place and time. Places were no longer visible reminders of what to say next to an audience (*topoi*), but rather rooms that could be filled by a variety of prepared lectures (*chora*). By the time of the medieval university, these lectures were commonly said to be 'contained' in the rooms, a dead metaphor that remains preserved today in the idea of the 'content' of a speech (Ong 1958). As for the timing of speech, what the Greeks called *kairos* evolved – or, I should say, devolved – from something that a speaker did to make his words bear on the concerns of his audience so as to prompt timely action, to a matter of decorous conduct that was dictated by events that took place prior to the speech, whose only purpose lay in recounting those events (Kinneavy 1986).

However, disembodying knowledgeable speech was one thing; ensuring that such speech was continued in perpetuity was something else entirely. It is here that the university as we know it starts to emerge. Academies in the Greek, Roman and Muslim worlds had depended on private endowments and state protection, either of which could change drastically with the slightest shift in the balance of power. To stave off this volatility, urban scholars in the twelfth century adopted a strategy that seemed to work for craftsmen, who persuaded overextended feudal authorities that they were capable of managing their own affairs. These affairs did not directly compete with affairs of state but centred on the application, transmission and refinement of a manual art that was deemed to have value above and beyond the livelihoods of the people who happened to practise it at a given time. Thus, the crafts received corporate charters that enabled them to control membership and draft by-laws in perpetuity. Indeed, the original referent for *universitas*, the Latin word from which 'university' derives, was a craft guild.

The scholars had a somewhat tougher case to make for their corporate status than the craftsmen did. You might think that it had something to do with the kind of labour in which the scholars were engaged. But that would be to import our own over-sharp distinction between intellectual and manual labour, one that did not apply in the twelfth century. In fact, the scholars were known to the general – which is to say, non-literate – public for their invention and deployment of various literary technologies, including pens and books, as well as sophisticated systems of dividing up, cross-referencing and indexing written matter. Indeed, the problem with granting scholars a corporate status akin to craftsmen was that the scholars spent much of their time not in reading and writing books but in deploying their technical skills to 'keep the books' (i.e. the financial records) of local secular and ecclesiastical authorities. In other words, scholars did not appear to be as singularly devoted to a calling as craftsmen. A lot of their work seemed purely instrumental. To grant a corporate charter to the scholars would thus be already to commit to the idea of a 'multiversity' that would permit, if not encourage, scholars to roam off campus periodically to perform 'consulting services' (Kerr 1963).

Of course, the scholars managed to allay enough of the suspicions about the impurity of their mission to receive the corporate charters that established the first universities. Yet, it was not without a cost. In order to advertise the purity of their vocation, the scholars attempted to cast themselves as much as possible in the mould of classical Athens, especially its spirit of dialectical engagement and its disdain for manual labour of any kind, including writing itself (Le Goff 1993: 104–5). Of course the 'Scholastics' (as they became known) continued inventing and deploying ever more sophisticated literary technologies, both on and off campus. However, they refused to take official notice of that fact in how they accounted for their activities – and we live with the consequences of that refusal.

In the short term, the Scholastics alienated themselves from fellow manual labourers who dwelled in the cities, which, in turn, led to some early instances of 'town-gown' hostilities. But in the long term the quest for the sort of autonomy promised by a university charter forced the Scholastics and their successors to repress the role that the material conditions of their labour played in their thought (Sohn-Rethel 1978: 108). A singularly striking example of this repression operating today occurs whenever a scientist, say, describes the totality of their work in terms of the vanishingly few hours per week they actually spend doing research in the lab or intellectually engaged with colleagues. This incoherence runs still deeper, and I think helps to explain some chronic problems of academic self-accounting, the significance of which we are all too inclined to dismiss as the ugly addition of philistine bureaucrats and politicians. In particular, why do we academics have such a hard time demonstrating that we are worth what we are paid, or even that we deserve to be paid at all, despite the fact that when judged by the standards of industrial labour, academics are engaged in a potentially endless work schedule?

The core of my answer turns on what I call the 'military-industrial metaphor' in scholarly conceptions of knowledge. This metaphor fuses two distinct ways of thinking about knowledge that do not sit well together. Yet, since the establishment of the university, we have come to use them interchangeably and unreflectively in explaining what academics do.

The military side of the metaphor represents knowledge as inquiry, which is to say a goal-oriented activity whose target is truth, a target which inquirers approximate to varying degrees. Of course, since the target is typically hidden from view, 'behind the appearances', no one ever scores a direct hit. Yet, as we saw in the case of classical Athens, inquirers can be judged by the artfulness of their strategies and tactics. Education, from this angle, is target practice, an activity that calls to mind the spirit of gamesmanship with which examinations are often taken. In its military guise, knowledge is leisured, sporting and crafty, revealing as little effort as possible.

By contrast, the industrial side of the metaphor refers to knowledge as a laborious process that displays much handiwork and issues in products of various sorts, usually with the understanding that more is always better than less. Indeed, there is no end in sight whatsoever to knowledge production, only an image of indefinite productivity. In the industrial model, education is a form of craft apprenticeship, whereby one acquires the tools and skills needed to produce more knowledge products – not to mention more knowledge producers. Today we experience the tension of the military-industrial metaphor at several different levels of university life: between humane learning and scientific research; between liberal arts education and professional training. The twelfth-century scholastics first experienced this tension as they sought to recover an essentially aristocratic rhetoric of inquiry to legitimate what had become a highly technical form of manual labour.

What exactly were the changes that the manual art of writing wrought on the scholarly consciousness? I do not want to recount here the familiar speculations of Marshall McLuhan and Walter Ong on the transformative powers of literacy. Rather, I want to focus on what the new technologies for dividing up, cross-referencing and indexing texts did to education and research, causing them to be linked indissolubly in the academic mind. Historians of accounting say that this was the innovation that Peter Abelard called *inquisitio*: the inquisition machine (Hoskin and Macve 1986). This consisted of a set of techniques, all second nature to us now, but marshalled together for the first time in the service of academic labour. These techniques broke texts down into components that could be compared and combined in any number of ways: books were divided into chapters, chapters into sections, sections into sentences and sentences into words. Thus was provided the technological 'push' for converting a scholarly community into a fully-fledged research and education factory. Opportunities for commentaries could be readily generated by comparing one part of a book with another, and then accounting for the difference in one's own writings. Of course, one could ask a student to account for the difference themselves, or, for that matter, to account for the difference between a part of a canonical book and a part of their own composition.

There are simple and complex ways of 'programming' the inquisition machine to resolve the tensions latent in the military-industrial metaphor. The simple ways are fairly benign and familiar. For example, education can be seen in industrial terms and research in military ones. In that case, the university is a place that produces students who are instructed on how to seek the truth. Certainly, this is how the scholastics would talk when they were trying to don the mantle of the ancients. However, every now and then, the scholastics turned the metaphor around and sounded considerably more modern in their orientation toward their work – if only by drawing attention to the fact that work was being done! In this modern mode, research is seen in industrial terms – the production of texts – and education in military terms – the examination of students.

The more complex resolutions of the military-industrial metaphor don't really become evident for several centuries after the founding of the first universities. What makes these resolutions 'complex' is that the military and industrial sides of the metaphor are no longer restricted to particular functions, but have been allowed to interpenetrate one another in both teaching and research. I will only touch on how this works in the case of teaching. Basically, the status of the examination shifts from being the criterion used for evaluating instructions to its being the very method of instruction. Consequently, students can be mass-produced by simply 'teaching to' the examination, in which case the quality of instruction is evaluated in terms of the number of students passed.

On the research side, we witness a couple of metaphoric resolutions. First, while texts are produced indefinitely, none is designed to be preserved indefinitely. In other words, each text is targeted for eventual replacement at the moment of its production. Planned obsolescence enters the knowledge system, and the result is the inquistion to which we have grown accustomed in the natural sciences. The second metaphoric resolution, more familiar to humanists of a deconstructive bent, enables new textual productions by undoing prior attempts at accounting for the differences between texts. In both cases, the inquisition machine is primarily in the job of making work for successive generations of academics. (Those who doubt this claim should ask why there have been so few cases, if any, of a research programme whose practitioners decided to call it quits because all of their programme's problems had been solved. In Chapter 8, we shall speak of 'cognitive euthanasia' in this context.)

The underlying strategy here is the one that was used on Tantalus, the Greek mythological source of the word 'tantalize': to render increased effort compatible with a receding target. Cursed with an unquenchable thirst, whenever Tantalus moved toward a juicy fruit, the wind blew the fruit out of his reach, causing him to redouble his efforts, only to have the fruit elude him yet again. His torture thus consisted of repeated frustration just at the moment of consummation.

The Reformation and the Enlightenment as the original anti-university movements

So far we have made it seem as though the history of the university can be told as following from the logic of the military-industrial metaphor. Yet it is only during the eighteenth century Enlightenment, a movement in active competition with the universities, that the logic becomes self-conscious. However, in the interim, another anti-academic movement intervened which first gave voice to the kinds of concerns that would later characterize multicultural critiques of the university. This was the sixteenth-century Protestant Reformation. Although the Protestant reformers and the Enlightenment *philosophes* located their opposition to the university quite differently, nevertheless they shared a common interest in recovering what they perceived to be a lost cultural heritage. In the case of the Reformation, the concern was to recover the image of 'Jerusalem', whereas in the Enlightenment, it was to recover the image of 'Athens'. Both images were pitted against that of 'Rome', which had come to stand for a variety of transgressions and suppressions, as will be discussed below.

The Reformation

The Protestant reform movements can be understood as a backlash against the false inclusiveness behind the idea of the one universal ('catholic' in Greek) Church. In this context, it is important to recall that the university-based scholastics operated with a unified approach to teaching and research that called for the continual reintegration of the disparate Graeco-Roman and Judaeo-Christian traditions into a higher, synthetic form of knowledge that would provide an intelligible basis for thinking and acting in the contemporary world.

Although there were competing syntheses, they all shared an interest in legitimizing the current shape of Christendom, which typically meant revealing the weak, or 'inchoate' character of political cultures that did not resemble the Church's dominion. Most notably aberrant was the Old Testament idea that the Jews were a people chosen by God for special treatment. The scholastics routinely dismissed the sectarian and seemingly genetic quality of the Chosen People concept as a 'primitive' or 'tribal' impulse that had been overcome by the more refined and ecumenical sensibilities voiced in the New Testament and in Stoicism, which, in turn, enabled the Romans to build the largest transcultural empire in history, whose dominion had been passed on to the Catholic Church.

From the standpoint of the Protestant reformers, the Scholastic narrative only served to occlude corruption and injustices that were tolerated, if not actively promoted, by the Roman Catholic Church. The Protestant strategy was to recover 'the stolen legacy' of Christianity, which was associated with the suppressed Hebraic tradition. The tactics subsumed under this strategy have served as the paradigm for later 'multiculturalist' efforts to retrieve the lost voices of Africans, Asians, the poor, women and homosexuals – those who stand for 'the other' *vis-à-vis* white wealthy male heterosexual European culture. The tactics included the following three items:

1 *A reversal of values*. Whereas the Scholastics regarded the Jews as primitive and tribal, the Protestants portrayed them as deep and pure. Moreover,

the Protestants recast the sophistication of classical culture so admired by the Scholastics as signs of pagan superficiality and lack of commitment.

2 *A reorientation toward language.* Whereas the Scholastics saw themselves as translating classical concerns into contemporary terms, and sometimes even improving upon them, the Protestants held that Scholastic sophistication strategically obscured the essential purity and simplicity of the original Judaeo-Christian message. Consequently, the Protestants practised a 'hermeneutics of suspicion' on authoritative Church accounts of knowledge and morals.

3 *An appeal to secular authority.* Whereas the Scholastics continued to justify the subordination of secular to ecclesiastical authority, ambitious secular rulers exploited Protestant doubts about the legitimacy of Church authority for their own purposes.

The Enlightenment

Two centuries later, the Enlightenment *philosophes* launched a second attack on the attitudes toward knowledge promoted by the universities. Certainly much more than the Protestant reformers could have imagined (or probably wished), knowledge production had become technologically mediated. It had been hard enough for the Scholastics to admit that their own professional identity was tied to a mastery of pen and ink, but over the next 500 years, the university had reduced the pursuit of knowledge to a set of social relations surrounding the production and distribution of texts, especially books. Knowledgeable communications underwent a profound transformation (Tompkins 1980). Writings were no longer judged as surrogate speech events by their ability to move a target audience to action. Rather, the written text had become a commodity – something produced either on demand (as in the case of student examinations) or in the hope of acquiring a demand (as in the case of original scholarly works).

It is worth recalling that when authors started clamouring for a larger share of publishers' profits in the eighteenth century, they pointed to the uniqueness and difficulty of their labours, but not to any proven ability to move particular audiences in particular ways. And so began the modern legal doctrines of copyright. A big part of the story behind the mystification of copyright into 'genius' in the early nineteenth century can be told in terms of the author losing *all* hope of identifying an audience that could be moved in desirable, or even predictable, ways. The reader appreciative of genius was thus cast as a rare and cultivated breed that an author might not find in his or her lifetime. For their part, ordinary readers understood their purchase of a book as a licence to make virtually any use of the text that they saw fit.

However, if the universities could not control these developments, they might attempt to shape their reception. Thus, eighteenth-century pedagogy was distinguished by its preoccupation with *criticism*, which could range from the cultivation of refined sensibilities to outright censorship. Unfortunately, the standards of taste promoted under the rubric of criticism varied widely across universities. This apparent lack of value consensus fostered in the Enlightenment *philosophes* the image of the university as an institution that had lost its focus, now that knowledge production had become so decentralized and (relatively speaking) democratized. The tyranny of Rome was quickly yielding to the proliferation of Athens.

Much of the Enlightenment critique of the universities suggested that 'teaching' was little more than a mechanism of conformity that prepared students to resist whatever ideas were taken to be the latest threat to the reigning orthodoxy. This image of the university as a reactionary force was sufficiently compelling to enlist the support of a secular ruler, Napoleon Bonaparte, who proposed to replace the universities with two sets of institutions, one devoted exclusively to teaching and the other to research. Of course, Napoleon's own interest was not in allowing the free flow of knowledge, but in conquering by division an institution whose traditionally conservative role could impede acceptance of his radical political reforms. The result was that, in the nineteenth century, French teaching institutions became high-grade vocational schools dictated by state need and market demand (*les polytechniques*), while research institutions became high-grade professional associations which subjected every new knowledge claim to an elaborate and often highly politicized voting ritual.

If Napoleon was correct in supposing that teaching and research were best pursued in independent institutional settings, then that would seem to undermine the Greek ideal of knowledge as something that emerges only through dialectical encounters with one's students. Indeed, the viability of the Napoleonic plan would even cast doubt on the basic idea of a 'cognitive content' common to the teaching and research enterprises. This idea, ultimately traceable to Aristotle, implies that while knowledge is gained from the nature *of* things, there is something common and hence 'communicable' that is learned *from* things (in research) which can then be transmitted to students (in teaching). Those of us who work in universities routinely take this idea for granted, and it informs most philosophical theories of knowledge. Yet Napoleon had issued a profound and practical challenge to this assumption, one that anticipated the 'end of knowledge' thesis elaborated at the start of this chapter. In the next chapter, we shall look at the last heroic effort to preserve the integrity of the university – the one to which all contemporary defences of the institution ultimately refer. Not surprisingly, it was written in direct response to Napoleon's challenge. Yet this response has itself been increasingly challenged by the cluster of movements associated with 'multiculturalism'.

4

Multiculturalism's challenge to academic integrity – or a tale of two churches

The modern salvaging of the university: the pre-history of multiculturalism

All modern defences of the institutional integrity of the university are trace-able to Wilhelm von Humboldt's 'On the spirit and organizational frame-work of intellectual institutions in Berlin' (Humboldt 1970 [1810]). This 1810 memorandum by the first rector of the newly-founded University of Berlin was a sustained plea for Prussia not to go the route of Napoleonic France. In making his plea, Humboldt drew on the only major Enlighten-ment figure, Immanuel Kant, who did not go out of his way to portray the university as the text-mongering bastion of tradition and superstition. Indeed, Kant spent his entire career in the university. Thus, subsequent generations have come to think of the university as the natural place for Enlightenment, even though most of the Enlightenment *philosophes* would have favoured Napoleon's 'end of knowledge' vision as the more realistic (Collins 1998: 647–9).

Humboldt's Kantian strategy was to revert to a fairly pure version of the Greek dialectical model of inquiry, albeit one where the dialectic is con-fined to the walls of the academy and not spilling into the public square. Plato and Aristotle would have recognized Humboldt's assimilation of all inquiry to philosophizing on subjects at greater or lesser degrees of gener-ality. Any principled distinction between education and research was erased as students entered the university as peripheral participants in ongoing debates, only to gain full status as researchers as their participation in, and ultimately their guidance of, the collective discussion increased. This rather idyllic picture of the university tried to get around the thorny problem of identifying the exact object common to research and teaching by pointing to a unity of *practice* in these two signature academic functions. However, the success of Humboldt's strategy must be judged in terms of the exigencies of his situation, two of which are of note here.

First, the Kantian injunction 'Dare to know' (*aude sapere*), so eagerly embraced by Humboldt, politically had more bark than bite. This point can be seen more clearly by considering the Enlightenment motto 'The truth shall set you free'. This motto never provided a political vision that threatened existing regimes because the sense of freedom entailed by 'Enlightenment' was purely negative – a freedom from prejudices of one sort or another. But no proponent of Enlightenment ever seriously demonstrated that the consistently critical inquirer could simply 'back into' the good society in the process of eliminating all the bad ones. And so, as long as criticism and critical frames of mind were all that the university was promoting within its walls, there was little fear that an alternative politics would be forthcoming. If such a politics were put forth, its failure to have been rigorously derived from the canons of critical inquiry would be duly noted by fellow inquirers, thereby pre-empting any need on the part of the government to censor or discredit the politicized professor. (Those who find this judgement too cynical should have a look at the various complaints that Max Weber lodged throughout his career against colleagues who 'abused' their academic freedom.)

The second exigency of Humboldt's situation is the one that has been most recently emphasized by historians of Eurocentrism (e.g. Lambropoulos 1993). Promoting the military side of the military-industrial metaphor – the dialectic – suited the traditional Prussian self-image, which had acquired a special relevance in the struggle against Napoleon. Whereas Napoleon drew inspiration from portraying France as an analogical extension of the Roman Empire, Prussia turned to Greece for its model of a purer, more original European spirit. This is, of course, the spirit of Aryanism that played such a large role in the consolidation of the German national identity in the late nineteenth century and early twentieth century, and whose implications for scholarship were recently subjected to systematic critique in Martin Bernal's (1987) *Black Athena*, the controversial character of which will be discussed below.

Despite these local tactical successes, the big long-term problem with Humboldt's strategy was that it only continued to exacerbate the scholastic repression of the industrial, productive side of inquiry, just as that side of the military-industrial metaphor was about to hit its stride in the nineteenth century. The overall result was the complex resolutions of the military-industrial metaphor that I mentioned in the previous chapter, as well as the incommensurable knowledge products and attitudes toward inquiry that can be found in the university today. Perhaps the most striking of these resolutions is the reversal of the relationship between teaching and research. The medieval institution of the *lecture* made research an extension of teaching, in the form of commentaries on the Bible, Aristotle, the Justinian Code and Galen's medical works. In contrast, the post-Humboldtian innovation of the *seminar* turned teaching to an apprenticeship in research, whereby students did not simply copy and rehearse the master's words, but instead attempted to apply his method to new contexts, as in recently unearthed archival materials. This has had interesting long-term consequences, especially for our own era, in which academics are forced to minister to increasing numbers of students per classroom session. Publishers continue to press the medieval imperative of writing teachable texts, whereas academic administrators encourage the subordination of teaching to marketable research.

The mention of academic administrators brings to mind that over the past two centuries they have evolved to shield academics from routinely having to confront the disparity between the ideology and reality of their practices. Specifically, administrators are charged with explaining, say, why a PhD is needed for teaching at the university, why publications are required for retaining one's teaching post, and why faculty are really doing the job that parents and politicians are entrusting them to do – not to mention why less grantworthy departments within the university should be partially subsidized from overheads garnered by the more grantworthy departments.

The class of people whose job it is to explain these things, and much else, is the university's administration. Recounting the developments in academic life that have taken Humboldt's model of the university in unanticipated directions (of which he probably would not have approved), Edward Shils (1992b) has focused on the proportional rise in the number of administrators to the number of faculty. For Shils, the emergence of a permanent administrative apparatus in the university betrays a lack of nerve on the part of faculty to participate fully in their own self-governance. They have simply allowed 'teaching' to sink into the remedial and vocational, while 'research' floats into the specialized and esoteric. Not even a Harvard president's best impersonation of Dr Pangloss is going to work much longer to paste over all the discrepant forms of accountability demanded of those employed in today's universities. Perhaps Napoleon merely anticipated the inevitable.

Perhaps the most historically sensitive way of framing this debate is as being over the exact attitude that the university should adopt toward the society in which it is located. Employed by the state (or, in the case of private universities, a board of trustees), professors do not qualify as Karl Mannheim's (1940) 'free-floating intelligentsia'. Consequently, arguments for the university's normative position must appeal to the institution's alleged social function. Three attitudes have emerged:

1 The university is a neutral receptacle that simply represents the divisions of thought and labour that already exist in society at large. As Max Weber and other German defenders of academic freedom realized at the turn of the century, this position permits considerable academic self-governance, while at the same time enabling the state to use the university as a vehicle for training the next generation of leaders and providing them with appropriate credentials.

2 The university is designed to complement or counteract certain biases and injustices that prevent society from living up to its own normative aspirations. So-called affirmative action legislation that enables women and minorities freer access to university posts is the most publicly visible consequence of this attitude, which generally speaking promotes a 'critical' style of scholarship that is represented as such in the classroom.
3 The university is entrusted with the job of resolving, at least at the level of theory, society's contradictions. This is the liberal arts philosophy of education that informed Humboldt's renovation of the university, which is still present among many humanists who see the role of higher education as 'completing' the human being. Defenders of this viewpoint typically bemoan the Napoleonic tendencies toward both vocational teaching and professional research.

In the next section, we shall consider the division within the multiculturalist ranks in American higher education. It pertains mainly to how (2) in the above list should be interpreted. In Karl Mannheim's terms, is the university's dialectical position 'functional' or 'substantive'? A functionally dialectical position would call for professors to be critical of any bias or injustice, regardless of the groups involved. Thus, professors would be more than simply the intellectual wing of, say, the feminist movement. In fact, if feminists were to engage in the same biases or injustices that have been visited upon them in the past, then professors would be compelled to turn their critical gaze to the feminists. In contrast, a substantively dialectical posture recognizes that oppression runs sufficiently deep in society that in order to mount a powerful opposition professors must become politicized, and hence ideologically committed to certain progressive movements. We shall find, in the next section's discussion of multiculturalism, that functional interpretation corresponds to a 'High Church', research-orientation, while the substantive interpretation corresponds to a 'Low Church', teaching-orientation.

Multiculturalism's shattering of the university's Enlightenment legacy

Because hostility to all forms of multiculturalism remains quite strong, especially from critics outside the academy, one has to look closely to find the internal disagreements. As suggested above, the main axis of opposition is between High Church and Low Church multiculturalists. If one follows the rhetoric of the two camps, there is, respectively, talk of 'hybrid politics' and talk of 'identity politics'. In feminist scholarship, it is the talk of Donna Haraway, a Yale-trained professor in the history of consciousness programme at the University of California, Santa Cruz, versus that of Mary Daly, who teaches feminist ethics in the theology department at the Jesuit-run Boston College. In Afro-American scholarship, it is the talk of

Henry Louis Gates, who heads the African-American studies programme at Harvard, versus that of Molefi Asante, who teaches in the communication department at Temple University in inner-city Philadelphia.

If High Church multiculturalists are integrationists and inveterate decentrists, their Low Church counterparts are separatists and, so to speak, 'recentrists'. In this camp would be included the politics of 'radical feminism' or 'gynocentrism', which argues for an essential, often biologically based, difference between women and men, a difference that sometimes implies the superiority of women. Also included would be the Afrocentrist movement, which attempts to transcend conventional university baggage by reviving students' interests in native languages, oral and musical skills, while at the same time casting doubts about the ultimate value of traditional academic scholarship to societal transformation. At a subtle level, Low Church multiculturalists tend to see the suppression of women and minorities as not simply the product of other groups gaining power in an ongoing struggle, but a reflection of a deeply ingrained fear and/or hatred that those groups harbour against women and minorities. Not surprisingly, then, High Churchers are perceived as overintellectualizing the problems surrounding multiculturalism, the solutions to which will require nothing short of a cultural revolution that is often portrayed in charismatic religious terms.

Given the current political climate, there is not much crossfire between High and Low Churchers, but every now and then, and with increasing frequency, some sniping does occur. In both cases, charges of *naïveté* are lodged, but of decidedly different sorts. In the footnotes of High Church tracts, remarks are made about the unreflective Low Church tendency to repeat the mistakes of 'centrist' thinking by replacing Euro- and androcentrism with Afro- or gynocentrism. From the High Church standpoint, the Low Churchers continue to reify the old binaries – white/black, west/east, male/female – but only now accenting the second term in each binary. Low Churchers usually return the charge more directly, sidestepping the scholarly trappings. As they see it, in a remarkable feat of false consciousness, High Churchers have mistaken the ease of their own academic assimilation for genuine social progress. Indeed, some Low Churchers would go so far as to argue that the High Church is the ultimate 'fifth column' of emancipatory politics, as it subjects every potential point of common cause to an endless trial by nuance.

In the midst of this crossfire we begin the see the seams that barely hold the university together, as both sides try to square the Enlightenment circle of converting radical critique to positive politics. Both the High and Low Church are forced to adopt the legitimation strategy common to academics since the early nineteenth century when it became clear that the universities could not effectively compete with the rest of society in the production and distribution of books and machines. Namely, the university would be the place to go to acquire the competence to deal with the 'artefacts' 'appropriately'. While this strategy largely conceded that the inspiration for academic work came from outside the academy, at the same time it left open the possibility that academics could have a reciprocal effect on the character of later books and machines. Thus, many interesting discussions of this issue could be found across nineteenth-century academic life, ranging from 'Can criticism improve the writing of literature?' to 'Can science improve the development of technology?' Without going into the various answers that have been given to these questions, suffice it to say that academics who gave optimistic answers tended to downplay the extent to which the distinct products of academic labour do not have a natural place outside the university.

Consider this point as a critical explanation of Marx: it is not simply that it is not *enough* to interpret the world if one wants to change it; rather, in order to change the world one must typically do something quite *other* than interpret it. This aspect of the Humboldtian legacy to the university – whereby the academic is 'always already' removed from the field of action – helps to explain the impatience that the Low Church has had with the High Church. Low Church academic labours naturally tend toward general education and civic activism, whereas High Church labours are concerned primarily with professional training and research. The Low Church wants to proselytize outside the academy, while the High Church wants to intensify its hold within the academy. Yet, both presume that the university is the power base from which any movement must be launched. In that sense, Low Churchers are no less children of the Enlightenment than High Churchers. However, each side bears the burden of that legacy differently.

A good case that makes this difference in burden palpable is the alternative interpretations given to the first volume of Martin Bernal's (1987) *Black Athena*, the book that has focused the internal multiculturalist dispute in the USA. This three-volume work systematically unearths the suppression of the Phoenician and Egyptian roots of Greek culture by classical scholarship since its inception in the late eighteenth century. Bernal is Professor of Government at Cornell, having been trained as a Sinologist, not a classical Greek scholar. (He also descends from John Desmond Bernal, the distinguished British X-ray crystallographer and Marxist science policy theorist, about whom more in Chapter 7.)

Much of what makes Bernal's book controversial is his contention that the Enlightenment values that Humboldt supposedly institutionalized in the structure of the German university were betrayed by the university's own employees. These classicists strategically suppressed evidence, skewed translations and oversimplified historical lineages in order to present a relatively autonomous 'Aryan' account of 'the miracle of the Greeks', one purified of African or Asiatic influences. Bernal shows that these scholars were quite consciously shaping a history of classical culture that would make contemporary Prussia the natural descendant – a meticulously empirical version of the Hegelian enterprise.

The division among the multiculturalists emerges upon asking what is the exact crime of which these Aryan scholars are guilty? Bernal answers in

High Church fashion, arguing that their crime was to let racial prejudice and nationalistic ambitions subvert Enlightenment values, which should have compelled the scholars to follow the truth wherever it led – even if it led to a much messier and interpenetrative account of the relationship between Europe, Asia and Africa. Bernal's conclusion is recognizable in the work of other multiculturalists. In feminist theory, Donna Haraway's (1990) attempts to forge a 'hybrid' or 'cyborg' politics of scholarship are a case in point. Instead of emphasizing the distinctness or superiority of women, Haraway argues for the interdependence, if not outright indistinctness, of such categories as 'man', 'woman' and 'machine'. Among Afro-American scholars, a similar sentiment can be seen informing K. Anthony Appiah's (1993) argument that 'Africa' is a construction that better captures European ignorance of the diversity of African cultures than a common source of identity for everyone who lives on the African continent.

The first scholarly milestone of multiculturalism, Edward Said's (1978) *Orientalism* argued a related thesis with regard to the perceived 'inscrutability' of Islam and other 'eastern' cultures. Said's High Church mentality is reflected in his ability to neatly separate his critical scholarship from his high profile efforts to promote an autonomous Palestinian state. One would think that, given Said's scholarly accounts of the long-standing cultural commerce between Europe and the Middle East, arguments on behalf of 'national homelands' would constitute disingenuous politics: wouldn't a different political vehicle be better suited to the complexities of the Palestinian situation? Said clearly believes the answer is no, given 'current political realities', yet at the same time these realities should not be allowed to contaminate critical scholarly concerns. Here it would seem that Said has reinvented Max Weber's notoriously sharp separation of science and politics. At least, such a suspicion has crossed the minds of Low Church multiculturalists. They believe that the High Churchers have been co-opted by the status quo as a result of having attained prominence in the university system. (For the debate over Said's commitment to multiculturalism, see Berman 1992.)

In contrast, the Afrocentrist response to Bernal's book shifts the argument to the collective psychological plane and in particular to unconscious racial hatred that may have motivated the near-seamless concealment of the black legacy to western culture. Interestingly, the Afrocentrists do not dispute *what* the legacy is. Indeed, they tend to valorize the very qualities and achievements that the West has traditionally valued in the Greeks. Rather, the nub of the dispute is over *who* deserves credit for the legacy. Thus, in a seminal work of Afrocentric scholarship, French-trained Senegalese ethnologist Cheikh Anta Diop (1991) takes as significant evidence for the stolen scientific legacy of Africa the fact that western historians have favoured the Babylonian over the Egyptian roots of Greek mathematics, even though the Egyptians were closer to the Greek interest in a 'pure' mathematics than the Babylonians, who really only had measuring and counting techniques but no overarching abstract number system. For his part, Bernal is taken to have added conclusively to this literature, redressing the inequity of past judgements against the Egyptians and thereby enabling the black peoples to regain their rightful place in world history and, by implication, in contemporary culture (Aune 1993).

The point worth stressing here is that both the decentrist and recentrist interpretations of *Black Athena* are indebted to the Enlightenment. The decentrists appeal to the supposed power of consistently applied critical inquiry, while the recentrists appeal to the equally supposed power of revealing hidden truth. The struggle over what to make of Bernal's text certainly has the whiff of politics and real-world effects, but it will remain in this irreal state as long as the struggle is staged behind a copy of Bernal's book. What is needed, instead, are more candid discussions with administrators and concerned non-academics about how to reform the university, taking into account the struggles and fissures in academic consciousness that I have highlighted, most of which have been so far articulated only at the level of theory. Admittedly, this would require that multiculturalists shed some of the university's 'protective colouration' by publicly airing their core disagreements – what, in the next section, I dub the 'fundamental embarrassment'. This strategy would finally take seriously the idea of the university as a historically specific social formation that can organize the terms of its own change without being forced by external political and economic pressures.

What women's ways of knowing have to do with women – and other embarrassing issues for multiculturalists

Entry to the High Church is assured when multiculturalists confront the 'fundamental embarrassment' – that is, once they recognize that the supposedly unique body of knowledge associated with a subaltern race, gender, class or culture has actually received considerable expression and development by members of the dominant counterparts. Put most provocatively: what happens if it turns out that, say, élite white European males have already justified forms of knowledge that are said to constitute black African female identities? For example, many feminists identify 'women's ways of knowing' with an emphasis on the entire human body as the interface between self and reality, which leads them to devalue abstract reasoning and even discursive modes of expression in favour of intuition, sensation and emotion (an excellent sophisticated introduction is Rose 1994). Yet, many significant men in the western philosophical tradition have put forward precisely this view, including Plato in some of his Socratic guises. Admittedly, the privileging of intuition, sensation and emotion remains a dissenting tradition in the West, but among its male advocates have been mystics, conservatives, authoritarians and irrationalists who advanced metaphysics and epistemologies that were otherwise inimical to women's interests. We are then faced with the following delicate question: When one claims that there are distinctive women's ways of knowing, does one mainly want to promote the status of women or the ways of knowing being associated with them?

Consider this question from the standpoint of a woman who enters university in order to develop a critique of the natural sciences, which, in various ways, are male-oriented (Laslett *et al.* 1996). Here are two ways in which she might express her motivation:

1 I enter university because I want to help the plight of women who are prevented from succeeding in science, and academia will provide the tools for that.
2 I enter university because I want to extend feminist epistemology to all domains of knowledge, and academia will provide the tools for that.

Let us call (1) the political motivation and (2) the ideological motivation. They are not the same. Someone may believe in feminist epistemology as a matter of dogma and wish to pursue it wherever it may lead, even if it does not appreciably improve the status of women in science. There may be some belief that in 'the long term', the status of women will improve by the spread of feminism, but any short-term failures will not be attributed to the weakness of feminism but rather to forces that interfere with it. In practical terms, (2) does a lot for women's studies programmes, but what does it do for the women *not* employed in them? In what follows, I shall take this question much more seriously than the flippant spirit in which it seems to be posed.

There is both an academic and a political objection to (2). From the academic side, it remains an open empirical question the extent to which feminist epistemologies have helped to advance the cause of women. No doubt these are subtle issues, the answers to which may vary according to time and place: e.g. what may have worked in the USA 25 years ago may not be universally applicable today. From the political side, there may be a question of putting the cart before the horse: one needs to ask whether expertise in feminist epistemology is the most direct route to helping the plight of women. The answer to that question will depend on what exactly this hypothetical student takes the 'plight' to be. If she thinks it is a matter of getting women into science courses and scientific posts, then feminist epistemology may be a circuitous and even counter-productive route. More conventional knowledge of science and politics may be of more help. But if she thinks the problem runs deeper, involving a reorientation of the attitudes of both men and women toward nature etc., then feminist epistemology may be quite illuminating. But at that point, the sense in which this is a 'political' project starts to become vague because the desired outcomes are less well-defined. And for that reason, the student might want to treat feminist epistemology as an exploratory tool that reveals its own limitations in the course of its sustained academic pursuit. To presume anything less is to fall into (2).

The 'fundamental embarrassment' marks a crossroads in social epistemology, a moment when one must decide whether a subset of humanity
(e.g. women) or a subset of human beliefs (e.g. what is called 'women's
ways of knowing') is of primary concern. There are two Low Church
ways of cutting this Gordian Knot. One involves taking a cue from the
theory of 'strong democracy' (Barber 1984) and arguing that directly em-
ploying women in the academy via, say, women's studies programmes is
in fact the best way to help the plight of women, for the simple reason that
there is no more reliable way of achieving long-term democratization than
by immediately easing the passage of these traditionally excluded elements
into powerful positions. Admittedly, this may make the expansion of feminist epistemology courses seem like welfarist make-work schemes, but then
why should anyone pretend that the initial stages of incorporating the dis-
enfranchised will be anything other then 'artificial' and 'forced' – but no
less necessary? (The reader should see my sympathy for this line of thought
in the light of my call for the taxing of social inheritance at the end of
Chapter 1.)

The second way of cutting the Gordian knot of 'women's ways of knowing' is simply by saying – to continue the example – that women are more
'authentic' representatives of intuitive, emotional and otherwise sensational
forms of knowledge than men because they are 'essential' or 'natural' to
women in a way they are not to men. Of course, this response courts
circularity, given that gender identity and a specific body of knowledge
would seem to be interdefined. Thus, a woman who does not espouse the
relevant knowledges would be seen as suffering from a form of false consciousness that disables them from speaking in their own voice. High
Churchers have pursued this line of thought at a more sophisticated
level, which involves arguing that a body of knowledge is something more
than simply a set of propositions or beliefs; it also includes the physical
presence and behavioural dispositions of the knower – what is often dubbed,
respectively, the 'embodied' and 'embedded' character of knowledge (Fuller
1993a: 15–17). That women look different, occupy different social roles
and respond to their circumstances differently from men means that even
if women and men appear to be espousing the same beliefs, the content
and import of those beliefs are substantially different. Depending on the
interpretation given, this claim could imply that the category in question
– gender in this case – is either a social construction or a part of material
reality. But in either case, the import is to blur the distinction between
the nature of the knower and the known, or between epistemology and
ontology.

High Churchers are typically dissatisfied with leaving the issue there
because the dynamic character of the categories in question remains
unaddressed. This dynamism is reflected not only in the subtle semantic
drift they detect across history and cultures, but also, and not least, in the
High Churchers' own mobile existences and plastic identities. For example,
as noted above, the leading representatives of subaltern perspectives in the

academy occupy positions just as privileged as their counterparts who represent dominant perspectives. Three general sorts of category blurring are worthy of note: (1) alternation; (2) hybridization; (3) restitution. It is important to realize that the processes associated with these terms are not the same and in fact have rather different implications for how one explains and deploys a category like race, gender, class or culture.

Alternation

Alternation accepts the phenomenological and sociological distinctness of, say, male and female or black and white, but proceeds to argue that the same individual may switch from one to the other, under the right conditions. This ability to 'pass' as an instance of either term in a binary opposition thus becomes a potential source of freedom and change in a world that continues to be defined in such polarized terms. Of course, alternation is not equally available to everyone in a particular society, but drawing attention to its occurrence is supposed to challenge the clarity and rigidity of the relevant categorical distinction more generally. The great heroes of alternation are thus impersonators, people who can alter their looks, voice and demeanour at will to acquire one or the other identity (Butler 1989; Sedgwick 1990).

Hybridization

Hybridization differs from alternation by the nature of the challenge it poses to categories of human identity. Alternation presupposes stable categories between which individuals pass, while hybridization implies that individuals adopt elements of both sides of a categorical distinction to forge a substantively new identity (Sardar 1989; Haraway 1990). Take the difference between someone who can pass as male or female, depending on the circumstances, and someone who goes through their entire life as an androgyne. Or, take the difference between someone who can pass as black or white, depending on the circumstances, and someone who goes through their entire life as a mulatto. In both cases, the former alternates between categories, while the latter hybridizes them. When the categories are class- or culture-based, rather than gender- or race-based, the difference between alternation and hybridization becomes less clear-cut. Take a civil servant in imperial India who was a utilitarian by day but a Hindu by night. Does this person have a hybrid identity or simply alternate between two pure identities? Does his lifestyle mark him as an innovative ironist or a captive spirit desperately seeking some manoeuvring space between two unyielding constraints in his life? A similar set of questions may be asked of someone who sports a middle-class accent and tastes in public settings, but then reverts to a working-class accent at home with the family; or, for that matter, someone who lectures in physics on weekdays but attends Mass on Sundays.

Restitution

From the standpoint of the third category-blurring strategy, restitution, the presence of clear binary oppositions marks the members of both the dominant and subaltern sides as alienated from a prior holistic state of being, which may be rooted in the historical past or in a more mythically grounded sense of origin. Often such arguments are made in the spirit of the early, Hegel-inflected Marx, featuring much talk of 'totality' and even a quasi-Christian fall from grace (Crosby 1992). Take the tendency to identify men's ways of knowing with discourse, especially argument, and women's ways of knowing with intuition and other non-verbal modes of expression. The restitutionist would say that privileging either of these ways of knowing results in a lopsided sense of human identity. Thus, the predominance of discursive males has rendered the western philosophical tradition so abstract and detached from the concerns of everyday life that only those capable of devoting their entire energies to mastering works of subtle and complex reasoning can undertake such an inquiry. Not surprisingly, these leisured males have typically pursued their calling in the absence of women, who in turn have focused their energies on household maintenance. Likewise, women have overcompensated for their absence from the forum by identifying too strongly with their restricted social and spatial mobility, which often leads them to suspect any attempt to generalize claims to knowledge from the immediate site of their production. The restitutionist would therefore say that the more men and women define their identities in exclusion from each other, the more mutually alienated they become.

Having examined the three ways in which the High Church tries to get around the 'fundamental embarrassment', what can we say is common to these strategies? Low Churchers would be quick to detect that they all threaten any clear sense of identity-based politics – indeed, in ways that are familiar from other developments associated with advanced capitalism. Seen through the metaphorical lens of capitalism, identity politics is based on strategies of production – namely that, say, gender- or culture-based distinctions are reproduced intact across generations so as to provide a continuing basis for both (internal) solidarity and (external) discrimination (Anderson 1983). In contrast, alternation and hybridization are based on strategies of consumption, whereby one selects traits from both sides of a categorical divide in order to constitute an identity that is affirmed through its reception by others. Consequently, Low and High Churchers can be distinguished by whether they regard identity-based properties as constituting a *capacity* or a *performance*: that is, a persistent source of production or an occasioned site for consumption.

The restitutionist strategy is more difficult to explain within the consumer capitalist perspective, largely because of its stress on a lost past that does not directly draw upon contemporary experience. Perhaps the closest analogue is the deep ecology movement (Naess 1974), whose pursuit of a human lifestyle more organically in tune with the rest of nature often turns out to be a covert call for the affluent to withdraw from the economic problems that face most people. After all, the project of reintegrating the human condition – be it defined in specifically gender terms or more globally environmental ones – presupposes that people have sufficient control over their sphere of action that they can undo centuries of ontological damage. Thus, gender roles can be more easily harmonized in households with considerable financial discretion over how the two partners devote their energies, and the land can be restored to an earlier, more 'pristine' state if one has the political clout to restrict public access and to install what are often expensive restorative technologies.

However, in the end, the aspect of advanced capitalism that may be most telling for understanding High Church multiculturalism is the technologization of labour, which as a general cultural tendency eventuates in a blurring of the distinction between human and machine. This prospect is most evident in the 'cyborg anthropology' associated with Haraway's (1990) hybridized multiculturalism. A less utopian version of this perspective grounded in more mundane technologies is sometimes called 'prosthetic culture' (Lury 1998). For its part, alternation offers an automated version of this technological future in the form of the famous Turing Test, a thought experiment designed to set criteria for distinguishing between the performance of an intelligent human and a programmed computer. One is presented only with outputs, from which the nature of their producer must be inferred. If, as the alternationists maintain, being boils down to how one is taken to be, then not only could a man pass for a woman, but also a machine might pass as well (Genova 1994). That humans may come to treat even demonstrably machine-like presences as human, even to the point of delegating rights and responsibilities to them, has animated the emergent branch of artificial intelligence research known as 'android epistemology' (Ford *et al.* 1995). Finally, a techno-restitutionist perspective would attempt to undo the difference between human and machine to a common denominator, the cash-nexus of ontology, as it were. Here we enter the realm of 'artificial life', a computer-simulation driven application of complexity theory that attempts to model not merely all the life forms that have ever been but all those that could ever be (Horgan, 1996: 198–201).

The challenge for politically active multiculturalists in the twenty-first century will be to shore up a sense of 'identity' amidst these ongoing erosions of the concept's definition. The next chapter addresses the main source of these erosions – namely, the alienation of intellectual work from its sense of purpose, caused by the intrusion of industrial capitalism into academic life. As we shall see, the grand euphemism that masks this development is 'complexity'.

5

The university as capitalism's final frontier – or the fading hope for Enlightenment in a complex world

The university's search for a republican identity: Enlightenment lost

To understand the tortuous route by which academics now find themselves harbouring a fragmented sense of identity comparable to that endured by industrial labour under capitalist regimes, we need to return to when academics first had to expand their sphere of accountability. In the original medieval universities, academics dedicated themselves exclusively to the cultivation of the intellectual virtues, which included decisions about who was mentally fit to undertake a disciplined course of study. But they did not minister to lay people's souls: they were monks, not priests. Priests, of course, were invested with just such a pastoral mission, which immediately expanded their sphere of accountability. They had to confront not only the Creator and their own colleagues, but also a lay constituency.

An important transition in the role of academics from monks to priests occurred with the twelfth-century controversy involving Bernard of Clairvaux and Peter Abelard. Whereas Abelard used his monastic independence as a basis for questioning the taken-for-granted assumptions of the devout, Bernard used it to unify Christendom in its Crusade against Islam under an emotional common denominator that specifically excluded Abelard's dialectical wranglings as 'impious' (Collins 1998: 466 ff.). An interesting comparison here is with the situation in Islam during roughly the same period. On the surface, Al-Ghazali and Averroes corresponded to Bernard and Abelard respectively, except by that point the priestly mission of knowledge producers was already taken for granted and Averroes was forced to defend (unsuccessfully, as it turned out) a disputatious approach to knowledge as a largely monastic enterprise (Fuller 1997: 114–21). While the distinction between the monastic and priestly roles of academics was easily ignored in the early days of the national university systems, it has become more pronounced as the 'flock' has come to be dominated by some rather large wolves in sheep's clothing – in particular, funding agencies supported by either the taxpayer or private business concerns. Under the circumstances, it is not surprising that a wedge has been increasingly driven between the alleged universality of the knowledge produced in such settings and the multiply-interested knowledge producers themselves. In other words, the tensions underlying civic ideals and public goods that usually destroyed past republican regimes have been regularly enacted in the history of the university.

These tensions were already present in the original period of Enlightenment (the eighteenth century) which resembled the Protestant Reformation in its attempt to retrieve the critical functions of inquiry from institutionalized captivity and return them to its clientele. For the most part, the champions of Enlightenment were freelance writers who regarded the universities as little more than propaganda ministries for *les anciens régimes*. They strove to free 'science' from its alleged 'scientists'. The university itself enabled such a clear distinction between 'product' and 'producer' precisely because, as a state function, knowledge was provided with a public character that opened it to scrutiny by those outside the immediate sites of knowledge production. In short, what enabled knowledge to serve some interests outside the university's precincts also enabled it to be criticized by others equally outside its precincts. It is a tribute to the Machiavellian genius of Wilhelm von Humboldt and the German architects of the nineteenth-century 'research university' that the Enlightenment was so effectively co-opted into the strictures of academic life, so that by the beginning of the twentieth century the critical impulse that had animated Voltaire and Marx had become safely sublimated in the cramped prose of Max Weber. Of course, the heirs to the Enlightenment spirit had actively conspired in their own co-optation by succumbing to the siren song of positivism. It is worth recalling these inconvenient facts, lest we be seduced by an airbrushed history of the university, one which suggests that the moment of original sin occurred only when academics tasted the forbidden fruit of the atomic bomb in 1945.

Moreover, we must do more than simply recall the lost history. We need to reinvent for our own times those aspects of the original eighteenth-century Enlightenment that have never found a place in the canonical histories of the university. What I mainly have in mind here is the belief shared by most correspondents in the Enlightenment's 'republic of letters' that the success of Newtonian mechanics as an empirically demonstrable form of knowledge had brought the major period of esoteric inquiry to a close, and that intellectuals had best spend their time ensuring that the 'new science' did not further consolidate into a secular priesthood more virulent than the one traditionally ensconced in the universities. In other words, the Enlightenment wits would have rejected wholesale Kuhn's popular puzzle-solving picture of 'normal science', whereby once anchored to a paradigm, scientists pursue an increasingly autonomous and narrowed range of inquiry. Some of the wits would have been attracted to the German finalizationist school of critical science policy, briefly in vogue when Juergen Habermas directed the Max Planck Institute in Starnberg in the 1970s (Schaefer 1983). Here the state steers the course of science in more practically relevant directions once a critical mass of knowledge has been reached.

However, perhaps the truest vision of Enlightenment science was the ideal epitomized by such American founding fathers as Benjamin Franklin and Thomas Jefferson, who practised science as part of living a cultivated life, just as one might also write poetry and play music (Cohen 1995). In this way, science is not merely downsized but integrated into each individual, thereby dissipating the mystique of 'divinity' that many British clerics and eulogists attached to Newton's original accomplishment. This truly democratized science would thus be science secularized, more about which in the next chapter.

There have been periodic stirrings of this spirit in the nearly two centuries since the research university embalmed the Enlightenment. However, a sense of the speed with which this embalming occurred in the early nineteenth century may be seen in the dubious place that Johann Wolfgang von Goethe occupies in the history of science today, despite having practised science exactly in the spirit cultivated by the likes of Franklin and Jefferson. Though now known primarily as The Great German Poet, Goethe spent most of his life as a civil servant and, were it not for the academic co-optation of critical inquiry in the nineteenth century, he may well have been remembered mainly as a distinguished intellectual descendent of that other great German civil servant, Gottfried Wilhelm von Leibnitz.

In the twentieth century, Ernst Mach, Otto Neurath, Karl Popper and Paul Feyerabend come to mind as representatives of this repressed tradition. For a sense of just how repressed this side of the Enlightenment has been, consider that, notwithstanding postmodern portrayals of the Enlightenment as the epitome of academic respectability, most of the eighteenth-century wits flouted scholastic writing conventions in open defiance of academic claims to epistemic privilege. Indeed, their attitudes toward inquiry exhibited much of the playfulness that postmodernists – especially cultural studies practitioners – claim for themselves today (Goldgar 1995).

At this point, let me caution against one interpretation of the Enlightenment legacy – namely, that the university should be in the business of mediating society's cultural clashes, *but* without taking a stand of its own. Allowed to take its course, this avowedly neutral form of mediation would effectively put the university in the business of increasing the complexity of an already complex world by inserting yet more layers of discursive mediation. To my mind this would undermine the university's republican potential. As the flagship institution of societal reproduction, the university is entrusted to distil the various cross-currents in a society's collective life into a 'heritage' that is worth imparting to its next generation. The very idea of a 'canon' may have become the object of much abuse in these postmodern times, but it stands metonymically for what the university is all about. Of course, the contents of a given canon (in, say, literature or philosophy) have tended to outlive their usefulness. However, with due respect to postmodernists, the solution is not to eliminate the canon and replace it with a plethora of cross-cutting discourses that either match or increase the level of societal babble. Rather, the solution is to revise the canon regularly so as to highlight aspects of social life that students might otherwise ignore or devalue in the normal course of their lives.

In short, the university should simply institutionalize oppositional consciousness (for a history of 'oppositional consciousness', see Frisby 1992). It should become the clearing house for all the voices that would otherwise be silent or muted beyond recognition, with the understanding that these will change as the power relations in society change. In that sense, 'affirmative action' would be built into the institutional design of the university, rather than simply being an unwanted temporary corrective to the status quo (Cahn 1995). Only in this way can the university continue to play a necessary role in the processes of societal reproduction – by reproducing dissent and difference – while retaining its independence. However, there is a price to pay for the university agreeing to this new social contract, which will be explored in Part 3 of this book.

Complexity as post-Enlightenment academic ideology

An important consideration in my thinking is that I believe that most of the alleged 'complexity' claimed for the postmodern condition has been manufactured by academics themselves, often unwittingly and in response to circumstances not entirely under their direct control. When I say that complexity is 'manufactured', I mean that it does not refer to something deep about the nature of a reality that is, in principle, independent of the collective activity of human beings. Thus, while we may have been caught off guard by the realization that we now live in an especially complex world, nevertheless the processes of 'intermediation' involved in constructing this complexity can, and should, be reversed.

Below I discuss four sorts of intermediation that together constitute the pervasive sense of complexity that haunts much contemporary discourse on the governance of science, and even society more generally. As we shall see in Part 3 of this book, reversing these forms of intermediation will force defenders of the university to take some hard decisions, yet ones that are necessary for the return of the repressed side of the Enlightenment, the side that would bring us back to civic ideals and public goods. I shall deal with the first two forms of intermediation only briefly, since I have already mentioned them in Chapter 2.

Economic intermediation

First, there is economic intermediation, which is encapsulated in the saying 'High entry costs make for high exit costs'. Once enough material and human capital have been invested in a line of inquiry, it becomes difficult to justify its discontinuation, especially if it reaps reasonable benefits for those pursuing it. Moreover, this continued investment lowers the chances that others will be in a position to contribute to the inquiry unless they enter through the already established channels. Here the sheer concentration of resources can easily provide the illusion that the field exhibits a level of complexity that can be fathomed only by the keenest and most dedicated minds. In fact, this complexity is often traceable to the ingenuity needed to translate legitimate areas of cognitive interest into the confines of obscenely expensive machinery and excessively narrow technical skills.

Functional intermediation

Second, there is functional intermediation, which results from the implicit social contract that science has made with the state in the twentieth century, whereby the research frontier is allowed to advance apace on the condition that scientists also contribute to the normative reproduction of society. However, the trajectories of these two functions increasingly diverged over the course of the twentieth century. Perhaps the clearest case in point is the continued use of thinly veiled intelligence tests as a social sorting mechanism, despite their methodologically suspect character. This dissonance in the knowledge system has opened a space for all manner of people to broker the difference through activities ranging from the writing of pop psychology to the conduct of so-called 'policy-relevant' research. (On the rise of functional intermediation in early twentieth-century German science, see Fuller 1994b.)

Temporal intermediation

Third is temporal intermediation. Sometimes a 'before and after' sense of history is invoked to highlight the complexity of the current knowledge system. On this basis, one influential multinational research policy manifesto (Gibbons et al. 1994) has heralded a 'new production of knowledge'. The advent of Big Science with America's World War II atomic bomb initiative – the Manhattan Project – is normally seen as the defining moment between an academically oriented 'Mode 1' and a user-friendly 'Mode 2' knowledge production. But as a matter of fact, the difference between the time the experimental natural sciences were regarded as sufficiently theory-driven to be deemed fit subjects for the university curriculum and the time they started to take the lead in forging links between the university, industry and the state in large-scale research projects is no more than one generation. In the case of the vanguard nation, Germany, this period spanned the third and fourth quarters of the nineteenth century. The start of this period was marked by the first nationally adopted textbooks in experimental physics, Kuhn's ultimate criterion of normal science; the end by the establishment of the first hybrid research establishments, the Kaiser Wilhelm Institutes. Thus, 'Mode 1' and 'Mode 2' knowledge production seemed to have been virtually joined at the hip at birth, not separated by several centuries and incommensurable world views. However, to hear the 'Modists' tell the history, Mode 1 and Mode 2 have quite distinct origins, the one in the remote past and the other in the recent period. Kuhnian paradigms had been in place at least since the founding of the first autonomous scientific societies in the seventeenth century (and maybe were present even in the ancient and medieval worlds), while the social hybridization of the scientific research agenda did not take root until the atomic bomb project (and really did not precipitate a crisis in knowledge production until the post-Cold War period).

What is going on here? In essence, the Modists present a 'stereoscopic' view of the history of knowledge production that creates an illusion of temporal depth by driving a wedge between two rather closely connected developments, and then reading the earlier one in terms of what might be plausibly said to have led up to it, and the later one in terms of what might be plausibly said to have followed from it. The result is the appearance of deep rupture where there is none. Ironically, the illusion is maintained because, despite talking a 'hard-headed' policy-relevant line, the Modists systematically ignore salient features of the institutionalization of inquiry.

To take just one example, it is misleading to classify a chartered scientific society and a publicly maintained university as 'autonomous' research institutions in the sense of Mode 1, if only because they are not accountable for their activities in the same way. More importantly, the Modists' stereoscopic historical perspective leads them to overlook that it became easy for academics to move into Mode 2 knowledge production processes once they identified the source of their 'autonomy' with their discipline rather than the university as such. Laboratory scientists were not included in either the medieval or the Humboldtian conception of the university as the natural home for inquiry. The corporate consciousness of scientists was rather modelled on such emergent nineteenth-century formations as professional associations and labour unions. For laboratory scientists, there has been always the sense that the university is a more or less hospitable space for doing business but is not constitutive of their identity as autonomous inquirers. Consequently, scientists who shifted from Mode 1 to Mode 2 have generally done much less soul-searching than might have been expected, given the alleged chasm that separates the two Modes.

Collegial intermediation

The last but by no means least form of intermediation is what may be called collegial intermediation. These days it is not sufficient to know about the world for oneself; one must first know about others who know about it. In crude terms, it is the problem of having to read what everyone before you has written before you are permitted to say anything for yourself. Much of the historical uniqueness that is claimed for the 'postmodern condition' is probably traceable to this easily taken for granted feature of academic life. It involves treating the expansion of the universities since the end of World War II as if it were in direct response to some profound change in our understanding of reality, if not the nature of reality itself. However, objectively speaking, the world is probably not changing 'more than ever before'. Rather, there are more academics looking at it, and because they are rewarded for their 'distinctiveness', as Pierre Bourdieu (1984) would put it, they have made their careers by adding new 'perspectives', probably beyond necessity.

These perspectives often correspond to substantive developments in specific disciplines. For example, the tendency to stress the unique and autonomous character of cultures is probably due more to the way in which anthropologists have had to stake their claims to knowledge (whereby a case study essentially establishes a right to intellectual property over a culture) than the nature of cultures as such. Nevertheless, given the benefit of hindsight, we would probably conclude that the postmodern tendency to regard people as having multiple cultural identities reflects more the inadequacies of an originally over-sharp conception of culture than a recent tendency for people to diversify their personalities. On the whole, then, I remain unconvinced that the world has become a more uncertain place in which to live – a common subjective indicator of contemporary complexity. What is incontrovertible is that the sheer availability of alternative perspectives has made it difficult to bring closure on matters that require a specific course of action. Not surprisingly, then, social movements that have rallied around the postmodern exposure of 'global uncertainty' are more effective in blocking the actions of others than in taking action for themselves.

Science without vocation in the 'knowledge society'

To put in perspective some of the previous remarks about the intermediation of academic life – especially at the economic and the collegial levels – let us revisit a well-known address to graduate students given by the classical sociologist most celebrated for his historical sophistication. Max Weber may have been more subtle than Karl Marx in his understanding of the relationship between economic and cultural change, but he would be an easy mark for today's academic administrators who promote a close fit between successful business firms and successful universities. Careful readers of the original 1918 'Science as a vocation' cannot fail to detect Weber's captivation by the ideology of enterprise that characterized the USA in the early twentieth century (Weber 1958: esp. 129–31). While he may have been careful to distinguish the calling of academics from that of politicians, Weber uncritically embraced the analogy between business and academia. Luckily, for his posthumous reputation, Weber's critics were equally oblivious, as they fixated on the physics-based model of inquiry that was in the process of replacing the humanist-based model of science. Thus, Weber's most incisive contemporary critic, the Latinist Ernst Robert Curtius (1989), objected to a definition of science that did not require inquirers to realize the ends of inquiry in their professional lives. Curtius harkened back to the liberal arts model of the unity of teaching and research that had lost credibility with the disciplinary fragmentation that had come to be institutionalized, even at the time of Weber's address.

Nowadays, equipped with 20/20 hindsight, we pretend to understand these matters much better than Weber did. But, of course, the cost of every error corrected is a new error committed. On the one hand, the spirit of enterprise that Weber found in the American academy was seen by Americans as itself a German adaptation, specifically of the Kaiser Wilhelm Institutes (today called the Max Planck Institutes) which were unique in their day in treating the research site as a crucible for forging together academic, state and industrial interests (Conant 1970: 69–72). On the other hand, in recent years, science policy gurus have forgotten this ancient history altogether, making it appear that the industrialization of science is a product of World War II, and, more importantly, that it has been largely for the better in fostering a spirit of interdisciplinary inquiry (Gibbons *et al.* 1994). Lost from this view of history is that the experimental natural sciences have been historically the main vehicle by which industrial and commercial concerns have permeated academia, largely in the face of resistance from the traditional liberal arts culture which disdained the presence of machinery and manual labour on university grounds. And the time-lag between the establishment of laboratories at major universities in Europe and the USA and the profusion of industrial concerns in campuses is approximately one generation: from the third to the fourth quarter of the nineteenth century. We are now completing the first century of this transition, which, to my mind, is more important than the so-called Scientific Revolution of the seventeenth century.

The result is that, in recent times, the academic community has embodied a paradox. On the one hand, we have persuaded many non-academics that history has recently entered a 'post-industrial' phase, whereby the endless production and accumulation of material goods are no longer the driving forces of the human condition. This is the so-called 'knowledge society' that we currrently inhabit. On the other hand, our professional consciousness remains very much captive to the old industrial mindset. Even an expression as innocuous-sounding as 'knowledge production', which freely tumbles from academic lips, immediately calls to mind the manufacture of products – specifically books and articles – the more, the faster, the better. To sound a familiar Marxist theme, the meaning of our labour has come to be identified with its products, the ultimate fates of which we are in less and less of a position to control. University administrators merely articulate this subtle form of capitalist alienation when they characterize the need to shift faculty energies from research to teaching as a reorientation of the academic enterprise from 'producing goods' to 'distributing services'.

I shall reflect on the origins and implications of our lingering industrial mindset, the new sense of marginalization that has resulted, and what we may do about it. To capture the spirit of my argument, consider the entry that 'knowledge society' would receive in *The Devil's Companion to Social Theory*:

Knowledge Society. n. What advanced capitalism looks like to intellectuals, once they have been assimilated into its mode of production – a classic case of what economists call the 'internalization of a negative externality'. Intellectuals specialize in two sorts of activities: moralizing and criticizing, which are typically deployed against the powers that be. However, with the right incentives, they can be just as easily deployed on their behalf. Thus, intellectuals may be made to moralize by appealing to norms that, at the same time, function as principles for reproducing the social order. They can even be motivated to criticize each other in ways that not only distract them from criticizing the powers that be, but also enable those powers to appropriate whatever survives the criticism. The roots of K.S. predate advanced capitalism, reaching back to the reconstitution of the university as the 'spiritual infrastructure' of the 19th C. nation-state, starting in Prussia. Faced with the inadequacy of the old feudal-clerical order's response to Napoleon, Wilhelm von Humboldt came up with the inspired idea of co-opting the intellectuals, many of whom had been sympathetic to Napoleon, by declaring the university the natural home of 'Enlightenment'. In one fell swoop, free-floating gadflies were flattened into civil servants (see Hegel, G.W.F). Over the course of the century, the critical spirit of Enlightenment metamorphosed into a guild right under the rubric of 'academic freedom', which was most definitely not to be confused with the sort of 'license' that would be routinely censured in the public sphere (see Weber, M.). An important turning point was the Franco-Prussian War of 1870–1, in which Germany's victory was widely attributed to the rapid conversion of its industrial base for military use, which was in turn attributed to its relatively high level of technically skilled personnel who could be mobilized at a moment's notice. This led to periodic calls across the industrialized world (usually made in anticipation of wars) to increase the level of scientific and technical training in the general public. The universities duly expanded to meet the new demand, and soon academics were in the business of administering 'aptitude tests', standardizing school curricula, and certifying the credentials of an increasing number in fields of employment. They became quality control checkpoints for the new military-industrial order. In addition, educational achievement became the 'democratic' principle of social structure that eroded traditional class and status barriers to social mobility. This principle was most celebrated as 'meritocracy' during the Cold War period of the 1950s–1970s, the time when K.S. is first formally identified (see Drucker, P.). However, with the end of the Cold War, K.S. ideology has begun to buckle under the strain of capitalist expansion. Two general signs stand out: (1) Credentials have gone the way of other forms of social discrimination. It is slowly becoming clear that just as race and class were never especially good performance indicators, neither is the possession of academic credentials. The point is not obvious because formal education has permitted social advancement for an unprecedented number of previously excluded groups, yet it has been at the cost of eliminating alternative paths of advancement, including on-the-job experience. However, if total war no longer seems likely and 'the market' gets its way, the credentials monopoly currently enjoyed by universities may be punctured by corporate-sponsored training centres, perhaps as part of an omnibus devolution of the welfare state to private sector agencies. (2) Ironically, a surfeit of academically qualified people has given the competitive edge to those who possess non-academic, specifically entrepreneurial, forms of knowledge. This is no more evident than in the sciences themselves. The 'expert' scientist enters and exits lines of research just ahead of the pack, invests in skills and equipment that are usable in the widest variety of projects, and constructs her knowledge products so as to extract a certain 'tribute' (be it an attribution in a citation list or a financial tribute in patent royalties) from their users. At the limit, 'knowledge engineers' design computers that simulate a field's expertise and thereby eliminate still more academic competitors. The raw material for the simulations are experts who gladly sell their knowledge in the face of eventual obsolescence. **Related Concepts**: 1. *Credential Society* – used somewhat cynically to refer to K.S. in its latest, decadent phase of credential inflation (see Bourdieu, P.; Collins, R.). 2. *Information Society* – used by both boosters and critics of K.S. to highlight technology's role in the construction of K.S.; boosters tend to focus on the high-grade (and very impersonal) knowledge it takes to programme computers and other electronic media, whereas critics focus on the low-grade (but very personal) knowledge that is collected and distributed on such media (see Castells, M.; Schiller, H.). 3. *Post-Industrial Society* – used somewhat obscurantistly to suggest that because Marx failed to predict the end of capitalism, he was therefore wrong about the relentless expansion of capitalist logic into every sphere of social life (see Bell, D.; Harvey, D.). 4. *Risk Society* – used to capture the management of uncertainty, be it in terms of distributing potential costs and benefits across various social sectors or created a generalized sense of risk on the basis of which authority is challenged (see Luhmann, N.; Beck, U.).

'I am cited, therefore I am': the politics of recognition in the modern academy

Higher education in the twentieth century has made great strides to incorporate people who have been historically marginalized on the basis of gender, ethnic background and ideological persuasion. In most of these cases, the marginalization had been more or less intended. However, the upscaling of the academic enterprise since World War II and especially during the 1960s and 1970s – i.e. the increasing numbers of people who have become professional academics along with the enormous resources that have been lavished on university-based pursuits (at least when compared with the past) – have brought on a more insidious form of marginalization; 'insidious' because it is an unintended consequence of the academy's new-found expansiveness. In fact, this form of marginalization is so insidious that it is now just as likely to affect straight white males from Oxbridge and the Ivy League as colleagues with contrary qualifications. I am speaking, of course, of the marginalization that results from one's published work going unread, undiscussed, uncited – and even when cited, cited in an omnibus fashion as part of a list of names whose company the author had perhaps taken great pains not to keep.

When Weber delivered 'science as a vocation', he stressed the subtle but real personal satisfaction one could derive from a life of scholarship, even knowing that one's work would be surpassed by future scholars. Of course, Weber was assuming that scholarly work would be *read*. However, this is an all too big assumption to make these days, a deceptive tale that we continue to relate to aspiring academics. Epistemologists who like to see the pursuit of inquiry in Darwinian terms are inclined to think that today's research is born into a world where survival depends on a process of critical scrutiny that resembles natural selection. It is expected that few pieces of research will survive intact across a variety of critical environments. But this is perhaps to misconstrue the relevant analogue. For, it would be truer to our current predicament to say that most of today's research fails to survive because it perishes once it is published – stillborn, as it were – never quite connecting with an environment long enough for other scholars to subject it to critical scrutiny. I resort to such grim metaphors in order to impress on the reader that being ignored is not a sophisticated form of criticism, however much our radical fantasies may tell us otherwise.

Pathologies of a dependency citation culture

As with so many of the other ailments of contemporary academic life, the natural sciences have displayed the most exaggerated symptoms of the marginalization I describe. But the social sciences and humanities are following close on their heels. Credit for uncovering these symptoms in the 1960s belongs to the sociologist Robert Merton (1973: Pt 5) and the historian Derek de Solla Price (1978). Unfortunately, they interpreted the emerging behemoth as speaking to the *health*, not the illness, of what Price called 'Big Science' (cf. Turner and Chubin 1976). To appreciate this point, consider the lengths to which Merton, Price and their followers have been willing to go to portray the pursuit of knowledge as a massive industrial enterprise – but one that exhibits only its positive, not its negative, features. Their most concrete legacy is the *Science Citation Index* (SCI) and the attendant use of citation counts as indicators of quality, relevance and influence. Even humanists and social scientists find it difficult to resist measuring their careers in terms of the droppings left at the foot of other people's articles.

SCI discriminates between research contributions in rather crude ways for reasons that have largely to do with the massive labour costs originally associated with compiling and processing the citations (Fuller 1997: 69 ff.). Normally attention is focused on the distribution of citations among those cited. Generally speaking, the harder the science, the more easily identifiable the research frontier, as an increasing percentage of citations concentrate on a vanishingly small group of authors, virtually all of whom are currently active contributors to the field. Yet, to understand the social psychology of the citation process, we must examine the role of *citers*, the vast majority of whom are anonymous and ultimately forgotten in the great mass of unread material to which their efforts unwittingly contribute. Regardless of how much they are cited by others, an author who cites 30 works in their article exerts ten times more influence over the final citation count than one who cites only three. This is a rather curious result for an enterprise like science, which has been periodically advertised as the paradigm case of democracy in action.

In most democratic theories of voting, whenever one can vote for more than one candidate, the votes are treated as fractions adding up to one, so that each voter formally exerts the same influence over the electoral process, and voters with distributed allegiances are not privileged. The only major exception is the system of multiple voting for university dons and graduates that John Stuart Mill (1977 [1861]) advocated until everyone met (what Mill regarded as) the basic educational requirements for full political participation. However, Mill would have been shocked by the kind of multiple voting permitted – and perhaps even encouraged – by *SCI* citation counts. In essence, authors who acknowledge a large number of scholarly debts – as measured by the citations they bestow on their colleagues – exert a disproportionate control over the structure of knowledge in their field. Imagine a polity that by its electoral system discourages its citizens from being economically self-sufficient and ideologically focused. This, then, is the sense of scientific self-governance implicitly promoted by *SCI*.

The reader may regard what I have just described as a formula for producing the kind of 'dependency culture' that is the dark side of the welfare state. Certainly, from an economic standpoint, a debtor-driven market looks less than rational. Whereas debts usually accumulate around those whose capital assets can be independently assessed, in science one's capital assets grow in proportion to the number of colleagues who perceive it in their interest to openly acknowledge a debt. This is an instance of Pierre Bourdieu's (1977) 'symbolic capital' at work with a vengeance: the size of your capital is determined exactly by the degree to which others recognize it. Of course, this is not entirely a case of backward causation and spontaneous judgements of whose work is likely to matter in the long run. There is a material basis, but it will remain obscure as long as systematic correlations between citation counts and research finances (including not only outright grants but also the fixed capital embedded in university infrastructures) continue to be regarded in poor taste. At this point, it is easy to imagine how Bronislaw Malinowski must have felt when he tried to present the Trobriand Islanders with naturalistic explanations for why rain dances seem to bring about rain (when they do).

Pathologies of a differentiating citation culture

Are less explicitly political accounts any more rational in their explanation of scientists' citing practices? I am afraid not. There is a school of thought that regards the bestowal of citations as less an act of affiliation than of differentiation. Though often associated with evolutionary theory, in practice it looks more like a mutant form of cell division theory – a 'carcinomic' model of science! Both the historian Thomas Kuhn (1970) and the sociologist Niklas Luhmann (1982) have had their names attached to such euphemistically entitled 'autopoietic' or 'self-organizational' models of scientific change. Central to the plot of both is that science becomes autonomous from the larger social environment sometime in its history (say, with the founding of the Royal Society) – not merely in the sense of science being protected from ambient social pressures but more importantly in terms of science's development being defined exclusively in the scientists' own terms. In practice, this means that the invisible hand of peer review miraculously discriminates important from unimportant research as the overall result of a set of privately taken decisions in referee's reports. Autonomy in this sense enables science to simulate the frictionless medium of thought that philosophers since Plato have considered ideal to the pursuit of knowledge. Consequently, neither Kuhn nor Luhmann has much to say about the material requirements of scientific knowledge. Rather, they present a seemingly irreversible, if strictly non-teleological, story of functional differentiation of the scientific enterprise, as inquirers encounter impasses in the day-to-day business of puzzle-solving that force them to divide their efforts in order to clarify the overall direction of their inquiries.

These impasses are registered as acts of differentiating oneself from previous researchers. And to be sure, the more citations you give to others in such an act, the more focused your own contribution to the knowledge system appears. But for that very reason, the less significant your contribution will likely appear in the long run, precisely because you have defined it so narrowly. Indeed, given the vagaries of institutional memory which collapses the complexity of the historical record of any generation into a few distinguished inquirers, the ironic long-term consequence of your careful efforts at differentiation will simply be to raise the citation counts of those from whom you distinguished yourself. Your own contribution will probably be lost in the process. The easiest way around this eventuality is to cite yourself a lot, and hope that self-promotion will drive others to promote you – at least by attacking what you cite so frequently! A subtler course of action is to become part of a mutual citation network: that is, to cite others who cite you. Once *SCI* defined the 'impact factor' of a journal in terms of the frequency with which articles published in the journal are cited, it turned out that *Social Studies of Science*, the premier journal in the sociology of science, scored consistently highest in this factor. Could this be because the editors decided to apply one of the field's key findings to the field itself? If so, it would provide further evidence of the time-honoured maxim that 'if you can't beat 'em, join 'em', since arguably the original aim of the sociology of science was to expose the sources of science's power to critique (for further elaboration, see Fuller 1999a: Ch. 7).

Most democratic theories presume that voters cast their ballots fully realizing that their vote is a scarce resource: to give to one is to withhold from another. Of course, scholarly citing practices are no less strategic, but scarcity does not play quite the same normative role. When each citation, but not each citer, is weighted equally, it becomes impossible to detect the deliberate enhancing or withholding of credit. The received view is that scientists cite simply because their knowledge claims demand that they do so. The implied image of the citing scientist is one devoid of agency, which in turn creates the impression that a science is a spontaneously self-organizing field of activity that can be monitored as one would any other object of enquiry; hence, the expression 'science of science'. Moreover, although *SCI* formally masks the strategic character of citing behaviour, once the citation counts are made public, the scientists can adjust their citing strategies. In a political system that enables one to cast a non-exclusive vote for a candidate, there will be a tendency to err on the side of voting beyond one's preferences – that is, to vote for every minimally acceptable candidate so as to ensure that someone tolerable is elected. The corresponding tendency is for scientists to cite anyone who might have a hand in the fate of their article (or anyone whom such people would expect to see cited), lest the article be ignored and their next grant proposal go unfunded. Here we find Merton's fabulously mystified 'communist' ethic, according to which scientists cannot tell the difference between protection money and selfless sharing. Be that as it may, by adhering to this norm, scientists end up inflating the citation counts of their colleagues who are regarded as even marginally powerful, which in turn enhances the power of those colleagues, as *SCI* indicators are fed into the larger science policy process.

Can anything be done about scientific citing practices to prevent Big Science's slender grip on democracy from dissolving into Mafiosism? My recommendation here is to make the analogy between citing and voting as explicit as possible, so that both authors and readers of scientific texts are clear about the strategic character of situating one's work in a body of research. This would include restricting the number of citations that authors are permitted to make, and forcing them to allocate a fraction to each citation's significance so that the fractions assigned to all the citations add up to one. (That authors are already disciplined to conform to word limits bodes well for this stricture.) I would even go so far as to urge that both positive and negative citations be allocated from this single vote, so that authors are forced to decide whether they wish to be counted more as supporting certain claims than opposing others. One obvious consequence of taking this advice to heart is that citations can no longer be used as an 'unobtrusive measure' of the overall trajectory of scientific research. However, as we shall now see, that might not be such a bad idea.

Science's 'economy of scale' as the ideology of self-sacrifice

Derek de Solla Price (1986) had no qualms about defining 'science policy' as investment strategies for producing the largest number of highly cited articles. Indeed, he conceded that science was a massive consumer of resources, thereby reversing the economists' image of science as exclusively a 'factor of production', a perpetual motion machine. This he did by noting that the clearest economic indicator of scientific productivity (as measured by number of papers published per scientist) is national electrical consumption (as measured by kilowatt-hours per capita), which is in turn related to economic productivity (gross national product per capita) by a power of 3/2 (Price 1978: 87; see Olsen 1992 for more recent confirmation). By drawing attention to consumption patterns, Price unwittingly brought into focus the question of *waste* in the scientific enterprise. Here it is worth recalling Michael Polanyi's famous definition of free inquiry as the ability to waste resources with impunity in the name of truth (Polanyi 1962). Moreover, these resources include not only money, paper, machines and energy but, most especially, *people*. This point is papered over by Merton's principle of cumulative advantage, which, like capitalism's 'invisible hand', is presented as a situation that appears cruel to individuals but eventuates in long-term systemic benefits.

As social Darwinists of science policy, Merton and Price never suggested that this tendency should discourage the recruitment of new scientists, which would in turn downsize the scientific enterprise so that more of its participants would have a better chance of having their contributions recognized. On the contrary, in terms familiar from Chapter 2, Price stressed 'economies of scale' as improving the overall quality of science. In other words, an ever-widening field of competitors would keep all scientists on their toes, which would in turn ensure their best performances, leading to an increase in the overall percentage of quality publications – but also an increase in the absolute number of unrecognized scientists 'wasted' by the system. Indeed, the difference between the initially advantaged and disadvantaged increases rapidly over time, such that two-thirds of scientists give up on publishing altogether after their first article. This is largely due to a combination of lack of response and lack of incentive to continue producing work, once the initial publication has secured academic tenure. We can even take the argument back a step to justify scientists acquiring PhD's before starting their careers. If credentials provide at least an indirect measure of likely achievement, and this fact is widely known, then all competitors will meet the highest standard they can, which of course will raise the quality of the average applicant while diminishing the advantage gained by having that credential. Merton (1973) went so far as to argue that if indeed genuine contributions to knowledge are likely to go unrecognized, disadvantaged scientists should try to get advantaged scientists to promote the findings as their own.

Perhaps the most striking pattern is that graduate training is devoted almost entirely to the development of cutting-edge research skills, with little, if any, attention paid to the interpersonal skills needed for teaching and administration. Yet, most science PhD's are employed in teaching-oriented institutions that often have a strong service component. And even if a freshly minted PhD is fortunate enough to be employed in a research university, the value of their hard-earned skills is bound to depreciate at a rapid rate, especially if they trained in a field with a rapidly advancing research front. This last point helps explain why scientists have traditionally done their best work before turning 40. For, unless scientists continually upgrade their skills, they become obsolete as researchers within a dozen years out of graduate school. Thus, most scientists conduct the bulk of their professional lives in teaching and/or administrative posts for which they have received no formal training. Interestingly, these well-known facts have yet to elicit outrage from scholars of management and labour (an exception is Stephan and Levin 1992).

On the contrary, the situation just described is often taken to be not merely normal, but exemplary of science as a self-organizing enterprise. Indeed, the clearest reasons that federal policymakers give for adopting a *laissez-faire* attitude to the allocation of research funds turn on an analogy drawn between science's internal means of picking its winners – the so-called 'peer review process' – and the 'invisible hand' of the capitalist market-place. The basic idea is that good scientists are in the best position to know, and to acknowledge, good science when they see it (Chubin and Hackett 1990). After all, are they not the primary consumers of scientific research? Thus, without any special prompting from the government, science would seem capable of stratifying its many practitioners according to the merit of their contributions. This stratification is more evident the more mature the science is perceived to be. For example, in the natural sciences with the clearest research fronts, it is not uncommon for 80 per cent of the footnotes in journal articles to go to 20 per cent of those publishing in the field. In addition, more than two-thirds of those who begin their professional careers by publishing research undertaken in graduate school will soon cease publication altogether, typically as a result of discouragement brought on by their failure to generate interest in the 'market-place of ideas'.

Lest the reader think otherwise, there is a strong positive correlation between initial research funding and the number of scientific publications subsequently generated. The most highly funded research universities produce the most professional papers. A similar tendency can be discerned at the international level, as nations with more lavish research budgets outpace the scientific publication of less endowed countries (Schott 1991). However, these facts address only issues of production, not of productivity, that is the amount of scientific bang one gets for each research buck. Even granting that those with access to the most resources generally have the largest impact on the research front, there lurks the more interesting question of the proportional impact of budget size on the course of inquiry. Unfortunately, there are no easy answers, largely because the question can be framed in two quite distinct ways: should scientists be seen primarily as adding to a potentially endless storehouse of knowledge, or should they be seen as inching ever closer to some ultimate cognitive goal, such as a unified theory of reality? When appealing for public support, scientists like to conflate the two images, typically by presenting a torrent of publications in some field as evidence for their closing in on nature's fundamental principles. This is the so-called military-industrial metaphor introduced in Chapter 3. However, closer examination reveals that the two images do not fit so neatly together. While there is evidence that the nations with the lion's share of research funding generate an even larger share of the total number of scientific publications, on the other hand there is also evidence that each additional increment in research investment advances the frontiers of knowledge a little less than the previous one. Thus, accelerating the rate at which scientific publications are produced is perfectly compatible with decelerating the rate at which consensus is reached on the solutions to a field's fundamental problems. In other words, science may suffer from diseconomies of scale (that is, 'bigger is worse'), especially if scientific inquiry is seen as aiming for the ultimately comprehensive account of reality. The overall image of the dynamics of scientific inquiry, then, would be one of a goal that seems to recede the more vigorously it is pursued.

The steady accumulation of professional papers serves to assuage the fears of those who worry about how scientists spend their time at work. Nevertheless, it is the image of scientists getting closer to unravelling the secrets of the universe that enables scientific inquiry to escape standards of accountability to which other productive enterprises are routinely held. Yet, it is precisely here that we find the familiar phenomenon of diminishing returns on investment. Indeed, an economic indicator of a 'mature' science is that more resources need to be invested in order to make comparable advances. The main reason, of course, is that mature sciences work on increasingly technical problems, the solutions to which call for the manufacture of sophisticated instruments and the extended specialist training.

Evolutionism as the mask of decline in a complex world

Things analysable by the categories of consumer culture are often faulted for debasing one or another value system – if not all value systems – in the name of 'commodification'. Should the same conclusion be drawn about Big Science's impact on the value of knowledge and its producers in our supposedly knowledge-intensive post-industrial society? And if that conclusion is drawn, then what should those of us concerned with the politics of the academy do about it (Fuller 1993a)? A life of inquiry is now officially available to more people than ever before in human history. However, the quality of life one leads in that pursuit is changing rapidly and probably declining, if the rise of contract-based research and teaching in universities is any indication. At the very least, we should critique narratives of progress, especially the seductive evolutionary models of knowledge production (Campbell 1988 is probably the best of the lot).

The persuasiveness of evolutionary models often rests on an ambiguity: is the evolution in question supposed to be unique or repeatable? For example, when Kuhn (1970) spoke of science undergoing a cycle of 'normal' and 'revolutionary' periods, was he trying to model the stages through which *the* history of science as a singular global phenomenon passes, or rather the phases through which specific sciences pass in any of a variety of times and places? If Kuhn intended the former, his model would have approximated a literal application of evolution to epistemology. But then he would have been forced to confront how the initial scientization of certain fields at certain times and places (specifically, experimental physics in seventeenth-century western Europe) set constraints on later developments, even in remote fields, times and places. In other words, how does the prior existence of certain forms of inquiry constitute the environment against which subsequent forms of inquiry are selected? Clearly, Kuhn has not been read in this way, but rather as having advanced a multiply repeatable, perhaps even universalizable, model of scientific change that is just as relevant to, say, sociological inquiry in the 1960s as physical inquiry in the 1660s. It is ironic, given Kuhn's reputation for having 'historicized' the history and philosophy of science, that his model should be applied in such a mindlessly ahistorical fashion.

Nowadays it is often assumed that because science does not follow the same path in all times and places, it must therefore follow different, unrelated paths that can be explained only by citing local factors. This inference, characteristic of the 'ethnographic' or 'postmodern' turn in social and cultural studies of science, constitutes a false dilemma. It overlooks that the evolution of scientific knowledge may be exactly like biological evolution in being a single and unrepeatable trajectory that encompasses the entire world. This is, of course, compatible with a considerable degree of variation across local environments, which can in turn be explained by the differential impact of earlier events of common ancestry. My model here is Lenin's theory of imperialism, according to which the logic of capital expansion know firsthand what is for sale and hence must rely on third parties. A situation of this sort arises in the 'informal economies' of the former Soviet Bloc countries, which have experienced the breakdown of socialism without yet installing market mechanisms that reliably transmit price information. Do we really want to call such a state of affairs 'functional'?

Evolutionary theorists of science have great difficulty envisaging the decline or corruption of science as a long-term consequence of science having been developed symbiotically with, say, capitalism or the nation-state. However, the pressures on governments today to divest their massive funding commitments to science suggest that we may not be so far from a world that would force this awareness upon us. In a fascinating essay on the collapse of the great ancient civilizations, the archaeologist Joseph Tainter (1988) argued that these societies eventually became too complex for their own good, as the cost of governance exceeded the benefit that accrued to either the governors or the governed. Collapse came in the form of either a simplification of the administrative apparatus or a fragmentation of the regime itself. If our highly 'functionally differentiated' science system is like one such ancient civilization that let its material development go unchecked, then we might expect epistemic collapse to come from, on the one hand, the elimination of disciplines and specialties (say, through the reorganization of the university) and, on the other, the privatization of knowledge in the form of intellectual property. These 'developments' are already upon us, and as critical intellectuals we have a duty to theorize them as signs of *decline*, not progress, in a hypertrophic knowledge system. As we have seen throughout this chapter, complexity once again proves to be a mark of pathology not health. Some approaches to a remedy are to be found in Part 3.

PART THREE

The secularization of science and a new deal for science policy

Nowadays it is common for scientists to treat with suspicion any attempt to understand science in terms of its social dimensions. However, this is due less to the motives of sociologists than to the peculiar social situation in which science finds itself today. After all, the features that had enabled science to function as the source of rational order in a secular world were themselves thoroughly social and staunchly defended by the classical sociologists. But over the past century, the social character of science has changed substantially in ways that have been discussed in the first two parts of this book. In Part 3 we turn to the reconstitution of the republican ideal of scientific inquiry, given that science has become a diversely interested, materially invested enterprise that reproduces both the strengths and weaknesses of contemporary democratic societies. In Chapter 6, I introduce the 'secularization' strategy that characterizes the entire argument. Like the secularization of religion, the point here is to divest the state's funding of scientific research, while at the same time promoting public access to alternative research programmes, each being allowed to find its own funding constituency. Secularization has many profound philosophical and political implications for the nature of inquiry, not least of which is the renewed significance assigned to teaching in academic life. Chapter 7 locates a precedent for secularization in the American 'New Deal' and examines the obstacles that calls for 'national competitiveness' pose to recovering that ideal in our own time. Finally, Chapter 8 lays out a dual strategy for democratizing science from 'within' and 'without'. In short, to realize the republican ideal of the open society in an era of Big Science, forums must be provided so that *all* professional knowledge producers can participate in determining the direction their fields take and the general public can influence the process in a manner that is commensurate to their interest in such matters.

6

Sociology as both sanctifier and secularizer of science

Science: from subject to object of secularization

Any proposals for the future governance of science must start by acknow-
ledging the profound historical irony that sociology has been both sancti-
fier and secularizer of science. Many scientists nowadays hold sociologists
responsible for science's current public relations crises. Sociologists have
certainly contributed to the public demystification of the natural sciences.
They have shown through ethnographic and historical research that the day-
to-day operations of the laboratory can be explained in the same terms as
any other highly competitive and highly funded activity. 'Truth', 'rationality' and 'objectivity' are metaphysical hypotheses that recent sociologists of
science do not require to understand how science works (Latour and Woolgar
1979; Fuller 1995). My project of social epistemology, illustrated by the
arguments pursued in this book, is concerned with how we should regard
contemporary society's most esteemed institution once it has been 'sociolog-
ized' in this fashion.

Yet, at the same time, sociology may also be blamed for originally plac-
ing science on the pedestal from which it is now being knocked. While
the natural sciences may be given credit for many things, one of them is
not their replacement of religion as the respectable repository for hopes
of salvation in the western world. That honour (such as it is) belongs to
Auguste Comte, who produced a body of thought – part philosophy, part
history, part prophecy – that anointed the natural sciences the successors
of the Roman Catholic Church as keepers of the key to the City of God
on earth. He called that body of thought 'positivism', and the discipline
embodying it 'sociology'. When Comte first embarked on his mission in
the 1820s, most practitioners of the natural sciences had not seen themselves

as worthy of anointment. Indeed, the 'natural philosophers', 'natural historians' and 'mechanics' whom we now lump together as 'scientists' did not even see each other as sharing a common mission. But by the end of the nineteenth century they had warmed to Comte's portrayal.

Comte came to sociology from historical and philosophical considerations of the role of systematic knowledge in society. This point of entry enabled him to drive a wedge between the substance of a body of knowledge and the function it serves in society at a particular time. That wedge was *secularization*, the process by which Christianity lost its traditional role as the source of authoritative knowledge and political power. However, Comte saw secularization as more than this separation of substance and function. For even after the substance of religious knowledge is discredited, the question remains as to which, if any, institutions will step in to serve its traditional social functions. Comte was convinced that the natural sciences were collectively suited to play the role of religion in the post-Christian era. But because Comte himself increasingly spent time worrying about which scientists would replace the Catholic saints in his secularized holy calendar, few commentators have been willing to admit openly that Comte's dream has largely come true.

Now we are in the midst of a second phase of secularization – that of science itself. Some details of the precedent set by the first phase are worth recalling here. The secularization of Christianity began with the seizure of Church properties by the emerging European nation-states in the seventeenth century, most notably after the Treaty of Westphalia in 1648, which ended 100 years of religious strife throughout Europe. The French term 'secularisation' implied that the jurisdiction of religious authority was restricted to followers of the religion in question. This legal fact had many interesting consequences. One was the revival of proselytizing as a strategy for attracting followers in what had suddenly become a 'market' environment for religion. The subsequent rise of evangelism reflected this competition for adherents, now that religion was no longer a protected state monopoly. Moreover, the signature doctrines of modern epistemology – rationalism and empiricism – were designed as alternative strategies for filling the vacuum of authority left by the divestiture of political authority from the Roman Catholic Church. Rationalists favoured an indubitable sovereign reason whose edicts were capable of silencing all dissent, whereas empiricists settled for experience as a relatively neutral court to which all factions could appeal for support. This turned out to be the difference between, on the one hand, René Descartes and Thomas Hobbes and, on the other, John Locke and David Hume (Toulmin 1990; Collins 1998: Ch. 11).

In retrospect, the legal separation of Church and state can be seen to have benefitted both parties. On the one hand, religious expression was protected from political interference by the state's refusal to grant one faith absolute authority. On the other hand, the state was able to stand above sectarian disagreements which in the past have been a source of political instability. However, over the next 150 years, second thoughts emerged about the overall benefits of secularization. In their different ways, the French and Industrial Revolutions had produced social dislocations of such magnitude that intellectuals were forced to reassess the Enlightenment claim that the true test of faith is whether it can be maintained after the material bases of its authority had been removed. Rather, it was now thought, long-term social stability lay in some other institution being accorded the indisputably sacred status that the Catholic Church enjoyed prior to the Reformation. To this day, when sociologists begin their theoretical enquiries by wondering about the grounds of social order, they are re-enacting this conundrum. However, the first sociologist, Comte, was clear that the grounds for a new social order lay in the natural sciences.

This was a genuinely new idea: In the seventeenth century, scientific findings had been used to flesh out the more enigmatic parts of the Bible as well as pagan texts whose obscurities hinted at access to powers that the Bible would have prohibited. *Prisca sapientia* ('pristine wisdom') was the name given to these original sources of knowledge, to which both Galileo and Newton appealed to legitimate what we now regard as their strikingly 'original' scientific innovations. It is far from obvious that these 'modern' minds would have been comfortable with the Enlightenment's self-appointed mission of demystifying religion. During the so-called Scientific Revolution, the natural sciences were aligned with military and industrial concerns that complemented, not competed with, religion (Proctor 1991). This was illustrated not only in the Charter of the Royal Society, which precluded its members from entering into religious disputes, but also in science's general lack of presence in the university curriculum until another two centuries had passed. By this time, the last quarter of the nineteenth century, under the influence of Darwinism, science had come to assume many of the features that made religion a source of authority in earlier times.

This uneasy mix of science's critical and dogmatic roles – its need to contain both the civil and the sacred within its institutional confines – is reflected in the debate that raged in the philosophy of science during the 1960s between Karl Popper and Thomas Kuhn, the implications of which were felt across many disciplines (Lakatos and Musgrave 1970). Popper argued that scientific theories are only as good as the illumination one receives from publicly testing them, whereas Kuhn claimed that the mark of a good scientist is that he or she persists with a theory in the face of much countervailing evidence. 'Commitment' and 'belief' are words that do not belong in a scientist's vocabulary, according to Popper, whereas they are essential for understanding Kuhn's account of science. Here we see the two sides of secularization in sharp relief: the side that eliminates religion (Popper's) and the side that replaces it (Kuhn's). Future historians will regard the debate between Popper and Kuhn as foreshadowing the secularization of science on which we are currently embarked. Nevertheless, science continues to occupy a sacred space in modern democracies.

Remapping science's sacred space in contemporary America

Generally speaking, modern democracies are hard to govern because they must balance issues of equity against those of efficiency among diverse and mobile constituencies (Barry 1965). The time it takes to deliberate over who deserves what (equity) works at cross-purposes with the need to deliver what is deserved in a timely fashion (efficiency). Small wonder, then, that democratic theorists have been willing to make trade-offs. On the one hand, market liberals have argued that equity will take care of itself as a by-product of private individuals tending to their own interests. On the other hand, proponents of the welfare state doubt this rosy, free market scenario, and prefer instead to ensure that everyone's minimal needs are satisfied, regardless of the inconvenience that this poses for some people. How does science figure in the democratic balancing act?

The general problem of democracy is compounded in the case of science because of the awe and mystery surrounding it. Witness the persistent failure of nerve and imagination modern democracies display in attempts to articulate the exact relationship between science and societal goals. In fact, 'more science' is such a pervasive part of the solutions proposed to standing social problems that few people have taken the trouble of thinking of science itself as a social problem (Restivo 1988). Billions of dollars are annually 'invested' in scientific projects, the ultimate value of which is assumed on a faith that largely goes unexamined. This faith is epitomized in the credo: 'Even if science never quite solves our social problems, nevertheless it is a good in its own right that can do no harm if left to its own devices'. And so, although the United States Constitution explicitly separates Church and state, science continues to occupy a sacred space in the American political system. In what follows I draw on two technical senses in which social psychologists talk about the experience of 'the sacred'. They bring out, respectively, the wishfulness and indirectness with which the sacred object, science is encountered in contemporary public policy.

The first concerns the blind eye that policymakers turn to science's frequent failures to deliver on expectations. Perversely, these 'failures of prophecy' often lead policymakers to be still more committed to the inertial tendencies in the scientific enterprise. Failures in the use of science as an instrument for public policy are often attributed to 'bad science', which is interpreted as a lack of knowledge that can be remedied only by a more generous funding policy for science. The thought that scientific research – at least as it is normally conducted – may bear no clear relationship to successful public policy of any sort is still regarded as controversial, even though the point has been made by leading policy theorists (e.g. Lindblom 1991) since the time of Lyndon Johnson's Great Society programme, as well as by historians of technology who have found little clear connection between the mere fact of technological innovation and economic progress (Rosenberg et al. 1992). Yet, like pouring libations upon the earth deity to ensure a good harvest, it often seems that great public expenditures for new research are needed to legitimate calls for action that could have been justified without the promised science.

The second sense of sacredness pertains to the diffuse character of the science policy process itself, which effectively prevents the national research agenda from ever being discussed publicly and in its entirety. Indeed, the US Office of Management and Budget appears to follow the common religious practice of referring to the sacred object – science – only under partial descriptions, namely as line items of the budgets of separate mission-oriented agencies (Office of Technology Assessment 1991: Ch. 5). These include the Departments of Defense, Energy, Agriculture, and Health and Human Services, the Environmental Protection Agency and the National Aeronautics and Space Administration. Unlike most nations today, the USA lacks a cabinet-level Department of Science and Technology. In fact, the only federal agency that specifically mentions 'science' as part of its mission – the National Science Foundation – ranks a mere fifth among the recipients of federal research funds. Add to this already diffuse image the fact that the most expensive and most glamorous scientific projects of the past decade (the human genome project, the Hubble space telescope, the orbiting space station and the Superconducting Supercollider) receive their funding directly from Congress, for the most part bypassing the usual agency channels.

Recent steps toward separating science and state

Despite these signs of science's sacred status, there are already indications that Americans are gradually getting used to the separation of science and state. The mentality that, say, led the US Congress to stop funding the Superconducting Supercollider in 1993 was motivated primarily not by any inherent distrust of science, but by budgetary burdens, as the state was forced to pick up the costs for social necessities that did not attract market-based solutions. Science, especially 'basic' or 'blue sky' research, must compete more directly for funding with other agencies whose relevance to human welfare is more evident. It is perhaps unfortunate that, in the case of the Supercollider, because weapons funding was possibly threatened by continued support for the Supercollider, the US Defense Department reversed its traditional pro-science stance and refused to intervene on the project's behalf (*New York Times* 1993). Needless to say, the scientific establishment used the defeat of the Supercollider as an opportunity to decry these forced encounters between scientific and non-scientific projects. However, given the ease with which scientists themselves have been willing to claim long-term, large-scale public benefits for their most expensive efforts, it is perhaps not so unreasonable that they be made to compete against other projects that claim similar consequences, be they proposed by the Defense Department or the Department of Health and Human Services. In any case, the material conditions that invite the divestiture of state support for science have little to do with any perceived failures or frauds on science's part. However, the fact that there have been such failures – e.g. 'the war on cancer', AIDS – and frauds certainly does not enhance science's status as a sacred authority.

The late epistemological anarchist Paul Feyerabend (1979) made a career out of suggesting that the formal divestiture of science from the state would be the best thing that could ever happen to science. Science has been such a destructive and threatening force in society only because the state has been able to concentrate so many resources on certain preferred projects. Without its resources so concentrated, science would be conducted on a smaller scale, one suited to the level of social accountability that can be reasonably expected of a community of enquirers. Clearly, a decentralized science would never have given us the nuclear arms race, just as a Protestantized Christianity in the Middle Ages would not have been able to mobilize the material and spiritual resources needed to field a series of Crusades against the Muslim world. Moreover, a decentralized science would enable the simultaneous pursuit of many different lines of enquiry without scientists feeling pressured to continue one line simply because so many resources had already been invested in it. In that respect, scientists would be less squeamish to propose fundamental criticisms of the dominant paradigm in their fields, since research would never reach a financial 'point of no return'.

Equally, the separation of science and state would benefit the state, or at least those who are subject to its rule. Just as religion was a source of fractiousness in sixteenth- and seventeenth-century European society, science is a destabilizing force in today's world. The dark side of accepting science's promise of universally valid knowledge has been to put *all* of humanity in a constant state of risk. Yet, there is little agreement on the nature of the risks involved – only that they are universal and 'real'. To cite just one vivid example, climatologists are now sounding the alarm of 'global warming', but less than 20 years ago some of the same people were predicting a 'nuclear winter'. I sometimes wonder if the so-called 'risk society' might be the result of our mistaking this instability of scientific judgement for some deeper, ontological insecurity (Giddens 1990; Beck 1992). That scientists should disagree publicly is, of course, not at issue here; rather, it is the idea that government policies should be tied so closely to the vicissitudes of these debates, and vice versa, that scientists should tailor their disagreements to appease one or the other constituency. Although politicians are just as likely to ignore as to obey what scientists say, the invocation of scientific findings – almost any findings will do – has turned out to be the most ideologically palatable means of coercing the populace available to democratic governments.

None of this is to say that the political sphere should shun scientific judgement altogether. Far from it. However, the state should separate its power to *distribute* scientific knowledge from its power to *produce* it. Crudely put, a secularized science would keep the former 'public' but make the latter 'private'. Among the 'distributional' functions of government that would be expanded, two stand out: (1) the testing of knowledge claims and products for validity, efficacy and safety, coupled with the regular mass publication of those results; (2) the institution of 'citizen education in science' that would empower students to critically engage with science-based issues in public forums, alongside the wider provision of such forums. The implications for such state-supported science facilities are, respectively: (1) the redeployment of laboratories currently pursuing 'original' research for purposes of conducting these critical tests; (2) the enhancement of laboratories that support science education at the undergraduate university level and below. In addition, one important way in which the state could expand public forums for the distribution of science-based issues is by officially declaring a period of debate and opinion sampling prior to a parliamentary vote.

Knowledge production as such would be left to corporations, unions, charities and other special interest groups, who should be offered tax incentives for foregoing exclusive rights to intellectual property and thereby keep the fruits of research in the realm of 'knowledge', strictly speaking. However, given the authorized character of any state-produced knowledge (which, in the past, underwrote much of what passed for science), the government should only fund research where it is required to address a problem in public policy. This proposal is less Draconian than it first appears, given that the agricultural and environmental sciences emerged as long-term effects of policy-driven research initiatives (Pavitt 1996). But history presents other precedents that should prepare us to wonder whether the conventional call for 'more research!' is ultimately oriented toward hastening or delaying certain known policy outcomes. Another important line of policy-driven research is on the effects of smoking on health. This has been promoted by the tobacco industry on the (often correct) assumption that scientists operate with such rigorous standards of causation that their 'trained incapacity' to assert any strong connection between smoking and cancer without an indefinite number of experiments serves as a bulwark against policymakers who would dare suggest that cigarettes be banned altogether.

As the state gradually divests its funding of scientific research, a period of 'science evangelism' may emerge comparable to that of the first wave of secularization. It would force scientists to actively court different sectors of society for support. 'Grantsmanship' would be sublimated into a proselytizing spirit whose precedents are to be found in the public demonstrations of science that marked the eighteenth and nineteenth centuries and among whose leading practitioners were Joseph Priestley and Michael Faraday (Knight 1986; Golinski 1992; Stewart 1992). It may mean that science acquires some of the 'customized' character of 'New Age' knowledges (Hess 1993), the validity of which depends on the meaning that a target constituency can attach to it. Consequently, the very principle of science funding may shift from *pay for effort* to *pay for results*. The former marks science as a relatively self-contained institution that operates on a system of grants based more on the scientist's credentials and previous work than the promise of the project as such, or whether the scientist is in an especially good position to exploit the project's potential. In contrast, a pay for results scheme characterizes an activity whose institutional boundaries are much more permeable. The paradigm case of payment is a prize awarded to the first person who solves a publicly announced problem by set criteria, regardless of that person's credentials or track record. The overall shift from prizes to grants in nineteenth-century science coincided with the onset of professionalization, and hence the need to provide payment for full-time scientific work. As science is increasingly secularized and thereby deprofessionalized, more economic arguments are heard for reverting to the old prize-based system (Hanson 1995). In Chapter 8, I sketch a comparable proposal that tries to model science competitions on spectator sports, but in the spirit of the republican ideal elaborated in Chapter 1.

Although my proposal for secularizing science so far seems drastic, it is comparable to instituting a principle of religious tolerance without authorizing a religious orthodoxy. Thus, the state's responsibility extends to exposing alternative scientific perspectives once they have been developed, but not to their actual development. A crucial presupposition of my proposal is that for most social and even scientific problems, there is already a sufficient knowledge base but its potential has not yet to be realized in public policy debate and implementation. In so far as there is a need for state-driven research innovation at all, it is in information science, so as to enable people to locate and utilize knowledge already available. Under the circumstances, the call for 'more research' should be understood as an attempt to delay our drawing upon current knowledge as a basis for action – a call that researchers heed in their need for new sources of income, given the increasing tenuousness of academic tenure. However, were these economic pressures removed, the issue would boil down to whether the existing body of knowledge is sufficient to license people trying out courses of action on themselves. The answer to that question turns on whether the society in question could absorb the consequences of those trials. A serious test for the plausibility of my argument is medical research, especially into the causes of disease. Here I would say that the importance of searching for causes has been greatly exaggerated, often in a way that delays policy implementation (as in the case of effects of smoking on health) and lets the bare promise of a cure divert valuable resources from the dissemination of preventative measures based on what is already known.

That 'endless innovation' is taken for granted as a desideratum of national science policy reveals the extent to which the public policy agenda has been subsumed by the competitive character of society's military and industrial sectors. These sectors orient their performance toward imagined zero-sum games based on international comparisons that bear tangentially on the welfare concerns of most citizens. To counter this tendency, the state needs to reassert its own ends, specifically to the quality of life of its citizens. The imperatives of military and industrial policies should inform national science policy only to the extent that they also advance citizen ends, without presuming that citizens automatically benefit from whatever benefits what C. Wright Mills (1956) called 'the scientific-military-industrial complex'. Here I am making a veiled critical reference to the most recent UK government White Paper on science policy, *Realising our Potential* (Chancellor of the Duchy of Lancaster 1993), which routinely conflates 'national economic performance' (an end of industry) with 'quality of life' (an end of the state).

Moreover, there is nothing intrinsically 'efficient' about the endless drive to innovate. The vast majority of research goes unread as it is, with duplicated effort providing a poor excuse for collective learning. Indeed, regarded as a personnel matter, it would seem that scientific talent is being deployed in the elusive race for 'original discoveries' when it might be better spent on improving library and other database search facilities that would make already existing (including indigenous) knowledge more readily available for use.

Interestingly, the military and industrial establishments tend to take somewhat opposite views of this plethora of effort in science. Once the Soviet Union was shown to have created a centralized scientific network that precluded the funding of proposals that duplicated previous work, the American defence establishment called for the creation of what turned out to be the Institute for Scientific Information, as a means of keeping track of the direction and intensity of scientific research (Fuller 1997: 68–70). This is the source of the *SCI*, discussed in the previous chapter. In contrast, industry looks more benignly on duplicated effort as part of the 'trial-and-error' learning that characterizes the spontaneously organized market for knowledge. In any case, there has been little systematic study of the impact academic journal-based research has outside academic forums, so the level of wastage in our 'social intelligence' networks may be much higher than is often suspected.

Science desacralized: questioning the quality of scientific life

This section has continued the previous chapter's critique of the interpretations given to capitalized Big Science. The critique ultimately turns on what I have called the 'normative underdetermination of social regularities' (Fuller 1996; 1997: 63–7). In other words, a pattern of activity that appears rational at the system level may be irrational at the subsystem level. For example, we saw that high scientific productivity was not merely compatible with, but an emergent consequence of, a high wastage of scientific talent. Whether this state of affairs is regarded as good or bad depends on the perspective adopted. Those concerned with maximizing such scientific 'outputs' as papers and patents – science policymakers and university administrators – would probably adopt the system perspective and approve the process, whereas those concerned with the fate of the scientific agents themselves would probably deplore the process.

The ultimate precedent for this schizoid evaluation is Marx's critique of the kinds of capital in *Das Kapital* (Vol. II, Ch. 11). Classical political economy, represented by Adam Smith and David Ricardo, divided capital into what remains fixed in the course of production and what 'circulates' in the sense of having to be continually replaced. Fixed capital includes land and buildings, while human labour constitutes circulating capital. Marx argued that this distinction was drawn from the perspective of bourgeois factory owners who encountered their workers as friction in the production process, as they regularly had to replenish their resources, especially in the payment of wages. In a fully efficient factory, these workers would be replaced by automated technology which would eliminate downtime altogether, thereby enabling circulating capital, which could be absorbed into fixed capital. This is the mentality of the science policymaker who believes that the biggest problem with our scaled-up knowledge enterprises is that the resulting plethora of publications impedes access to the truly 'quality' items and hence needs to be supplemented by a computer-automated 'search engine' (or 'knowbot'). For his part, Marx redrew the fixed/circulating distinction in terms of constant versus variable capital, or the potential versus the actual source of value in production. Although land and buildings provide the opportunity for the production of goods, no goods will be actually produced unless human labour is engaged – and, by no means, can this engagement be taken for granted. By analogy, an emphasis on the status of the scientist in Big Science could easily call into question the quality of intellectual life, so to speak, that is promoted under this regime. This point will be explicitly addressed in Chapters 7 and 8.

Secularizing the legitimatory function of the history of science

At the end of Chapter 1, I proposed a general strategy for enabling individuals to overcome the principle of cumulative advantage: a social inheritance tax. However, alongside that strategy must be a demystification of the very idea that, in the long term, some tradition or line of inquiry is bound to dominate, simply by virtue of the advantages it will have accumulated over its rivals. In the case of science, this idea appears most clearly in historically based doctrines of progress. No matter how postmodern we claim to be, the idea that science progresses by retaining the wheat and shedding the chaff of the past remains an article of faith in the public sphere. Indeed, both liberals and communitarians have no problem endorsing the idea: the former by the invisible hand of Merton's principle of cumulative advantage, the latter by the much heavier hand of a Kuhnian paradigm focused on normal science. However, republican scruples compel us to rework this common faith by capitalizing on historically unrealized possibilities. Specifically, I propose to reinvent the distinction between the contexts of discovery and justification of scientific knowledge. For some, this call will bring back unpleasant memories of logical positivism, with its strictures against letting the idiosyncratic psychosocial origins of a knowledge claim interfere with the publicly inspectable means by which its validity is determined. The former – the realm of discovery – was by implication irreducibly irrational, and the latter – the realm of justification – steadfastly methodological. The distinction can be traced to William Whewell, the early Victorian polymath who coined the word 'scientist' as the name of a professional whose practice called for specific academic credentials (for a fuller story, see Fuller forthcoming: Ch. 1).

In the 1830s, Whewell realized that virtually every major scientific innovation with industrial applications over the previous half-century had been made by people without university training. Whewell was concerned that if the humanistically oriented universities did not incorporate experimental inquiries into their curricula, they would be eventually forced to yield their authority to the emerging vocational schools and polytechnics which typically trained these innovators. Consequently, Whewell argued that scientific innovations were not fully understood unless they could be explained as the natural outgrowth of an evolving body of theoretically grounded knowledge. The ability to provide such explanations was the mark of a 'scientist', as opposed to the amateur inquirer. Thus, the medieval institution of the university received a new lease on life as the provider of justifications that went beyond the simple fact that a given innovation yielded immediate practical benefits.

A hundred years later, the discovery/justification distinction exchanged these elitist origins for more populist ones, with the invention of the 'genetic fallacy' as philosophy's first line of defence against the Nazis. (The first textbook to feature the fallacy was Cohen and Nagel 1934.) When the Nazis argued that the ethnic origins of a scientific innovator contributed to an innovation's validity, the logicians struck back that valid knowledge claims can come from any number of sources, thereby rendering an innovation's origins irrelevant to its ultimate validity. However, with the passing of the Nazis, the urge to stamp out the genetic fallacy has weakened. Indeed, the discovery/justification distinction is often said to have been definitively deconstructed in the 1960s and 1970s by the 'historicist' strain in the philosophy of science, as represented by Thomas Kuhn, Imre Lakatos and Larry Laudan. According to these historicists, a research tradition justifies its continuation by the number of robust discoveries that are made under its auspices. In this way, a research tradition enjoys intellectual property rights over the knowledge claims it originates. Thus, if a scientist working in, say, the Newtonian or Darwinian research tradition happens to make an important finding, then the finding counts as a reason for promoting the tradition, and soon the impression is given – especially in textbooks – that the finding could have been be made *only* by someone working in that tradition. In other words, priority quickly becomes grounds for necessity.

The historicists clearly presupposed a highly competitive model of scientific inquiry that gravitates toward the dominance of a single paradigm in any given field. They rarely countenanced cases in which knowledge claims originating in one research tradition had been adapted to the needs and aims of others. One important reason for this oversight is that ultimately the historicists believed that alternative research traditions are little more than ways of dividing up the labour in pursuit of some common goals of inquiry, such as explanatory truth or predictive reliability. Thus, they presumed that there is some automatic sense in which a discovery made by one tradition is 'always already' the property of all, though access to this supposedly common property requires that one first exchanges theoretical allegiances.

Consider the treatment of Darwinian evolution and Creation science as mutually exclusive options in the American public school curriculum. Although two-thirds of Americans who believe in evolution also believe that it reflects divine intelligence, such compatibility has yet to be seen as a philosophically respectable option, and consequently has no legal import (Carter 1993: 156–82). But what exactly would be wrong with teachers trying to render biological findings compatible with the Creationist commitments of most of their students? One common answer is that the presupposition of a divine intelligence or teleology has retarded biological inquiry in the past and has not contributed to evolutionary theory since the time of Darwin's original formulation. Yet, the contrary presuppositions of mechanistic reduction and random genetic variation have equally led to error (see the interviews with maverick biologists in Horgan 1996: 114–42).

In this context, the republicanism advocated in Chapter 1 emerges as a pedagogical issue: should students be forced to accept the current scientific canon as a paradigm (in the Kuhnian sense of a total ideology) that would deny the legitimacy of whatever larger belief systems they bring to the classroom? Or, should students learn how to integrate science into their belief systems, recognizing points of compatibility, contradiction and possible directions for personal intellectual growth? If we favour the latter 'citizen science' perspective of republicanism over the former 'professional science' perspective of communitarianism, then we need to reinvent the discovery/justification distinction.

Reinventing the contexts of scientific discovery and justification

According to the old distinction, an ideally justified discovery would show how anyone with the same background knowledge and evidence would have made the same discovery. The role of justification was thus to focus and even homogenize the scientific enterprise through a common 'logic of scientific inference'. In practice, however, 'the same background knowledge and evidence' understated what was actually needed for people to draw the same conclusions – namely, involvement in a particular research tradition. In contrast, the new distinction I propose conceptualizes scientific justification as removing the idiosyncratic character of scientific discovery in a deeper sense than the old distinction pursued – not simply the fact that a discovery was first reached by a given individual in a given lab, but the fact that it was reached by a particular research tradition in a given culture. In other words, the goal of scientific justification would be to remove whatever advantage a particular research tradition or culture has gained by having made the discovery first.

This project would safeguard scientific inquiry from devolving into a form of expertise, whereby, say, one would have to be a card-carrying Darwinian before having anything credible to say about biology. It would also have the opposite effect of the old discovery/justification distinction, in that it would aim to render a discovery compatible with as many different background assumptions as possible, so as to empower as many different sorts of people. Models for this activity can be found in both the natural and the social sciences. In the natural sciences, there are 'closed theories' (e.g. Newtonian mechanics) and 'dead sciences' (e.g. chemistry), which can be learned as self-contained technologies without the learner first having to commit to a particular metaphysical, axiological, or perhaps even disciplinary orientation. In the social sciences, conceptual and technical innovations originating in one tradition have been typically picked up and refashioned by other traditions, so as to convey a sense of history as multiple parallel trajectories (Deutsch *et al.* 1986). It is just this cross-fertilization that gives the social sciences the appearance of a field of unresolvable ideological differences which, from a republican standpoint, is a good not a bad thing.

But perhaps the historically most interesting models of this renovated sense of discovery/justification at work are the hybrid forms of inquiry that have emerged as defensive responses to western colonial expansion. In Fuller (1997: Ch. 6), I consider the cases of modern Islam and Japan. In both, the instrumental power of the natural sciences has been neither denied nor anathematized, but rather systematically reinterpreted so that these sciences become a medium for realizing the normative potentials of their respective cultures (Sardar 1989). Along the way, some telling critiques of the historicist perspective on science have been made. Whereas Islam has criticized the West for not anticipating the destructive and despiritualizing consequences of the 'science for its own sake' mentality, Japan has lodged the opposite complaint that the West superstitiously clings to the stages undergone by its own history as a global blueprint for the advancement of science.

Clearly, the relationship between the contexts of discovery and justification needs to be reconceptualized. Whewell originally imagined the process of scientific justification as akin to a major river into which many tributaries flow. Each discovery (by analogy, a tributary) is treated as an unexpected challenge that must be rationalized in terms of the dominant paradigm (by analogy, the major river). Once justified, discoveries lose any sense of their unique origins, having been homogenized in a common body of knowledge. The alternative model implied in my secularization account is that, as a matter of fact, the origins of scientific discoveries are not usually

Table 6.1   Redrawing the contexts of the discovery/justification distinction

	Liberal/communitarian science	*Republican science*
Metaphor guiding the distinction	Convergence: tributaries flowing into a major river	Divergence: a major river flowing into a delta
Prima facie status of discovery	Disadvantage (because of unexpected origins)	Advantage (because of expected origins)
Ultimate role of justification	Concentrate knowledge through logical assimilation	Distribute knowledge through local accommodation
Background assumption	Discoveries challenge a paradigm unless they are assimilated to it	Discoveries reinforce a paradigm unless they are accommodated to local settings
Point of the distinction	Turn knowledge into power (magnify cumulative advantage)	Divest knowledge of power (diminish cumulative advantage)
Definition of contemporary science	Present is continuous with the future – the past is dead and best left to historians	Present is continuous with the past – the future is open to the retrieval of lost options

Source: Fuller (forthcoming).

obscure but rather are already attuned to the dominant trends in science (otherwise, it would be difficult to recognize them as 'discoveries'). The aim of 'justifying' knowledge claims would be to integrate the discovery within any number of background beliefs and practices, thereby removing any advantage that may have accrued to the discoverer's original culture. This may even mean presenting evolutionary theory as compatible with divine creation. Thus, Whewell's analogy is turned on its head. Instead of tributaries leading to a major river, the relationship between the contexts of discovery and justification is envisioned in terms of a major river (the biased discovery) issuing into a delta (its multiple justifications). It is captured in Table 6.1 (adapted from Fuller forthcoming: Ch. 8).

Secularization as university policy: towards a new asceticism?

As in Whewell's day, universities today are crucial to implementing the standards by which claims to knowledge are justified. But it is equally clear, based on considerations raised over the previous three chapters, that universities must revisit their 'Enlightenment' mission as the locus of critical thought and citizen education – as the institution responsible for applying 'affirmative action' to the soul by sensitizing students to perspectives that complement, and sometimes contradict, the dominant values of the time. Universities will satisfy this lofty mission only by rekindling their ties to the welfare functions of the state and taking advantage of their role as the sole provider of systematic understanding and democratic empowerment in an increasingly fragmented and segmented world. In short, 'teachability' will need to be made a criterion of good research. This will appear to be an especially radical proposal in national educational systems like Britain's, where teaching and research are subject to very different evaluative regimes.

In other words, a new finding that cannot be made readily available to competent students operating with radically different assumptions should be seen as problematic until proven otherwise. I do not wish to deny that students may enter the classroom believing things that are so opposed to what is on the curriculum that only a conversion experience will enable them to make progress. But if students have already demonstrated competency in one or more other academic subjects, but find themselves stymied by, say, their biology instruction, then that is, on the face of it, grounds for wondering whether the teaching of biology is not geared more towards keepers of the current paradigm than those removed from that circle who nevertheless wish to make use of biological knowledge in their own lives. In terms of the social sciences, I would say that sociology is currently more 'teachable' than, say, economics or psychology because it tends to present the richness of social life independently of particular theoretical accounts, thereby potentially opening the space for many different accounts to explain the same phenomena, without denying that each such account must reach a certain minimum level of academic respectability (Fuller 1999).

In the modern period, the state has been the vehicle through which most western intellectual movements have had major societal impact. This point has been obvious to natural scientists from the founding of the Royal Society, which received a charter from the then newly-reinstated king of England. As the secularization of science proceeds apace, universities may relate more symbiotically to the state by distinguishing their own interests from those that involve the promotion of specific disciplines whose research agendas may be strongly influenced by external funding. For, while a specialized field may be captured by special interests, it is unlikely that an institution resolutely devoted to the pursuit of inquiry *as such* would be susceptible to such co-optation. If the state continues to define its identity in potential opposition to the forces of global capitalism, then it will retain an interest in supporting an institution like the university, which is involved in the distributional functions reserved for secularized science policy, as described in this chapter. My discussion of the American New Deal in the next chapter provides an example of what it is like to think of knowledge production in these terms.

The overall picture I am painting is of a university that reunites the performance and evaluation of teaching and research, which in turn implies that both would operate with the generalist in mind as the target audience. For most institutions of higher learning, this would probably mean a renewed focus on undergraduate education. It may even involve the withering away of specialized graduate science programmes and the divestiture of intellectual property rights. Indeed, the science-secularized university would be an institution whose relative financial independence – albeit bred more by asceticism than wealth – enables it to regain its critical independence (see Cook 1991: 91–140 on the politics of asceticism). In sum, I propose that the university recover its Enlightenment promise by becoming, so to speak, a medium of 'disintermediation'. The university would thus aim to reduce the complexity of the social world as part of an overall strategy of empowering citizens to pursue common ends. In terms of the four forms of intermediation introduced in Chapter 5, the university would be committed to the following:

- *Economic disintermediation*: the university discourages the pursuit of research the enormous cost of which would compromise the institution's critical independence. But if such research is pursued, then a principle of 'epistemic fungibility', as discussed in Chapter 8, would need to apply, whereby the cross-disciplinary relevance of a project would have to increase with its overall cost.
- *Functional disintermediation*: the university limits the role it plays in reproducing and normalizing the social order, which implies that it either divests many of its current credentialing functions or requires that credential-based programmes incorporate a 'canon' underwritten by a university-wide curriculum committee that may well challenge the knowledge claims presupposed by the credentials – e.g. the canon may include Marxist works that contradict what the student is taught in a business management course.
- *Temporal disintermediation*: the university rejects the Mode 1/Mode 2 narrative introduced in the previous chapter, which is designed to capture the allegedly irreversible rupture in the history of academic life caused by Big Science and the more general introduction of client-based knowledge production. Instead, the narrative is regarded as a self-fulfilling prophecy that ought to be resisted, especially given that the relative openness of higher education to external imperatives has varied cyclically across history (Collins 1998).
- *Collegial disintermediation*: the university reorients its incentive structure so as to discourage academics from trying to gain recognition simply by distinguishing themselves from their colleagues in a narrow disciplinary field. Instead, academics are encouraged to link their claims to non-academic interest groups, so that disputes which are supposedly 'internal' to the university are seen to represent positions that are in conflict within the larger society. The discussion in Chapter 4 of the High versus Low Church split in multiculturalism captures the type of issue that needs to be foregrounded in the university at large.

While stripped-down by the standards of today's 'multiversities', this ascetic renewal of the university's mission would enable the institution to speak *to* power without having to speak *for* it. In this sense, the university's republican promise would start to be realized, as it begins to regain control over the material conditions of inquiry. An inchoate version of this strategy is already at work in academic accounting schemes that incorporate overhead costs for purposes of internal resource reallocation. In terms of the above four proposals, a primitive version of the first operates in what is essentially a surcharge that universities impose on research funding agencies in order to raise revenue for lines of inquiry that are less likely to be self-supporting; hence, American humanities and social science programmes are often funded on the back of large natural science grants by adding 20–40 per cent to the actual research costs specified in the grant. In the case of the second proposal, the concept of overhead functions more metaphorically as an educational toll imposed on degree candidates – that is, students cannot serve their own vocational interests unless they have also served the larger issues of critical citizenship promoted by the university.

The main objection to the asceticist strategy is that it renders universities too user-*un*friendly, when compared with privately operated institutions that expressly aim to provide clients with the epistemic capital they need – be it embodied in patents or people. These institutions do not impose extraneous requirements, especially ones that cut against and perhaps even undermine the projects that their clients are trying to pursue. Must the ascetic university, then, as a matter of principle, cede the bulk of the demand-driven knowledge market to specialized 'knowledge businesses' (Hague 1991)? On the contrary, I believe that universities should adhere to the American football maxim that a good offence is the best defence.

The offence would be two-pronged. First, the university should hold its ground as the most credible site for critically testing knowledge claims. This remains the most powerful basis for state regulation of market-based activities, especially once the results of these tests are publicized. Clearly, both industrial firms and the consumers of their goods have an interest – albeit one rarely admitted – in quality control checks, including the anticipation of major problems and unintended consequences. The second prong is that universities should extend their auditing regimes to determine what portion of publicly funded education and research is merely privately appropriated. When James R. O'Connor (1973) first raised this issue as 'the fiscal crisis of the state', he meant mainly the ways capitalist firms had managed to get the general public to pay for replenishing and extending their sources of capital accumulation within a given nation. However, these concerns have acquired greater poignancy with the globalization of capitalism. Thus, academic auditors need to address the following questions:

- Do all regions of the nation proportionally benefit by increased provisions for higher education?
- Is there a 'brain drain', such that other nations turn out to be the main beneficiaries?

- Does the nation that registers a patent sufficiently benefit, if the registering firm then manufactures and markets the patent-based products overseas?
- If there is indeed a 'trickle-down' effect from public investment in capital that is, in the first instance, privately appropriated, then exactly how would one detect and represent this supposely salutary trickling?

Notwithstanding all this tough talk in defence of the university's integrity, it may come to pass that economically insecure universities revert to a more demand-driven, trades-based curriculum, much like the institutes of higher learning that competed with Oxbridge in the nineteenth century when laboratory-based training was still regarded as unfit for the liberal arts curriculum. However, given our post-industrial economic base, the relevant jobs are now more likely to be found in management than manufacturing. It is conceivable that these institutes, especially when largely under the thumb of a single corporation, will be more efficient providers of job training than traditional universities. Perhaps the 'management training programme' most familiar to British broadsheet newspaper readers is the 'special relationship' that Manchester Metropolitan University (a former polytechnic) has with the Sainsbury's supermarket chain. (At the time of writing, Lord David Sainsbury is the Labour government's spokesperson for science and technology.)

It may then make sense for the institutes to lose the not-for-profit status traditionally accorded to universities, since they would be primarily devoted to cultivating the 'human capital' needed for maintaining specific business concerns. Moreover, if traditional universities wish to continue competing with industry by engaging in research designed to yield patentable products, then they too may deserve to lose their not-for-profit status, or at least be taxed for the royalties accrued to those inventions. While it is in the public interest for universities to 'reverse engineer' inventions in order to determine how they work, so that they may be made more widely available, it is not clear that the public interest extends to what normally passes as 'original discoveries' – especially when they have the potential to concentrate wealth and increase the vulnerability of the more disadvantaged members of society (e.g. by rendering their jobs redundant). We turn to this point in the next chapter, when discussing the historical precedent for secularized science policy set by the New Deal, President Franklin Roosevelt's policy for the economic reconstruction of the USA after the Great Depression of the 1930s.

7

The road not taken: revisiting the original New Deal

The original rise and fall of New Deal science policy

Nowadays one risks uttering a platitude when saying that research priorities, funding levels and accountability mechanisms have been distorted by national security concerns during the Cold War. But what would it mean to remove those distortions? First, it would mean recognizing their full extent. The last time this was done was immediately after World War II, during the debate surrounding the establishment of the US National Science Foundation (NSF). But few realize just how many wartime science policy practices were actually normalized by the version of the NSF that came into being (Kleinman 1995). Therefore, we shall have to explore the road not taken in the founding debates, the road that would have led back to the New Deal policies that were abruptly diverted once America entered the war.

Before the two world wars caused the state to take such an active interest in scientific research, academic scientists were primarily teachers who were more concerned with opening students' minds than with pushing back the frontiers of knowledge. Innovative work was, in turn, to be found in the industrial labs and corporate foundations, both of which fostered interdisciplinary work that had no clear place in the university curriculum (Kohler 1991). In those days scientific innovation implied that the novelty had to have some relatively immediate practical uptake. Indeed, until Hiroshima the average American's conception of a 'scientist at work' was either the self-taught Thomas Edison or a white-coated industrial chemist – not an academic at all (La Follette 1990: 45–65). The success of the atomic bomb project changed all that by vividly demonstrating what leading academic scientists could accomplish when given enormous resources with minimal political oversight. The urgent needs of war easily explained this combination of heavy expenditures and high levels of secrecy. Nevertheless, after the war, Vannevar Bush (1945) and the other architects of America's post-war science policy refashioned these conditions as characterizing something called 'basic research', the supposed foundations of the scientific enterprise. What had previously been regarded as 'unprecedented' research conditions were now normalized as providing the basis of 'autonomy', that most sacred of scientific virtues. Ironically, one of the most attractive features of this sort of research, interdisciplinary character, was dropped from the design of the NSF in favour of discipline-based, peer-reviewed research.

However, it would be a mistake to conclude that Bush simply took advantage of an opportunity. In fact, the concept of basic research was integral to the emerging image of the 'security state' whose primary activity was preparation for war. Indeed, Bush and his allies were more successful in diminishing science's public accountability by having much defence research reclassified as 'basic' than by boosting actual research funding (Reingold 1994: 367–8). Because the 'applied research' championed by industry was increasingly consumer-oriented and market-driven, Bush and his colleagues concluded that a business would invest in research only to the extent that it would be likely to increase its market share. Products too ahead of their times are just as unprofitable as products that fall behind consumer demand. Thus, industry had little incentive to make major revolutionary breakthroughs in research. In contrast, the national security state was dedicated to mastering and overcoming the military capabilities of the Communist Bloc through the design of ever 'smarter' weapons, whose potential for 'mutually assured destruction' would supposedly be a sufficient threat to end war altogether. This search for what might be called 'the military sublime' was the very antithesis of the run-with-the-pack market mentality of business, but was well suited to the sense of ultimate ends that has always animated the basic research mindset. By contrast with society's short-term vision, the military was concerned with technologies that coincided with science's own long-term vision.

Moreover, based on the performance of academic scientists during World War II, the defence establishments of most western powers seemed content to continue to allow scientists to work with minimum oversight. In this way, the military became the main external supporter of basic research in the Cold War era, with 20 per cent of all scientists worldwide working in defence-related research by the 1970s (30 per cent in the USA and UK) (Proctor 1991: 254). Given this background, the market-oriented science policy analyst should recommend that, in the post-Cold War era, the supply of researchers be reduced to match demand. For, the current plethora of researchers is not a 'natural' outgrowth of the search for knowledge but a vestige from the upscaling of universities that accompanied the Cold War. This point is often overlooked because Big Science was being 'naturalized' – that is, grounded in a rewritten historical sociology and political economy of science – as it was coming to fruition in the 1960s (see Shils 1968; for a systematic critique see Fuller forthcoming).

However, Bush's greatest legacy was probably the idea that research funds should be allocated according to the quality of the researcher, a judgement which, in turn, could only be made by other distinguished researchers. Peer review would probably have never enjoyed its sacred status had it not been used to construct the team entrusted with building the bomb. Threatened in common by the Axis powers, the Allied physicists put aside their theoretical differences and focused on collecting colleagues who were most likely to help complete the task in the shortest time. This was a novel use of peer review that Bush and others thought was relevant to resource allocation issues in peacetime.

To be sure, peer review had always been used to evaluate research for professional publication. But to entrust scientists with dividing up the available resources for research, especially once they were no longer focused on a common goal, was to reopen the door to a kind of partisanship that would compromise the integrity of science. The sorts of self-serving judgements that scientists routinely try to suppress when weighing the merits of completed work would arguably re-emerge when evaluating the prospects of work yet to be done and hence compromise the resulting judgements. In historical terms, most of the scientific outsiders whose work was readily recognized by their peers upon completion – certainly Einstein and maybe even Darwin – would have been initially passed over for peer-reviewed funding because of their prior lack of accomplishment and potential threat to established research programmes. Michael Faraday is an especially interesting case because, fully aware of his disadvantaged background, he early volunteered his manual services to Humphry Davy at the Royal Institution's chemistry laboratory, and through apprenticeship managed to rise up within the establishment, so that he became an 'institutionalized radical' (Morus 1992).

Bush's moves to extend wartime science policy practices into peacetime did not go unchallenged in the few years that separated the end of World War II and the start of the Cold War. However, the failure of those challenges continues to be felt every time criticism of peer-reviewed funding procedures is answered by moralizing about the evils of 'earmarking' or, worse still, 'pork barrelling'. A project is 'earmarked' if its funding comes from outside the official competition, while an earmarked project is 'pork barrelled' if it comes specifically from a politically sensitive constituency. These currently reviled terms harken back to an honourable alternative world of science policy that is worth revisiting as a prod to the contemporary imagination, one that specifically targets scientific developments to constituencies who might otherwise fail to achieve them.

The continuing legacy of the New Deal

Even before the end of the war, many American state university heads had begun to worry that peer-reviewed funding procedures in peacetime would exaggerate existing resource differences between élite and non-élite institutions that had arisen from selective corporate research and development investment before the war (Mills 1948). As it turns out, the concerns about élitism have been well placed. In recent years, 50 per cent of federal science funding in the USA has gone to 33 out of over 2000 institutions of higher education, virtually the same 33 that receive the lion's share of corporate sponsorship (Office of Technology Assessment 1991: 263–5). One way of forestalling this situation would have been to follow the advice of Chauncey Leake, then provost of the University of Texas, and institute a system of checks and balances (modelled on the US Constitution itself) to prohibit the same scientists from serving on the governing boards of the major journals, professional societies and private and public funding bodies (US Congress 1945). In effect, a wider cross-section of scientists would have been brought into the governance of their fields, creating a broader sense of scientific 'peerage'. This jury duty model would democratize peer review by counteracting Merton's principle of cumulative advantage, whereby academia's rich get richer and poor get poorer.

More radical proposals would have banished peer review from the funding arena altogether. Peacetime science policy would have resumed the comprehensive welfare programme initiated by the New Deal. One scheme in this vein, favoured by Edwin Land, the inventor of the Polaroid camera's self-developing film, called for the federal government to grant scholarships to science students as seed money for potentially lucrative inventions. Others suggested an 'affirmative action' programme for the traditionally disadvantaged southern and western regions of the country, whereby they would receive a disproportionally larger fraction of the funds than regions that had traditionally benefitted from private endowments. There was even talk of a national service programme that would set aside scholarships for clever students from impoverished backgrounds to matriculate at the major universities, on the condition that they would then staff technical training and research facilities in the nation's economically underdeveloped regions (Kevles 1977).

All of the above proposals merit a second look today. Especially noteworthy at the time was the claim that science was a suitable site for redistributionist policies precisely because its modes of enquiry, in principle, could be known and done by anyone. Any differences in scientific performance among universities or regions could be attributed to differences in the quality of the training and research facilities at their disposal, not the quality of the people staffing them. Even opponents of the democratization of science needed to explain how it was possible for many of the greatest scientific achievements to be made by people who were considered 'slow' in their day, such as Darwin and Einstein. Rather than allowing only the intellectual élite to pursue scientific careers, it might be better to promote a spread of intelligence so that radical but underdeveloped ideas were not rejected out of hand by the quicker wits equipped with all the 'standard counter-arguments'. However, this analysis only proved persuasive as long as the the fast-paced, high-tech research that characterized World War II was considered an aberration that would be redressed in peacetime by a science policy sensitive to the rate at which scientific innovation could be assimilated by society at large. Unfortunately, the Cold War was declared soon after the Allied victory and this required the rapid deployment of technically trained personnel, a policy that clearly favoured scientists already at the major research centres.

Ironically, despite their claims for being far-sighted thinkers, those who today defend the maintenance, if not increase, of basic research spending neglect the fact that, over the past century, science funding has been subject to recurrent cycles of mobilization (for war) and post-war conversion (for the USA see Reingold 1994: 367). Indeed, it is often forgotten that in the original NSF (National Science Foundation) hearings, the head of Bell Telephone Laboratories and president of the National Academy of Sciences, Frank Jewett, argued that the state should roll back all of its research investment to pre-World War II levels. The public should then be encouraged to treat scientific research programmes as charities, contributions to which could be the source of tax relief (US Congress 1947). Whatever else one thinks of Jewett's scheme, it would certainly have provided an incentive for members of the public sufficiently wealthy to have incurred a significant tax burden to acquaint themselves with competing research programmes.

The idea of deliberately slowing the pace of scientific progress may seem unthinkable today, but it was treated as a live option when the New Deal sought ways out of the Depression. In that context, science was perceived as a regulatory monster. On the one hand, scientists contributed to a volatile financial climate because their inventions often failed to match their investors' hopes. On the other, when science did deliver on its promises, there was the even greater fear that its results would be monopolized by firms with the power to hold the rest of society in their grip. This problem has re-emerged as transnational corporations have found it in their interest to promote more comprehensive intellectual property rights (Drahos 1995). Moreover, once the Depression was in full swing, scientists were chastised for developing new forms of automation that cut the production costs of firms by making workers redundant. Consequently, a key provision of New Deal industrial policy was to curb chronic unemployment by restricting the amount and type of such innovations that could be introduced into the workplace. Some especially zealous regulators went so far as to suggest, on the model of farmers being paid not to raise crops, that scientists be paid not to do certain kinds of socially disruptive research (Proctor 1991: 238). A couple of related ideas would be relevant to our own time. One is that instead of regarding a patent on an innovation as an exclusive (albeit temporary) intellectual property right, the innovation may be taxed in order to discourage the tendency to innovate faster than society can assimilate. The other, of course, is to divert scientists' efforts from research to teaching, given the mass of unread publications that could benefit from more direct exposure.

I have so far neglected one important proposal that was favoured by much of the scientific community to help the state normalize science's relation to the rest of society: unionization. It received considerable attention up to World War II but little afterward. American scientists first acquired a collective identity fighting on the same side in World War I. However, after the German defeat, the career patterns of scientists drifted according to the centrifugal demands of the market, which left the peacetime economy increasingly destabilized. Some scientists took a page from Marx and cast themselves as exploited high-grade workers to whom a union would give the voice to ensure that the fruits of their labour did not do more harm than good. Given that most scientists at the time were themselves from working- to lower middle-class backgrounds, the call for unionization seemed ideologically credible.

Britain provided the exemplar that American scientists followed in the 1920s and 1930s. An especially influential figure in the latter period was the X-ray crystallographer and Marxist historian of science, John Desmond Bernal, whose view of science policy as a form of labour-management relations was influenced by Alfred Mond, head of Imperial Chemical Industries (Jones 1988: 6–14). However, suspicions of latent Communist sympathies slowed the unionization process, until World War II intervened, causing scientists once again to rally around the flag – only this time with some of them co-opted into the management side of military operations, most notably the atomic bomb project (Kuznick 1987). After the war, these scientist-managers became the architects of post-war science policy, the official conduits between science and the public. Although few really believed that the likes of Vannevar Bush spoke for all scientists' interests, florid state-subsidized employment opportunities and a growing economy were no cause for complaint.

Time for a renewed New Deal? The deskilling and casualization of academic labour

The conditions that encouraged scientists to see their research interests tied to national military and industrial policies have rapidly changed since the Cold War came to an end. In one important sense the climate has become potentially more conducive to unionization. A good case in point is physics, the standard-bearer of Cold War science policy, which in recent years has been the discipline most strongly pressured to treat its degree holders as 'stakeholders'. In January 1991, the Council of the American Physical Society (APS) adopted a public position on funding priorities for the first time in its 93-year history, one that favoured broadly-based physics research over the more glamorous but élite Superconducting Supercollider (Office of Technology Assessment 1991: 159, n. 40). Three years later, two write-in candidates who worked outside physics were elected to the Council: Kevin Aylesworth and Zachary Levine. Their platforms called for restructuring physics education to match the new labour market and for the APS to adopt policies that explicitly represented the interests of all its members. Given that PhD production in physics was still growing at Cold War rates of 10 per cent per year, Levine (1994: 17) went so far as to call for 'limit[ing] the growth of the physics community in the USA to sustainable levels', and 'help[ing] young scientists who wish to make a transition out of physics'. This, in turn, sparked a more general debate about whether science degree programmes were broadly enough gauged to enable young scientists to function in work environments that were increasingly inter-disciplinary and non-academic (Holden 1995).

It is worth underlining the fact that the depth of the problem of inter-disciplinary understanding means that it needs to be addressed during initial training, not simply by 'on-the-job experience'. A currently popular argu-ment for state-supported research is the 'collective store of tacit knowledge' that supposedly results from scientists working with people in other discip-lines, government and industry (Science Policy Research Unit 1996). How-ever, the fact that such knowledge emerges from the research environment after the scientist has already completed his or her education may simply represent a deficiency in training that could be addressed much earlier and hence made more intelligible than the expression 'collective store of tacit knowledge' suggests. An experimental paradigm for the promotion of inter-disciplinary understanding involved medical students and social work stu-dents in a 'shared learning' programme during their final year of university study, in which they were required to work together in groups to solve problems of common concern. Being still students, their professional iden-tities and status sensibilities had not yet solidified, which enabled them to succeed at the task at hand and to be receptive to cooperative ventures with members of the corresponding group in the future (Carpenter and Hewstone 1996).

As the state increasingly devolves its research funding functions to the private sector, scientists are returning to the role of economic 'wild card' that they played in the 1920s. The vicissitudes of today's biotechnology and cyberspace industries in the world's stock exchanges prove that we are in the midst of encountering a Scylla and Charybdis rather like the one that the New Deal's industrial policy was designed to circumnavigate. But perhaps most significant of these recent developments is the extension of automation beyond the factory shop-floor into the post-industrial heartland of scientific workspaces. Computerized expert systems, the products of the 'knowledge engineering' business, are slowly but surely absorbing the work of medical diagnosis, chemical analysis and engineering design – to name just a few tasks that have traditionally required scientfically trained personnel. It is still an open question whether these machines will take a permanent sizeable chunk out of the scientific workforce or, for that matter, whether they will deskill the workers who remain. A renewed union sensibility in this context might align scientists with technical and support personnel who, despite their different credentials, nevertheless come to have similar experiences with computerized expert systems in the workplace (Fuller 1994c). That we are now in a position to address these matters openly suggests that science is on the verge of becoming a normal part of public policy.

To develop this point more fully, consider three senses in which scientists are becoming 'deskilled':

1 Scientists lose part of their sphere of discretionary judgement, which, practically speaking, means that they no longer have the final say on the disposition of their own research.
2 Scientists are held accountable to more publicly-oriented standards that are neither of their own creation nor necessarily those most likely to promote the interests of their professional community.
3 The kind of knowledge that is lost in (1) is not comparable to the kind that is gained in (2). Administratively designed formal procedures are perceived as a shallow replacement for the scientists' own deeply in-grained and historically sedimented expertise.

All of these concerns have already been extensively articulated in the another context, namely the replacement of factory and office workers, as well as professionals, by a kind of computer – the expert system – that can simulate the reasoning processes by which the relevant humans issue judge-ments in their domain of expertise (Dreyfus and Dreyfus 1987). The emo-tionally charged debates surrounding this issue typically take it for granted that the promotion of meaningful human labour entails the cultivation of personalized expertise. Yet, such a requirement prevents discussion about the kind of society in which meaningful human labour is to occur. For example, the political theorist Benjamin Barber (1992) has argued that the goal of a democratic society may be better served if each person were encouraged to perform a number of different jobs in his or her lifetime rather than to cultivate obsessively – and to identify exclusively with – one form of labour. In that case, 'merely competent' performances subserved to a higher end would be favoured over a jealously guarded expertise pursued as an end in itself. Marx, for example, seemed to have something like this in mind as the utopia of post-revolutionary communism.

Politics aside, another possibility is that the competent/expert distinction has been given more psychological weight than it deserves. Is it so clear that there is a distinctly 'cognitive' component to expertise that is, in some sense, sacrificed in the civil society that Barber and other radical democrats envisage? I think not. Scientific judgement appears 'expert' only against a certain social background, a major part of which includes a public that allows the scientists virtually complete discretion over how and when they account for their activities, such as whether they explain deviations from normal practice as 'errors' or 'genius' (Fuller 1994a).

This background also includes supportive, or at least non-obtrusive, peers. Indeed, expertise depends to such an extent on the appearance of consensus among peers that the gloss of expertise can easily invite public scrutiny once two similarly credentialed scientists contest each other outside strictly professional forums. For this reason, scientists who circumvent the peer review process and seek vindication in the media are rarely accepted fully back into the scientific fold (Nelkin 1987). Just as physicians often refuse to testify against their colleagues, one could imagine similar resistance from scientists invited to debate openly the relative merits of their research proposals. In both cases, the motivation would be clear. No matter whose claim to knowledge turned out to be vindicated, the entire discipline's credibility would suffer from public exposure.

Scientists realize that just as credibility is built on circumspection, it is also spent through overexposure and popularization. Likewise, the proliferation of machines that are persuasively portrayed as performing the tasks of experts contributes to an erosion of expertise. This devaluation is often subtle but it can be seen to have operated over a long period. A good indicator is the long-term shift in the image of what it means to 'do science'. Certain practices, especially those associated with sensory observation, have been removed from the core image of science as they have become mechanized and automated. For example, the need to have a 'good eye' for field and experimental work is now an anachronism in most disciplines (Fuller 1993c: 137–42). Such mechanized operations are treated as ancillary to the actual conduct of inquiry, the locus of which has shifted to whatever the human continues to do with minimal instrumental mediation. And with the advent of expert systems capable of modelling multiple causal interactions, automation may soon reach the inner sanctum of scientific reasoning – the process of hypothesis-testing (Langley *et al.* 1987).

The history of science and technology is full of alarmists who argue that the removal of restrictions on some jealously guarded form of knowledge will lead to the decline of civilization. However, to put these claims in perspective, it is worth remembering that, for almost every oppressed segment of society, it has been argued that even the spread of literacy would lead to the collapse of authority (Graff 1987). What has been true about these dire predictions is that the relative value of certain forms of knowledge has changed. Once a previously esteemed form of knowledge is made readily available, either because people know it for themselves or it is embodied in technology, the knowledge becomes commonplace and hence irrelevant in determining social worth. Indeed, scientific knowledge is an instance of what the economist Fred Hirsch (1976) originally called a 'positional good' – that is, a good whose value is primarily tied to others not having it. In recent years, Hirsch's idea of positional goods has itself been popularized by the French sociologist Pierre Bourdieu (1984) as the differences in training between groups that become the bases for other forms of discrimination. A group is empowered to the extent that the knowledge of its members enables them to do things that members of other groups would like to do but cannot. In Chapter 1, I spoke in terms of possessing social capital, which produces 'multiplier effects' as it circulates through the knowledge economy.

Following Hirsch and Bourdieu, then, the net effect of democratization and mechanization is to level old distinctions, invariably spurring new attempts to restrict inquiry by creating new domains of knowledge that, in turn, will provide new opportunities for discrimination. Every deskilling is thus a potential reskilling. For example, value hierarchies are typically so restructured after a scientific revolution that a new paradigm may offer few job prospects for scientists clinging to the old traditions, while providing new opportunities for their more adaptable colleagues. But such a trans-formation may also come about by more mundane means. With the com-puterization of the medical workplace, it may soon no longer matter that a diagnostic expert system fails to reproduce the complexity of a physician's reasoning, provided that the system offers good enough diagnoses. Why? Because the shift in the sources of authoritative knowledge – from human to machine – will have been accompanied by a shift in the standards for 'worthwhile' knowledge. To put it bluntly, we may decide that we have better things to worry about than the perfectibility of computer performance in that particular domain. If such a response were to become typical then the last half-century of debates over the ability of computers to simulate certain forms of human thought (e.g. Dreyfus 1992) would become beside the point.

How technology may end up redressing the balance in academia

My discussion up to this point suggests that expertise is nothing more than a kind of procedural knowledge whose sphere of application has been mystified by those enjoying exclusive access to that knowledge. If so, it would seem to follow that the areas of expertise most vulnerable to the positionality effects noted above are those having the most articulate pro-cedures, perhaps because they are routinely given extensive treatments in textbooks. These areas of expertise form the core of scientific and profes-sional establishments (Hales 1986).

By contrast, among the areas of expertise least vulnerable to problems of easy access are two groups that currently enjoy little respect in science policy forums – namely, people whose knowledge is of too recent vintage to have yet been standardized into procedures and people whose know-ledge is too embedded in a specific locale to be of much use as a generalized set of procedures. Speaking abstractly, *novelty* and *locality* are the qualities most resistant to the knowledge engineer trying to design an expert system. Perhaps not surprisingly, these two features of knowledge are valorized by the 'postmodern' turn in cultural studies. Indeed, Jean-Francois Lyotard's (1983) seminal essay, which popularized the term 'postmodern', originated as a policy study on the likely implications of information technologies on cultural production. Although Lyotard acknowledged Daniel Bell's (1973) 'post-industrial' vision as a benchmark for such considerations, it is clear that Lyotard's own image of 'knowledge work' in the postmodern condition is one of increasingly politicized knowledge brokerage, and not one of politically sanitized technocratic facilitation. Here I concur with Lyotard, and would suggest that Bell's technocratic ideal is vulnerable to the proliferation of expert systems. A somewhat better image of the emerging knowledge worker is Robert Reich's (1991) 'symbolic analyst'.

Speaking concretely, novelty and locality are epitomized by, on the one hand, the growing number of recent PhDs whose status as itinerant post-doctoral fellows has earned them the title of 'unfaculty' and, on the other hand, the technical and administrative support personnel whose experience with the day-to-day nitty-gritty of the research site typically exceeds that of their more highly credentialled supervisors. These unsung heroes of the research process are underpaid and undervalued, yet they often make all the difference between success and failure: what if the project secretary is unfamiliar with the work rhythms of the researchers, or the lab technician has not been consulted on the overall scheme of the project, or the postdoc's judgement is trusted only in matters of technique but not theory? Just as consumers should be incorporated into decisions taken at the level of production, so too should these 'implementers' at the level of project conception. The case of the 'unfaculty' is especially acute, as they threaten to become the *Lumpenproletariat* of academia. In 1991 they comprised one out of five academic posts in America's research universities (Office of Technology Assessment 1991: 214–15); by 1998 the proportion had doubled in comparable British institutions (Thomson 1998). Now such staff, who are technically defined as being on 'fixed-term contracts' are routinely described as 'casualized', as if to draw specific attention to their dispensability.

Economic competitiveness as the continuation of Cold War science policy by other means

We are on the verge of continuing Cold War science policy by other means, as 'economic competitiveness' has become the new battleground in the post-Cold War era. For example, Britain's place on the front lines has been ensured by the Office of Science and Technology's inclusion in the Department of Trade and Industry. Not surprisingly, this has been followed by a spate of calls for the state to concentrate its research funding on the universities best equipped to make the biggest international splash, including the National Academies Policy Advisory Group (NAPAG), a consortium of the country's most venerable scientific societies. NAPAG has reckoned the number of British universities that are internationally competitive over a broad range of fields to be 15 out of around 100. They have recommended that research funding be restricted to the most competitive departments, thereby openly endorsing Merton's principle of cumulative advantage, as discussed periodically throughout this book (*Times Higher Education Supplement* 1996). But will this prove to be a sound strategy?

Ironically, the best argument against making competitiveness the premier goal of national science policy comes from Robert Reich, former secretary of labour in the Clinton administration. Reich notwithstanding, the
USA has been otherwise the world's biggest promoter of the competitiveness model. (The main ideological defence of national competitiveness is
probably Porter 1990.) Reich criticizes the model for presupposing that a
nation's inhabitants necessarily benefit from the economic success of firms
nominally headquartered within its borders (Reich 1991: 122–5). Applied
to science, it follows that the number of papers published or patents registered by a country's leading firms and universities does not automatically
translate to benefits for either the scientific community or the larger public
of that country. That will depend on the full range of its people's skills,
attitudes and employment settings. Arguably, in the last quarter-century,
Japan and Germany have made better use of the knowledge produced in the
USA and UK than the Americans and British have. To be sure, scientists already on the 'cutting edge' will always benefit, but that just reinforces
the élitism that the competitiveness model breeds. A nation often gains
ground on its international competitors at the cost of polarizing its own
residents.

This problem can be tackled from either the demand or the supply side
of science. The demand-driven strategy is to adjust the training, incentives
and rewards of scientists (and science students) to enable them to appear
more attractive to foreign and domestic firms. Despite the lip service often
paid to this strategy, its implementation would be prohibitively expensive.
This point contributes to the 'realism' of NAPAG's approach to research
funding. But even with adequate economic resources and political will, the
sheer provision of highly skilled, appropriately motivated scientific professionals does not guarantee their gainful employment in what has increasingly become a buyer's market for brains. As the scientific infrastructure of
former Second and Third World countries develop at a rate that outpaces
the rise in labour costs, firms and universities have seen fit to 'outsource'
substantial research projects to scientists from these regions. Even First
World countries have benefitted from this 'globalization of research and
development', as when high-grade skills are combined with marginally
lower labour costs. Here the USA and UK may enjoy an advantage over
Japan and Germany (NSF 1991: 110).

However, the demand-driven strategy to peacetime science policy suffers
from enormous presumptuousness, which in turn reflects the lack of voice
that rank-and-file scientists and technical support staff have in setting national
science policy. Specifically, the scientific community has never been consulted on its commitment to 'competitiveness' as a goal of its activities, be
it defined in military, industrial or even scholarly terms.

The first step toward a supply-driven response to the competitiveness
model of science policy would be just such a periodic inventory of the
competences and attitudes of the scientific community, including tertiary
sector science students. Without such systematic information, even leaders

of the scientific community have been prone to stereotype their constituency. A striking example is the 'cry of alarm' issued by the president of the American Association for the Advancement of Science in 1991, which called for the federal government to double its non-defence spending on science. To make his case, he restricted himself to surveying the opinions of tenured and untenured faculty at the top 50 research universities in the USA (Lederman 1991). Before it was disbanded by the Republican-controlled Congress, the Office of Technology Assessment had begun to take stock of science's missing voices by highlighting statistical data on groups that did not fit the stereotypical scientist: graduate students, women, ethnic minorities and the 20+ per cent of the scientific workforce that was migratory and contract-based, otherwise known as the 'unfaculty' (Office of Technology Assessment 1991: 205–30). Although these data only scratched the surface, they still suggested that the scientific community was not uniformly sold on the idea of competitiveness as a peacetime goal.

More indirect support for a New Deal for science policy comes from a Carnegie Foundation survey on the effects of the publication-oriented, resource-intensive research university model on academic work conditions across the entire tertiary sector, including private and public universities, liberal arts and community colleges (Boyer 1990). The imperative to become more 'research competitive' was shown to be a pervasive source of stress in academics' lives, especially in the harder sciences, as they were drawn away from their preferred image of scholarship as pedagogically relevant, open to interdisciplinary influences and less focused on sheer productivity. The survey found that while academic identity was tied more to disciplinary than specific institutional affiliation, the type of institution in which academics worked shaped their sense of what constituted appropriate scholarship in their discipline. On that basis, accrediting agencies and professional associations should cultivate a plurality of mechanisms for evaluating and promoting academic work that avoids polarizing faculty into a two-tier funding structure that inevitably ranks research over teaching and relegates public service to the sub-intellectual. This would mean, in the British context, that the Office of Science and Technology should be relocated from the Department of Trade and Industry to the Department of Education and Employment.

Contemporary problems often rest on maintaining distinctions that at an earlier point in history did not make a difference. The New Deal approach to national science policy did not presume as strong a distinction between scientists and non-scientists as operates today in, say, the contrast between 'peer reviewed' and 'earmarked' research. Rather, the idea was to extend scientific peerage, not simply by recruiting more scientists, but by ensuring that science's full constituency was represented on governing boards and policy forums. Were this principle in operation today, it is unlikely that we would witness the repeated complaints that federal science panels are 'biased' and 'narrow' (Cordes 1996). Public involvement would not seem so alien to scientific autonomy if a wider range of scientists sat on such panels in the first place. In the twentieth century, élitism in science has been driven primarily by military preparedness and, more recently, economic competitiveness. The twenty-first century offers an opportunity for science to regain the lost legacy of the twentieth, whereby science would be driven by the *entire* community of enquirers. With that in mind, let us finally consider the elements for a new constitution of the scientific polity.

8

Elements for a new constitution of science

Introduction: the two models of constitutionalism

The eighteenth century was the heyday of 'philosophically designed order', or *constitutionalism*, the closest that a deliberately undertaken social contract has come to being the real basis for social order. The Norwegian political theorist Jon Elster (1993) has performed the useful service of critically comparing the two main constitutions of the period, the American and the French, which were drafted only two years apart and under many of the same Enlightenment influences. Elster shows that they exemplify alternative models of collective decision making. On the one hand, the Americans who participated in the drafting of the Constitution in 1787 were remarkably similar in their Enlightenment cultural sensibilities and bourgeois economic interests (Beard 1986 [1913]). Moreover, they conducted their deliberations in private, which minimized the impact that any unrepresented 'others' might have had on the proceedings. On the other hand, the French Constituent Assembly of 1789–91 represented a broader range of class and ideological perspectives and conducted their meetings in public, which encouraged the delegates to present their arguments so as to appeal to the largest constituency possible, if only out of fear that otherwise they might be assaulted upon leaving the assembly hall!

The resulting founding documents bear the marks of their origins. The US Constitution's preoccupation with separating powers through 'checks and balances' presupposes a rather cynical view of human nature that would hardly play to the gallery. In contrast, the vague and abstractly worded French *Declaration of Human Rights* was written to be just such a crowd pleaser. The consequences of these differences could not be more striking. Over the last two centuries France has gone through a dozen constitutions, whereas the USA has simply amended the original one from time to time.

Nevertheless, in spite of its relatively limited efficacy, the French constitutional context arguably promoted a more literal sense of democracy, as the delegates were forced to think beyond their immediate interests in order to enrol a wide constituency. A contributing factor here was that the French delegates officially represented 'estates' – which is to say, functionally differentiated parts of the same society – while their American counterparts stood for geographically discrete 'states' whose interests were presumed to be naturally opposed (cf. Fuller 1993a: 48–9). This contrast is worth bearing in mind, as we consider the terms on which a constitution for science can be forged. Scientists generally represent themselves as working in the same or complementary, but not conflicting, fields: that is, akin to the French model. However, as we shall see, a truer representation of the scientist's situation may be closer to the American model: that is, one of internal division that promises no easy resolution.

Representing science: from trickle-down effects to workplace politics

In the previous two chapters we have observed the schizoid character of American attitudes toward science. Despite the periodic calls for Americans to 'take back' their government, the public's reach has failed to grasp the governance of science. On the one hand, Americans are clearly dissatisfied with a trickle-down economic policy that relegates most workers to the status of consumers of whatever investment opportunities the government happens to encourage in the rich. On the other hand, the USA has yet to question its even longer-standing policy of trickle-down science. This is a policy that reduces most citizens to willing – or not so willing – consumers of machines, potions and symbols, products the design of which they exert little control over. The difference is a lesson that has come hard in the economic sphere and remains unlearned in the science sphere, namely that the aims of policy should focus more on the employment of people than the manufacture of products.

Typical of the trickle-down thinking that still dominates science policy is a recent Carnegie Commission report (Carnegie Commission on Science, Technology and Government 1992), which calls for an independent 'National Forum' consisting of representatives of various groups that have a stake in the research agenda of tomorrow. The federal government has already set a good precedent for including women and ethnic minorities in other agenda-setting forums, but science policy introduces classes of stakeholders, most of whom have yet to be properly heard. These classes are not neatly categorized as either 'clients' or 'consumers' of scientific research. Their impact on the production and distribution of scientific knowledge is rather direct. Who, then, are these missing voices?

The Carnegie Commission provides an instructive negative example in answering this question. It speaks of the need to incorporate both 'top-down' and 'bottom-up' approaches to science policy (Carnegie Commission on

Science, Technology and Government 1992: 30). On close inspection, however, these approaches correspond to the familiar groupings of Washington politicians and policymakers, on the one hand, and eminent scientists and engineers on the other. Underscoring the exclusionary cast of these proceedings is the report's recommendation that safeguards be taken against the National Forum becoming a vehicle for groups traditionally hostile to science and technology, such as environmental activists. Yet, these troublesome groups are not about to disappear. If they are excluded from the policy process at the outset, their voices will only be heard later, and perhaps more loudly. Their response will come in the form of resistance to new scientific knowledge products. The annals of big business are littered with cases in which ideas that looked great on paper died stillborn because they were alien to the needs and interests of potential users.

Upon turning to Big Science, a subtle variation on this theme can be detected. Here we see, not a few backward souls, 'nature lovers' who fail to appreciate the gifts bestowed by modern science and technology. On the contrary, a bigger threat to cutting-edge scientific research is the passive opposition of science educators who teach in institutions of higher learning that are themselves not primarily devoted to research. These institutions include both community and liberal arts colleges, as well as most state university campuses. In fact, this group may include nearly every teacher of science outside of the 30 universities that have shared 50 per cent of federal research dollars in recent years. What interest do such teachers ultimately have in supporting research, little of which is ever likely to make its way into the undergraduate curriculum? Only a trickle-down mentality would assume that there is a natural fit between the research carried out in those top 30 schools and the teaching carried out in the other 2500 institutions of higher learning in America.

This last point receives indirect support from Ernest Boyer (1990), the late chair of the Carnegie Foundation for the Advancement of Teaching (not to be confused with the Carnegie Commission, though sharing the same private benefactor). Boyer formally identified and analysed one of the open secrets of higher learning, namely that the scholarly perspectives of the most prestigious members of an academic discipline do not represent those of rank-and-file practitioners. Although the average faculty member strongly identifies with the discipline in which they were trained, the skills and qualities that they associate with their discipline will depend on their place of work. Thus, physicists working in research universities tend to believe that cutting-edge research is what their field is all about, whereas physicists in community colleges believe that teaching is the core of their field. It would seem that the teaching-oriented faculty are far from eager consumers of research. Rather, teachers are increasingly forced to adapt their work habits to the research mode, as their home institutions seek greater academic status. If anything, Boyer tried to discourage those institutions from evaluating their scholarly missions by the standards of the large research universities; hence the title of his report: *Scholarship Reconsidered*.

Such an élite-driven yardstick is bound to prove frustrating for all concerned – administrators, faculty and students – and may even lead to a backlash effect, whereby teaching-oriented institutions would effectively boycott cutting-edge research, say by refusing to subscribe to the expensive scientific journals that typically publish such research.

Why, then, should the National Forum foster the truncation of higher education's diverse scholarly missions by including only faculty who define their work in terms of cutting-edge research? Instead, it would seem that the Forum should include representatives of faculty in community and liberal arts colleges, as well as in comprehensive teaching universities. They should be given a voice alongside faculty in research universities.

Behind these hypothetical deliberations is the delicate question of how a scientific discipline should be represented in the National Forum. Do all members of the faculty of physics departments count equally as contributors to the discipline of physics? The answer is clearly no, if we focus on who has the biggest impact on the research agenda of the physics community. But is that where we should focus? Boyer suggests that if each physics professor were to count for only one vote, the majority would call for research that is more teachable to students and more transferable across disciplines. For all its surface reasonableness, this point actually goes against the grain of contemporary academic scientific self-governance, whose sociological character most closely resembles that of an élite gerontocracy. This point was first forcefully raised in science policy circles by the philosopher Stephen Toulmin (1964) in a critique of Michael Polanyi's (1962) influential vision of the scientific community as a 'republic of science'.

Between the democratic tendency to represent scientists by their place of work and the élitist tendency of having scientists represented by their most distinguished colleagues, it may be argued that scientists are better represented by their professional associations. In many cases, professional associations challenge the self-serving research priorities proposed by a field's most prestigious practitioners. One highly publicized case centred on the the physics community. As we saw in the previous chapter, in 1991 the Council of the APS wondered aloud about the wisdom of tying up so much money in the multi-billion dollar Superconducting Supercollider, given the needs of other areas of basic research. However, lest we have an unrealistic view of the democratic potential of professional associations, we would best see bodies like the APS as operating much as political parties do. They serve constituents who will maintain and strengthen their numbers in the local precincts of higher learning. Sometimes the associations do a good job of representing the interests of the rank-and-file disciplinary practitioners, but sometimes they cave in to the special interests of the more élite practitioners. Thus, Daryl Chubin, then a senior analyst at the US Office of Technology Assessment, coined the expression 'quark barrelling' to characterize the self-serving arguments used by physicists on behalf of the Supercollider (Office of Technology Assessment 1991: 159, n. 40). Given the latter possibility, it is important that faculty also be represented in a National Forum according to the type of institution in which they work and the kind of work they do.

The same applies to the need for non-faculty representation. Indicative of the neglected state of non-faculty voices is that the Carnegie Commission report called for the revamping of university research facilities without saying a word about the people who would staff these facilities to ensure that projects proceeded according to plan. Indeed, the trickle-down science policy mentality has been all too often linked with a top-down research management style, in which the sheer brilliance or utility of a project idea is supposed to call forth the appropriate personnel. This linkage has, in turn, been propelled by romantic images of research teams inspired by visionary directors. Back on earth, however, studies of corporate management style show that the cult of the irreplaceable individual is a formula for megalomania, rude awakenings and failed enterprises. If the actions of any one individual, even the scientific 'genius', are seen as disproportionally more significant than those of anyone else, then that typically means that work and responsibility are not distributed in a way that makes optimal use of the talents of all the members of the team.

Admittedly, deliberations at the National Forum may take an unexpected turn once academia's *Lumpenproletariat* – secretaries, technicians and postdocs – are allowed representation. In particular, they may not want to lend their opinions and, implicitly, their approval to the science policy process until the status of their labour and the terms of their employment reflect the seriousness with which they would wish to be taken. While some scientific traditionalists may balk at the introduction of these issues, they nevertheless follow from the realization that in an experimenting society that is truly democratic, the success of science policy must be measured not merely by the quantity of the goods that science produces, nor even by the quality of those goods, but by the quality of the interactions of the people, all of whom are needed to get the job done.

Three strategies for democratizing science

In Chapter 2 I explained why science, despite its having served as the West's most compelling model for democratizing society, has failed to apply the democratic spirit to itself, and hence has failed to realize the promise of a genuinely 'experimenting society'. In what follows, I try to get beyond this impasse by starting from the assumption that scientists themselves constitute part of the lay public for every branch of knowledge that goes beyond their speciality. And if it is true that each scientist knows 'more and more about less and less', then scientists share a sphere of ignorance that increasingly approximates the epistemic state of the non-scientific lay public (Fuller 1993a: Chs 2 and 8). Moreover, if democracies work best when there is no obvious locus of authority, then any science policy decision that entertains alternatives to allowing a field to pursue its current research trajectory invites democratic participation. For, no matter how expert a scientist is in their own field, they are never expert in evaluating that field in relation to others.

This point is often overlooked because while the attitudes and competences of non-scientific adults and pre-college science students have been subject to extensive and periodically updated surveys, comparable data are lacking for scientists themselves. Indeed, we have a more finely-grained sense of the level of general scientific literacy among non-scientists than among scientists. As it turns out, on average worldwide, the public is three times more interested in science-based issues than they are knowledgeable of them (NSF 1991: 450). The US National Science Foundation's biennial *Science & Engineering Indicators* contains cross-national comparisons of the educational attainments, employment categories, income levels and career patterns of scientists, but nothing about their attitudes towards their work and whether these are adequately represented by their professional spokespersons and policymakers (as opposed to the media, scientists' attitudes toward which have been surveyed on a regular basis for years). Thus, although the USA exhibits a larger discrepancy between the public's interest in and knowledge of science than most countries (roughly, 5:1 vs. 3:1), there nevertheless seems to be a uniform 10–15 per cent of the citizenry who are knowledgeable of science, regardless of country (NSF 1991: 466). Moreover, scientists are trusted *less* in countries that are widely regarded as leaders in the production of scientific knowledge, such as Japan and Germany (NSF 1991: 464).

The most natural way to construct a democratic science policy regime is by specifying the grounds on which a choice between competing proposals should be made in a resource-scarce environment. The cynically minded may regard the following three policy regimes as 'science-termination' strategies. However, none of them is the least bit hostile to the pursuit of science as such. If anything, these strategies have been proposed in the spirit that science itself should be governed by the principles scientists use to govern their inquiries into nature. Thus, they should be understood as contributing to the general Enlightenment aim of extending the critical attitude of science to a wider sphere of social life, in this case to the policy forums where the research agenda is set. Given our standpoint of science policy as labour policy, it is worth stressing that these institutionalized forms of 'cognitive euthanasia' are designed to terminate scientific fields, *not* the scientists whose careers have been built in them.

Finalization

The first strategy, popular among West German leftists in the 1970s, is called 'finalization', a term meant to evoke the idea that a mature science coasts on its own inertial tendencies, unless it is explicitly given direction, and in that sense, 'finalized' (Schaefer 1983). The strategy was born during Juergen Habermas's directorship of the Max Planck Institute in Starnberg.

Staffed with politically motivated young scholars trained in the history and philosophy of science, the Starnberg Institute embarked on a programme designed to counteract what Kuhn (1970) regarded as an eventuality of all scientific paradigms, namely diminishing returns on investment as research becomes increasingly specialized. A finalization policy would thus empower a state agency to monitor the growth of the various scientific fields. Once a field had progressed to the point that its theoretical base was consolidated and most of its practitioners were solving technical puzzles, the agency would offer financial incentives to divert the practitioners away from continuing work on such puzzles and toward participating in interdisciplinary projects that addressed outstanding social problems.

Although no country has yet adopted the German plan as a general science policy strategy, cancer research, both in the USA and Europe, has proceeded largely in this fashion over the past quarter-century. Its pluses and minuses are thus reasonably well documented (Hohlfeld 1983). When scientists from different fields work well together, breakthroughs come more easily than if each scientist were left to the devices of their own discipline. Far from being an unmitigated good, scientists who have grown accustomed to the norms of their own disciplines often overlook research angles that appear quite plain to scientists operating from a different disciplinary perspective. This mutual correction of disciplinary bias turns out to be one of the biggest benefits of working in an interdisciplinary team.

More generally, scientists tend to underestimate the extent to which practically oriented, 'applied' research has been the source of major innovations in theoretically driven, 'pure' or 'basic' research. The impacts of agricultural and medical research on the development of biology and chemistry in the nineteenth century provide the clearest cases in point (Schaefer 1983: 290–3). In fact, only in the twentieth century does the causal arrow become regularly reversed, as basic research increasingly drives innovation in the applied sphere. And even then, this is true only of the natural sciences, not the social sciences. In the latter case, practical problems remain the royal road to theoretical innovation (cf. Deutsch et al. 1986).

Of course, the possibility of fruitful interdisciplinary activity is predicated on scientists working well together, which is easier said than done. Highly specialized and accomplished scientists typically find it hard to adjust to an environment in which research standards and strategies need to be negotiated on a regular basis. Consequently, even the most serious of social problems (e.g. AIDS) require large financial incentives to divert topnotch scientists from their normal research trajectories; yet, the likelihood that a team of such scientists will enjoy a fruitful collaboration over the long haul remains quite small. The class of exceptions that proves the rule is the remarkable feats of interdisciplinary research done by all sides during the two world wars. The stake was survival itself, and the objects of concerted inquiry were the 'ultimate' instruments of destruction. Ironically, however, the 'success' of these projects was credited less to the value of interdisciplinary teamwork and more to the ability of scientists to deliver on a Herculean task when allowed maximum discretion to dispose of abundant resources (Kevles 1977).

Before concluding our look at finalization, we should note its resemblance to Campbell's (1988) original vision of the experimenting society, as discussed in Chapter 2. It is science *for* the people, but not necessarily *by* the people. In this regard, it shares the ideological cast of J.D. Bernal's original 'socially responsible science' movement in the UK (Elzinga 1988) and is open to the criticisms that Frank Fischer (1992) has raised of clientelism in advocacy research. In short, finalization leaves open the possibility that public problems will simply be replaced by 'clarified' scientific ones (Fuller 1988: Ch. 12). A good case in point is provided in the following passage by the historian and physicist, Gerald Holton (1978: 229) who claims to be endorsing a modified version of the finalization principle:

> basic researchers in the physical and biological sciences have only rarely looked for their puzzles among the predicaments of society, even though it is not difficult to show that the lack of relevant scientific knowledge in such 'pure' fields . . . is among the central causes of almost any major social problem. (For example, a better understanding of the physics, chemistry, and biology of the detailed processes of conception is still fundamental to the formulation of sounder strategies for dealing with overpopulation and family planning.)

Advocates of a more democratized science policy, such as Commoner (1971) and Ravetz (1971), would regard Holton's call for more research into conception (and presumably, contraception) as a diversion from the real issue, which is to determine who stands to benefit and who stands to lose from diagnosing global environmental problems in terms of 'overpopulation', since, technically speaking, the earth has enough resources to support many times its current population. Of course, many millions remain ill-fed and ill-housed, but that problem is unlikely to be solved by the production of new natural scientific knowledge – though admittedly that is what natural scientists are most used to doing. Rather, the solution lies in the design of political and economic institutions capable of efficiently and equitably distributing existing resources. Typically, these institutions are portrayed as replacing key functions of the state. What we have here, then, are deep problems of social, not natural, science. Thus, if finalization is to contribute to the conversion of science into an experimenting society, care must be taken not to reproduce the old asymmetries between scientists and the public they 'serve'.

Cross-disciplinary relevance

A second strategy for terminating expensive research was originally proposed by Alvin Weinberg (1963) when he was director of research for the US Atomic Laboratories in Oak Ridge, Tennessee. Weinberg's funding principle was a simple one: the more expensive the research proposal, the more value it must have for fields outside the principal investigator's field. This principle has had considerable appeal for federal science policymakers (e.g. Office of Technology Assessment 1991: 139–40), though it has been actively opposed by senior figures in the scientific establishment, including the (unrelated) Steven Weinberg (1992: 59–60).

The principle makes sense at several levels. In the first place, it applies to science policy the economic principle of opportunity costs: that to invest resources in one course of action is, at the same time, to foreclose other opportunities for investment. Thus, even if a research programme is likely to succeed once it receives a certain level of funding, the value of that success must be weighed against the value of the competing programmes that had to be terminated because of their failure to receive those funds. Armed with Weinberg's principle, policymakers make funding decisions with an eye to the beneficial by-products that a given research programme might have for inquirers not directly contributing to the research.

This point about the opportunity costs of funding decisions dovetails with a deep point about the history of science. Major scientific break-throughs tend to come obliquely, often as a result of people trained in one field migrating to another one, or of one field borrowing ideas and tech-niques from another (Hoch 1987). The inclusion of cross-disciplinary rele-vance as a criterion in science policy decisions would highlight such oblique paths of influence. Pursued to its logical conclusion, Weinberg's line of reasoning suggests that the field officially receiving a large research grant need not reap the largest benefits from the research done under that grant; rather, the benefits may accrue to some third-party field whose own methods and theories are revolutionized by drawing on that research.

This conclusion may strike the reader as perverse. Nevertheless, the fact remains that no revolution in science has ever required the vast initial cap-ital investment that is nowadays routinely sought for the most expensive and glamorous research projects. Neither Newton nor Darwin nor Einstein ever sought large research grants, and justifiably so. What government agency dedicated to the promotion of institutionalized science would find it in its interest to support research that promises, if 'successful', to displace the career orientations of most of the people working at the cutting-edge of a large number of fields? That was, after all, the downside of the revolu-tions associated with these three scientists. After Newton, astronomers had to be knowledgeable in mechanics; after Darwin, biologists and geologists could no longer ignore each other's work; after Einstein, no physicist would be taken seriously without a theory of measurement.

It is worth recalling the consequences that scientific revolutions have had on the value of scientists' labour (specifically, the changes wrought on the value of existing scientific knowledge and skills) to appreciate that when supporters of the Supercollider touted the 'revolutionary' character of its expected findings, they were not proposing a shift in world view equival-ent to the shifts attributed to Newton, Darwin or Einstein. Rather, the Supercollider advocates trumped up the value of their high-energy physics puzzles to a level that was commensurate with the amount of funding that they sought from Congress. Thus, upon completion, the Supercollider would have enabled the performance of the crucial experiments that would decide between rival accounts of the fundamental forces of nature. But if history is our guide, a set of 'crucial experiments' of the sort proposed using the Supercollider would have only yielded still more ideas for experiments requiring yet more customized equipment. Thus, plans were already afoot for a Super-duper-collider!

In fact, one would be hard-pressed to find a scientific research programme that ever died a natural death – that is, as a result of having solved all its own problems to its practitioners' satisfaction. (None of this should surprise those who are used to the self-perpetuating tendencies of social welfare programmes long after their effectiveness has expired.) In short, according to Weinberg's principle of cross-disciplinary relevance, if a scientific revolution were to have occurred in the aftermath of Supercollider research, it would probably have been in any field *but* high-energy physics, as both the field's internal power structure and its balance of power *vis-à-vis* other scientific disciplines could only be strengthened by the level of funding that Congress was asked to commit to the Supercollider.

This is not to say that scientific revolutions come cheap. They are certainly labour- and capital-intensive affairs, but the requisite investments are rather diffuse both in terms of their sources and their recipients. Only a relatively small part of the overall labour and an even smaller part of the capital is invested in the designated 'genius' of a given scientific revolution. In the policyspeak of 'research and development', more needs to be invested on 'development' (i.e. the networking of interests that enables an innovation to spread) than on 'research' proper. Contrary to the common view that traces development's dominance of research to the rise of Big Science, this tendency can be found throughout the history of science (Cockcroft 1965). In this respect, the history of science is no different from the history of technology (Rosenberg *et al.* 1992). Scientific revolutions acquire seemingly miraculous qualities only because historians fix their narratives on the revolutionary genius to such an extent as to suggest that one person's efforts could move the world in a way that entire armies could not. In this context, it is sometimes claimed that truth is efficiently revealed to the honest scientific inquirer, whereas the artifice of politics requires constant coercion, manipulation, and, in any case, *work* (Latour 1989 provides a burlesque demonstration of this point in the case of Pasteur). However, the case of Isaac Newton, perhaps the greatest of all scientists, shows that this distinction simply does not hold up under closer scrutiny.

Living before our current 'Age of Grantsmanship', Newton earned a modest income as a mathematics professor at Cambridge University. Because his now classic *Principia Mathematica* was a rather hefty tome with pages upon pages of arcane geometric proofs, no publisher thought they could profit from printing it – that is, until Newton's friend Edmund Halley (of Halley's Comet fame) subsidized the entire operation. But Newton realized that publication alone would not achieve the desired effect, since his advanced mathematical formulations were enough to intimidate even potentially sympathetic readers. He therefore embarked on a campaign of instructing likely reviewers of *Principia* in how they might represent his main arguments without including the higher mathematics. Newton also went out of his way to invite challenges from scientists throughout Europe, especially France, whose major scientific societies sponsored competitions throughout the eighteenth century to refute this or that Newtonian claim (Cohen 1980).

The amazing powers imputed to Newton's mathematical vision of physical reality grew in direct proportion to the number of groups, both scientific and non-scientific, who found it in their interest to subscribe to the Newtonian way of seeing things. These alignments had less to do with prolonged exposure to Newton's own text and more to do with the work of intermediaries who translated 'Newtonianism' into a variety of idioms, including pedagogical, theological and political. Even a philosopher as sceptical of the prospects of experimental science as David Hume came to fashion a 'moral science' resting on an analogy between, on the one hand, a theologically inspired conception of free will and a secularized conception of social and natural forces, and on the other, Newton's principle of inertia and his law of gravity. Because, in Newtonian mechanics, 'inertia' refers to a body's motion before it has been subjected to an outside force, it was easily assimilated to the idea of intrinsic human agency, which in turn helped to reduce 'social mechanics' to an elaborate network of pushes and pulls on people. (Good critical histories of this development, which extends well into the twentieth century, are Sorokin 1928; Mirowski 1989.)

All told, the relationship between *Principia Mathematica* and the ensuing 'Newtonian Revolution' is no different in its successes, failures and vagaries from the relationship between, say, *Das Kapital* and its implementation in Marxist regimes. Although Newton is unique in the extent to which he orchestrated the revolution that bears his name, his example illustrates the number of levels on which activity must occur in order for a revolution to succeed. Less outgoing 'geniuses' such as Darwin and Einstein were fortunate to have in their corner such first-rate advocates as Thomas Huxley and Max Planck, who commanded considerable cross-disciplinary audiences. Otherwise, they too would have joined the multitude of intellectually ambitious and technically proficient scientists whose works sank without a trace because of their inability to attract the support of a broad enough constituency. While no government agency need be in the business of fomenting scientific revolutions, it can foster the sorts of destabilizing situations that characterize such revolutions by encouraging certain rivalries, both within and between disciplines, as well as cross-fertilizations.

Epistemic fungibility

The third strategy promises to be the most democratic by demanding the most changes in how scientists put forth their research agendas. It starts from the observation that science policymakers typically find Alvin Weinberg's criterion of interdisciplinary relevance very difficult to put into practice. The main source of the difficulty is that research proposals are ordinarily evaluated by peer review, which means that scientists are encouraged to write their proposals with an eye toward impressing experts in their own field, each encased in its own standards and jargon. Thus, a given proposal is judged for its ability to advance the frontiers of knowledge in the particular field. The peer reviewer is not invited to ask larger questions having to do with whether the particular field of knowledge itself is worth promoting indefinitely: is there a point at which we would better off shifting our investments from high energy physics to molecular biology? Because there are no opportunities for raising a question of this sort, proposals end up being accepted or rejected largely on grounds of 'technical proficiency'. In other words, the cross-disciplinary comparisons that are needed to implement Weinberg's criterion simply never arise in the normal course of events. Indeed, without a complete overhaul of the science policy apparatus, the disciplinary structure will simply be reproduced year after year, as each field allots its share of the available grants to technically proficient scientists.

However, the situation would be quite different if scientists from different fields were required to defend their proposals to one another in an open forum, such as before a legislature's appropriations committee or perhaps even a university symposium. Historians, philosophers and sociologists of the scientific enterprise could be called in initially to design procedures for publicly examining the scientists' claims. Once provided with an incentive to interrogate each other's claims, the scientists themselves would be in a position to intensify the investigation, stripping away gratuitous jargon, overstatement and all-around obfuscation that might otherwise mystify non-experts. Thus, what originally appeared to be the incommensurable knowledge products of two disciplines – such as the theoretical benefits of a branch of physics and the practical benefits of a branch of biology – would be rendered comparable, by virtue of their claims being articulated outside the confines of their original disciplinary discourses. They would have collaboratively spawned a pidgin language, which if reinforced and extended over time could develop into an interdisciplinary lingua franca (Fuller 1993a: 44–8). Such a metamorphosis would be grist for the mill of the social epistemologist, who holds that most of the seemingly 'deep' differences in subject matter between the sciences result from the absence of open communication channels across the corresponding disciplinary communities. In a nutshell, bad communication habits make for deep ontologies by allowing distinctions in words to mark differences in things (Fuller 1988; 1993a; 1993c).

Were disciplinary communities made to be routinely accountable to each other, then much of the aura of expertise and esoteric knowledge that continues to keep the public at a respectful distance from scientists would be removed. (For the tactics that scientists currently use to appear authoritative before policymaking forums, see Wells 1993; for the counter-tactics used to challenge those displays of authority, see Martin 1991.) Here, three points are worth recalling. First, scientists themselves constitute part of the lay public for every branch of knowledge that goes beyond their specialty and are bound to perform just as poorly on a 'literacy' test of those areas as any 'ordinary' member of the public. Second, when scientists received a more rounded education (i.e. until World War II), they were sufficiently steeped in the histories of their fields to demystify each other's claims by revealing the persistence of deep conceptual problems that had been obscured by mounting empirical successes (Fuller forthcoming: Ch. 2). Third, to call for science to be conducted in a 'civil tongue' is not to end all disagreements among scientists. However, interdisciplinary turf wars are likely to yield to the negotiated standards of adequate scientific performance that draw on the critical resources of logic, methodology and statistics without privileging a given set of facts or theories (Albury 1983 provides some good examples of this strategy in practice). Together these points offer hope for the success of the deliberative democracy schemes associated with republican politics, as discussed in Chapter 1.

Good models for thinking about criteria for evaluating competing claims in our science policy forum may be found in welfare economics. Of particular relevance are schemes for income redistribution based on competing ways of compensating the losers in a policy debate. These schemes have been given widespread currency in one of this century's leading works of political theory, Rawls (1971). According to Rawls, in the just society, people will tolerate income inequalities only if they believe that the poorer members of society can somehow derive benefit from the income of the wealthier members. This idea is common to all modern theories of public finance, ranging from the investment tax breaks favoured by the Right to the higher tax rates on the wealthy favoured by the Left. The problem of public finance is central to modern democracies that operate within a capitalist economic framework: how can everyone benefit from wealth that remains concentrated in relatively few hands? Modern science is implicitly forced to ask a similar question, given the vast disparity in costs and benefits across the disciplines. A useful way of thinking about this disparity is through the concept of 'epistemic fungibility' (Fuller 1993a: 295).

In economics, 'fungibility' refers to the ease with which one good can be exchanged for another – and hence the ease with which it can serve as a means of satisfying the ends of its owner. A fungible good is one that can be had in different amounts without destroying the good's integrity. For example, a half-bag of groceries may provide half the nourishment of a full bag, but a half-automobile will not get you halfway to where you want to go. Thus, only the groceries are fungible, not the automobile. By calling this kind of fungibility 'epistemic', I am stressing the fact that the goods in question are forms of knowledge. Clearly, some forms of inquiry are more 'epistemically fungible' than others. Below we shall consider the difference between the high-energy physics research that would have been done on the Supercollider and the psychological inquiries regularly conducted by means of public opinion surveys.

The Supercollider was presented, even by its proponents like Weinberg (1992), as a scientific instrument expressly designed to test certain theories in physics. No other discipline was likely to benefit directly from working on the Supercollider, as no other discipline requires particle accelerators for testing its theories. In addition, the dimensions of the Supercollider were clearly non-negotiable: one did not countenance 'big' or 'small' versions of the Supercollider, and it made no sense to speak of 'half' or 'three-quarters' of a Supercollider. The decision whether to construct the instrument was thus an all-or-nothing matter, and perhaps the main source of the controversy that surrounded its funding. Together, all of these features rate Supercollider research low on epistemic fungibility. In contrast, public opinion surveys are common to a variety of disciplines in the social sciences, so that even if most of the work is initially done by psychologists, sociologists and political scientists may stand to benefit and subsequently contribute to that line of research. Moreover, one can tailor the scope of the survey to the amount of funding available. While surveys that question more people are normally regarded as more representative of an entire population, one can determine the 'statistical significance' of findings reached on any sample size. These opportunities for negotiating the dimensions of the project make survey research more epistemically fungible.

If policymakers regularly thought about science funding as a branch of welfare economics, they would require scientific teams to draft proposals not only for accomplishing their own goals but also for compensating other scientists with whom they are competing for funds. Moreover, the burden to provide compensation would be greater in relation to the amount of money that the teams sought. Imposing such a requirement may cause certain disciplines to scale down their funding demands, as they reckon that the intrinsically esoteric nature of their inquiries precludes the incorporation of practitioners from other disciplines into their proposals. Of course, the other alternative available to these non-fungible fields would be to seek full funding from industrial and philanthropic concerns in the private sector. In that case, if the trend toward increasing specialization in science is truly irreversible, we should see the 'privatization' of science, which, some predict, will incline society to think about the products of scientific research much as we think about works of art today. In effect, a privatized scientific enterprise would convert all knowledge to intellectual property (Ezrahi 1990: Ch. 12).

Not surprisingly, many scientists have balked at the prospect of privatization. Historically speaking, most of the power that élite groups have been able to derive from specialized knowledge is directly traceable to that knowledge being shrouded in secrecy or in some other way rendered inaccessible to most people. Privatization, it is feared, would only increase that tendency, as certain wealthy 'patrons of the sciences' could emerge as majority shareholders in the knowledge produced by particular fields, resulting in a state of 'information feudalism' (Drahos 1995; Fuller 1998). To stave off this unsavoury possibility, it is reasonable to suppose that some scientific communities would start to reconceptualize their practices so as to increase the fungibility of their fields. For example, high-energy physicists may decide that rival theories in their field can be just as effectively tested on relatively inexpensive computer simulations as on the $10+ billion Supercollider. After all, geneticists, psychologists and economists have long used computer simulations for analogous purposes as they have tried to get around the moral and practical barriers to staging direct tests of their theories (Horgan 1996). Here it is important to recall a point first raised in Chapter 2, that nothing in the formulation of a scientific theory dictates the method by which it must be tested.

However, perhaps truest to the spirit of welfare economics would be for high-energy physicists to try to persuade a coalition of inquirers from different disciplines to participate in some successor to the ill-fated Supercollider project. For example, social scientists interested in understanding large-scale organizational behaviour in isolated settings would find the community that surrounds the Supercollider an ideal site for study. (The Supercollider required an 53-mile underground oval tunnel that was to be built under the town of Waxahachie, which is relatively near the University of Texas, Steven Weinberg's home institution.) In fact, some of these social scientists may be already seeking grants to investigate different communities that have similar characteristics. If the physicists were willing to take the trouble, they could persuade the social scientists to join their team instead. Such an invitation would not only save money but it would also eliminate much of the rancour and mutual suspicion that currently accompany interactions between natural and social scientists – interactions which all too often have threatened the fate of innovative interdisciplinary research (e.g. Traweek 1988).

Of course, as with all compensation schemes, the wealthy would have to pay, which, in this case, would mean that the physicists would lose some of their privacy as they allowed the social scientists to roam around the Supercollider facility, regularly recording observations and asking questions which would strike physicists as ranging from the pointed to the pointless. Indeed, in the not too distant future, one could even envisage the social scientists remarking on ways in which the scientific worksite could be improved. (This development would help assuage fears that the social scientists have been co-opted into the physicists' schemes.) Such are the first painful steps towards a democratic science. Of course, this scenario assumes the desirability of chunking science policy in terms of mega-project-sized appropriations, which I take still to be a very open question.

The reader who still feels that the principle of epistemic fungibility is a creature of political expedience with no discernible benefit for science as the search for knowledge has probably missed the fundamental changes that fungibility entails in our understanding of the 'cognitive' dimension of science. Fungibility does not presume that there are separate well-defined domains of inquiry for each discipline; instead, it presumes that any potential site of inquiry is a contested space defined primarily in terms of available resources and potentially subject to a variety of jurisdictions, each corresponding to the agenda of a particular discipline or even an interest group in the wider society. If science is to be remade into an 'experimenting society' of the sort discussed in Chapter 2, then science policy must weigh the opportunity costs incurred by turning these resources over to the physicists as opposed to other possible projects, including ones that integrate natural and social scientists. Indeed, this last prospect suggests that the long-standing scientific goal of 'integration' may be best achieved not by unifying the finished products of each science, but rather by coordinating the labour of variously trained scientists in a common workplace. In the scenario above, integration is something in which both natural and social scientists participate, not simply a theorist's *post facto* accomplishment on paper.

A sample proposal for constituting science as a democratic polity

What might all these proposals for democratizing science look like as part of a single social contract? At the very least, it would provide a clear sense of public access to science's decision-making processes. As we saw at the end of Chapter 2, a scientific literacy campaign may make science more understandable but not necessarily more accountable. The accountability issue can be directly addressed only if science is treated as a species of politics – though a species that retains vestiges of traditional notions of inquiry. For example, 'accountability' itself may be seen as a reformulation of the verifiability or falsifiability conditions of a knowledge claim, but now with reference to particular groups who have a stake in the validity of the claim. Below I translate three features of politics in an era of Big Democracy (Dahl 1989: Chs 15–21) into criteria for accountability in an era of Big Science.

1 *Coalitions* Political theorists from James Madison to Joseph Schumpeter have described the dynamics of Big Democracy as an endless 'circulation of élites', by which is meant the often temporary alliances that need to be forged among disparately interested parties in order for any political programme to succeed. In so far as most scientific research today is made possible by an alignment of university, government and corporate interests, coalition politics is already the implicit norm, though one that scientists are still inclined to treat as 'merely expedient' and not essential to their knowledge-producing functions, however much time and energy they may spend on building and maintaining such coalitions. In contrast, I would propose to make this norm explicit, by having scientists avail themselves of the media that politicians typically use to take their cases to

the people. In short: treat research programmes as party platforms. One intellectually salutary consequence of this practice would be to force scientists to reflect on the multiple ways in which various constituencies might come to have a stake in the outcome of scientific research. Moreover, as people see themselves as potential components in a scientific coalition, they are likely to become more self-conscious about the ends of knowledge production: what are the costs and benefits of pursuing one research programme rather than another? This could initiate an ongoing public debate on the topic of ends, long obscured by philosophical assurances that the 'truth' is the end of inquiry. In any case, more broadly accessible knowledge products are likely to result, products capable of persuading a wide range of people that they are getting their money's worth.

2 *Contestation* Big Democracies are defined by their forums for managing conflict. The sudden democratization of Big Science would pose formidable problems in terms of the public's ability to judge between competing coalitions, given both the ambivalence caused by the heterogeneous interests associated with any given coalition (e.g. military and environmental interests may be behind the same project) and the complexity of the technical issues on which the competing coalitions would differ. Under the circumstances, it is tempting simply to split the difference by allotting each side a certain amount of legal and economic space in which to do their work. However, this solution has the potential for generating still greater problems. It would discourage coalitions from thinking that they have to account to the entire population. After all, if a coalition needs only a modest plurality to receive adequate funding, why should it aim for knowledge products that would be accessible to the society at large? Unfortunately, such purely interest-based thinking runs the risk of severing accountability from responsibility for consequences that affect those outside the coalition. Thus, even if the resources were available to diversify research investments, it would be dangerous to fund a research proposal simply because it enjoyed the support of several interest groups. Rather, several such alternatives must be subject to comparative evaluation in an open forum. Instead of having the public engage with the technical details of these alternatives, competitors could confront each other through televised episodes of formal cross-examination. As the competing research proposals would often represent quite disparate fields and the television audience would consist of a wide range of interests and areas of expertise, the resulting debate would bring to light the sorts of unclarity, hyperbole and deception that would otherwise remain hidden in the technical language of the competing proposals.

3 *Elections* The importance of elections in Big Democracy testifies to the reversibility of all political programmes. However, much traditional philosophical thinking about science resists the idea of periodic elections in which the fortunes of research programmes can be substantially reversed. Big Science remains fixated on the image of inquiry as proceeding by a

natural trajectory, unless subject to interference. Admittedly, philosophers frequently reconstruct the history of science as a series of 'theory
choice' episodes, in which one of the options constitutes a radical departure from the reigning orthodoxy. But on most accounts, even the radical
successor must approximately save the phenomena of its conservative
forebear, thereby suggesting continuity at least in the data that need to
be explained. This sense of continuity is reinforced by the idea that the
primary aim of science is The Truth, which, in turn, has tended to reduce
normative questions about inquiry to disputes over the appropriate means
to this already agreed-upon end.

It is no accident that the philosophy of science has been primarily
concerned with something called 'methodology' rather than 'axiology'
(an exception is Laudan 1984). The same continuity may be detected in
the narrative structure of research grant proposals, which stress a path of
increasing specialization and elaboration in the solution of persistent theoretical problems. Even when sociologists of science have doubted this
narrative's adequacy to actual scientific practice, they have typically replaced it with another tale of continuity, often one that depicts scientific
progress as being driven by the need to exploit the investigative potential
of expensive laboratory equipment. Big Science is most perilous when
any of these continuity arguments and stories are taken to underwrite
what might be called 'techno-fatalism', the idea that science must proceed either in its current state or not at all. By requiring that ongoing
projects account for themselves on a regular basis, science elections would
enable alternative coalitions to propose novel ways of configuring available intellectual and material resources.

The most utopian feature of the above tripartite scheme is its assumption
that citizens in Big Democracy are already sufficiently engaged in politics
to be able to add scientific research as one more issue around which coalitions can be formed and elections fought. Unfortunately, nothing could be
further from the truth (cf. Dahl 1989; Yankelovich 1991). The biggest
obstacle facing Big Science's public accountability is not the public's lacking competence but its lacking a clear stake in the outcomes of research. To
be sure, when the stakes are made clear – as in most cases surrounding
biotechnology – the public is quite prepared to engage with highly complicated and technical issues. Indeed, the success of 'citizen juries' that are the
mainstay of experiments in deliberative democracy testifies to this point
(Stewart et al. 1994). Moreover, there is an arena in which the public has
no difficulty evaluating a set of complex rules and skilled performances,
following running commentaries and statistical indicators abstracted from
those performances, and identifying its own fate with possible outcomes –
even to the point of regularly betting on those outcomes when permitted.
That arena, of course, is *sports*. Recalling the etymological origins of dialect-
ics in jousting discussed in Chapter 3, perhaps it is not so surprising after all
that the Greeks so closely associated inquiry with gamesmanship.

The fact that people around the world can intelligently engage with sporting events yet increasingly fail to be galvanized by democratic politics highlights the extent to which traditional philosophical fears about the prospect of 'socialized knowledge' have been seriously misplaced. Recalling the worst nightmares of 'proletarian science' deployed during the Cold War, philosophers often act as if Big Science needs to be protected from a public that is all too eager to get its hands on the research agenda – a public that could do irreparable damage to that agenda, were it so commandeered. This perhaps explains why those epistemologists who have been most receptive to a social characterization of knowledge have also been interested in promoting the doctrines of epistemic 'expertism' (Stich and Nisbett 1984) or 'paternalism' (Goldman 1991) in order to provide rational grounds for the lay public deferring to scientists' judgements under normal circumstances (cf. Fuller 1988: Ch. 12). Once again, my response is that these safeguards are beside the point, in so far as people are already unwittingly disposed to follow such philosophical advice, but more out of boredom with anything political (*especially* science) than out of any admission to their cognitive shortcomings.

In short, transcending the utopian status of my proposal would involve importing to science the sorts of things that make sports so compelling for so much of the world's population. What would get people sufficiently interested in the conduct of science that they were driven to increase their stake in it? Here I follow a long line of subjective probability theorists, including Frank Ramsey and John Maynard Keynes, who have measured the strength of one's belief by one's willingness to bet on the belief being true (for historical background, see Hacking 1975; Daston 1987). But, clearly, with the exception of pathological gamblers, people are quite selective about what they are willing to place bets on. Sporting events typically have three features, examined in more detail below, that make them especially attractive to 'rational gamblers'. These features are notoriously lacking from the scientific enterprise, not to mention politics more generally.

1 *An easily accessible canonical accounting procedure* Just as daily newspapers run statistical breakdowns of all the teams in a sports league, one could imagine similar data – perhaps more along the lines of '*Consumer's Reports*' – regularly gathered and published on the officially recognized coalitions, component interest groups, level of support, current projects and output to date as some function of input. Potential bettors would thus have a clear sense of the affiliations and track records of the contestants. For, as it now stands, even the state must struggle to figure out the nature and level of research support in the private sector, as well as to prevent missed opportunities and overkill from happening in the public sector. Intellectual property law (patents, copyrights and trademarks) does a reasonable job of registering and policing (though not publicizing) completed knowledge products and processes, but a comparable system for 'works in progress' has yet to be developed. Here it is worth recalling

that while the highly ramified character of intellectual property law is traceable to the commodification of knowledge, copyrights and patents as such merely formalize the traditional marks of value in works done under the rubrics of 'arts' and 'sciences' respectively – namely, originality and priority. In that sense, intellectual property law derives legitimacy from a pre-capitalist sense of individualized merit in knowledge production.

2 *Fair and explicit rules of the game* As people have increasingly come to realize the mythic character of 'cognitive norms' and 'methods of science', a common response has been to become mystified and ultimately disengaged from the conduct of science. Thus, the public continues to marvel at the latest breakthroughs in research, but very much in the manner of an entertaining fiction that operates in ways that cannot be fully fathomed without destroying the illusion (cf. Postman 1986). In this sense, the demystification of method has led to a decline in the public scrutiny of science, as scientists retreat behind the special effects produced by their technical expertise. The remedy is to provide incentives for scientific coalitions to challenge each other in an open forum. For example, one coalition may bet part of its research budget that it can achieve its goals before another coalition achieves theirs. Targets may be chosen strategically, so that a coalition behind an upstart molecular biology programme may challenge a long-standing programme in nuclear physics that is beginning to exhibit diminishing returns on investment. Contests featuring such widely divergent foes would help accustom the public to comparing the research potential and products of different disciplines, especially as they try to decide where to place their own bets. Notice that the type of contest described here bears a closer resemblance to boxing than to baseball, in that the occasions for a contest are determined not by a schedule set independently of the degree of interest in the contest but rather by parties sufficiently interested in mounting a challenge that the size of their wager attracts the champion into the ring.

3 *Something worth contesting* This is perhaps the only condition that makes politics more publicly scrutable and more attractive to gamblers than science. Nevertheless, the condition is a significant one. It raises the general question of which features of science are worth betting on. If we envisage that research programmes covering quite different fields can challenge one another, then among the more fruitful debates would be one over which programme is more likely to generate the more desirable knowledge products, given the resources at stake. Philosophers of science should recognize this strategy as involving the 'context of pursuit' (Laudan 1981) and 'heuristic appraisal' (Nickles 1989). Stockbrokers call it, quite aptly, 'speculating on futures' (cf. Hanson 1990). The two sides could cross-examine each other about their track records, subject to the sort of procedural rules that a judge typically monitors in the courtroom. One side may succeed in showing that the other side does not deserve credit for part of the track record that it now wants to use to justify its claim to resources. Presumably, this would disincline people from betting

on that side in the future, perhaps leading to the breakup of the coalition that had so far supported that side.

My proposal makes at least two quite controversial general assumptions, which cannot be defended here. First, not only is there a standard procedure for collecting bets and distributing winnings, but also procedures governing scientific contests can be made sufficiently transparent – perhaps even scored on points – that the judgements of the referees and the viewing public will coincide on most occasions, just as they do in sports. Thus, after one such contest, there would be a straightforward way of establishing the winner. (The intuitive implausibility of this prospect may simply testify to the public's current alienation from the scientific enterprise.) Second, science elections can be highly adversarial without turning into zero-sum games, in which the contestants (and their supporters) feel that there is no middle ground between vanquishing and being vanquished. In this context, a judiciary body can be charged with holding research teams responsible for the consequences of their actions (including the ease with which they make their products available to others). Even when the consequences are irreversible, the victims may nevertheless be compensated. Proposals of this sort are already being discussed by lawyers concerned about the decisive role that 'junk science' often plays in underwriting risk assessments (Huber 1991).

Conclusion: is there an unlimited right to be wrong?

Critics of the 'the right to be wrong' as the cardinal principle of science policy have tended to make the same counter-argument. To be sure, the principle is necessary in a world where academics are afraid to speak their minds for fear of losing their jobs, forums and funds. But what about those academics whose protected perches enable them to offer advice with impunity, often leaving clients in a much worse state than had they not taken the advice?

The textbook case of this problem is the economist Jeffrey Sachs, whose bold advice to the former communist regimes of eastern Europe to 'open up' their markets was followed to the letter, only to eventuate in widespread misery and greater economic and political uncertainty (Bryant 1994: 60–2). Should not Sachs – or the university (Harvard) that permits him to offer such consultancies – be held liable for the consequences of his poor advice? In Sachs's defence, it has been argued that while he failed to anticipate the immediate fallout, nevertheless he was meant to be offering a long-term strategy, not a short-term fix, and that indeed some of the economies have now begun to stabilize. The defenders further claim that had Sachs not been implicitly protected by a right to be wrong, he would have been discouraged from offering what may still turn out to be the best advice that could have been given at the time. This kind of case is decisive to the prospects for republican science policy because it challenges the possibility of drawing a principled distinction between staking a thought and staking its thinker. Are there any precedents for adjudicating this matter?

As it happens, the US Supreme Court institutionalized a 'right to be wrong' for journalists in the 1964 case of *The New York Times* v. *Sullivan*. The Supreme Court ruled that journalists would be inhibited from reporting controversial matters were the burden of proof set so high that virtually any error could be made a source of litigation. Unfortunately, the permissive reporting environment opened up by these noble sentiments was immediately enveloped by the market forces governing newspaper rivalries. Consequently, newsrooms came to regard the cost of checking stories as yet another 'factor of production' that could be undercut in the never-ending quest to provide the news as soon and as cheaply as possible. In a field governed purely by market forces, it makes sense for an individual to maintain high (i.e. expensive) probative standards *only* if everyone else can be held to them; if even one individual breaks from the fold then it is in everyone else's interest to break as well.

Although Sachs would no doubt dislike the analogy with deadline-hungry newshounds, it is probably fair to say that had he not advised the eastern Europeans, an economist from another distinguished university would have easily filled the consultancy vacuum. At the very least, this point warns us off the liberal presuppositions of research ethics, critiqued in Chapter 1, which would make Sachs himself the exclusive locus of accountability. The problems here are much more systemic, implicating the universities as institutions capable of affecting the stability of the societies with which they interact.

Writing from a broadly communitarian perspective, former NBC law correspondent Carl Stern (1998) has argued that the Supreme Court should partly reverse its original ruling by awarding damages to parties whose reputations are ruined by misreporting. However, Stern would put a ceiling on the damage settlements, lest journalists be discouraged from investigating controversial matters. At the same time, he calls for regular public announcements of media reliability, as measured by the aggregated outcomes of libel cases brought to trial. Stern envisages that fear of the adverse publicity resulting from a poor investigative track record (e.g. loss of commissions to journalists, advertising to newspapers) would instil a greater sense of self-discipline than the liberal regime currently allows.

However, Stern's proposal may have exactly the reverse effect – namely to encourage risk-taking, since where limited damages are awarded a reputation for overall unreliability may not be such a high cost, if every so often a highly visible success is scored. This is certainly the principle that seems to govern tabloid newspapers, which gladly negotiate cash settlements with aggrieved parties out of court without substantively changing their reporting practices. That these papers are occasionally correct in one of their many outlandish reports is usually sufficient to motivate large numbers of regular subscribers. This lottery-like mentality among consumers is an unintended consequence of 'credential libertarianism' (Collins 1979), ostensibly an attempt to demystify claims to competence by publicizing track records. Yet, one can imagine that even knowing the relatively poor track record of a noted development economist's views, a desperate country's leaders may nevertheless decide to implement the economist's radical proposals on the chance they might work just this time.

While it is impossible to make people foolproof to their own credulity, measures can be taken to ensure that the combination of a hard-selling consultant and an impressionable client does not end in complete disaster. However, from a republican standpoint, these measures should enable consultants to continue to peddle their wares, while potential clients remain free to purchase them. One way to meet these conditions is for the university to engage in some creative cost-accounting of consultancies done under its auspices, specifically by demanding overheads that are then ploughed back into a fund to compensate the victims of poor policy advice. In short, the university would function as an 'epistemic insurance agency'. The resulting higher consulting charges might influence the nature of the advice given and taken.

The attractiveness of this course of action would depend on legally requiring consultants to specify the time-frame within which their advice is designed to produce the expected outcomes (see Fuller 1992b, where this procedure is used to remedy the ambiguous character of pragmatism's justification of belief by its 'consequences'). As it stands, it is virtually impossible to distinguish between a policy that works 'in the long run' simply because it was right and a policy that works because the clients managed to persevere until something vaguely resembling the expected outcome was realized. Similarly, how does one tell the difference between a policy that fails simply because it turned out to be wrong and one that was undermined in rather specific and deliberate ways? The world-historic precedent for raising this sort of test case for the open society is the Marxist 'prediction' of a proletarian revolution, for which there is evidence of both wishful thinking by those who have wanted it and strategic pre-emption by those who have not.

Nevertheless, some will maintain that these institutional innovations are insufficient to ensure that the right to be wrong will be exercised responsibly. Here the history of policy-oriented genetics research, culminating in the drive to map the human genome, rears its ugly head. The mere allowance of such research on grounds of 'free inquiry', so goes the argument, constitutes a threat to groups that are likely to appear in a disadvantaged light, especially non-whites, and in some cases women. However, the reasoning behind this concern suffers from the presumption that the mere pursuit of a particular research programme carries certain necessary policy implications. This presumption is often made because, as it happens, the people pursuing the research exhibit a clear ideological bias (e.g. Murray and Herrnstein 1994). Yet, those who conduct the research rarely determine the full range of its uses.

To be sure, when the ideology stems from the funders rather than the researchers themselves, the concern becomes more legitimate. But even here, steps can be taken to sever the conditions under which research is done from those under which it is applied. The model for dealing with this matter was raised in Chapter 6, as part of a revival of the philosophical distinction between the contexts of discovery and justification, where the point of justifying knowledge claims would now be to diversify, rather than mainstream, their potential applications. A sense of the full sweep of history offers the best appreciation of how seemingly 'hard' scientific findings, such as those grounded in genetics, can be insinuated in a variety of opposing policy regimes. Indeed, the forthright use of genetics as a political technology, or 'eugenics', has been remarkably ecumenical in its ideological appeal in the twentieth century (Hasian 1996).

Consider the difference between Left eugenicists such as Karl Pearson and the Fabian movement in Britain, and the racial scientists who fuelled right-wing Aryanism in Germany. The Left tended to treat apparently genetically based differences via economic incentives that encouraged the breeding of superior stock and inhibited that of inferior stock, whereas the Right licensed the superior stock to cull the surplus production of inferior stock through infanticide, war or genocide. In Darwinian terms, the Left manipulated the variation side and the Right the selection side of the evolutionary equation (MacKenzie 1981; Proctor 1988).

Interestingly, these policy orientations are the exact opposite of the advice most closely associated with the Left and Right when the biological character of human beings is *not* considered relevant to how one should deal with persistent inequalities in endowments. In that more familiar, purely economic context, the Left would have the surplus wealth of the rich culled and redistributed to the poor through progressive taxation, whereas the Right would offer incentives to encourage the rich to invest in ways that would indirectly benefit the poor, say, by such 'trickle-down' means as job creation in regions where the start-up costs for new factories are low. Were these policies interpreted as alternative measures for promoting the evolution of the economy, the social democratic state would be seen as diverting excess wealth *à la* natural selection, and the neo-liberal state as seeding new wealth *à la* genetic variation.

The biological and economic versions of these policy regimes reveal the metaphysical constants in the Left's and the Right's approach to politics: the former respects the integrity of individuals by virtue of their endowments, whereas the latter respects the endowments that individuals happen to bear. Yet, as we have just seen, how this metaphysical difference is put into practice depends on whether the policy context is defined as 'eugenic' or 'fiscal'. In other words, not only can the same scientific ('eugenic') perspective be used to support opposing ideological agendas, but also the same ideological agenda can back alternative policy interventions, depending on the scientific perspective that is used to frame the intervention. Thus, the Left is more likely to intervene *ex post facto* when the policy frame is defined as fiscal and *ex ante facto* when it is defined as eugenic, whereas the Right's interventions exhibit the exact opposite tendencies.

In short, in matters relating to 'inheritance', to name the concept common to both eugenic and fiscal frames, we live in a time when policymakers expect science to yield a univocal perspective that is otherwise lacking in the political ideologies that vie for their affections. Unfortunately, whenever this expectation seems to have been met, the frame of reference defined by political economy has been subordinated to that of the latest geneticized behaviourism that passes for 'sociobiology'. Over the past half-century, advances in biology and uncertainties in economics have undoubtedly contributed to this effect. (For a discussion of inheritance where the balance between biology and economics is more even, see Wedgwood 1939.)

From the standpoint of the republican ideal of science as the open society, as advocated in these pages, the problem with this state of affairs is *not* the significance that policymakers assign to biology in the particular decisions they take, but rather their tendency to construe the legitimacy of alternative scientific sources for policymaking in terms of their reducibility to biology. This has Janus-faced consequences, which together sufficiently narrow the space for political possibility so as to undermine the right to be wrong. On the one hand, policy-oriented social scientists are encouraged to join the bandwagon of biologization to ensure approval for their findings, while on the other hand those immune to sociobiology's charms revert to an ostrich-like stance towards any involvement in the policymaking process.

In this chapter, I have proposed some concepts and strategies designed to regain the republican ideal in an era of Big Science. My overarching approach is 'constitutionalist', in that the fundamental problems facing the governance of science today rest on issues of representation: both how science represents its own interests and how it represents the public's epistemic interests. Answers to these questions can be given only once we specify who can participate in science, and how. This, in turn, depends on the social dynamics of knowledge production one presupposes. In this respect, the traditional image of inquiry as 'the search for truth wherever it may lead' is not so much wrong as uninformative, since it is compatible with any of the sociological formulations of knowledge production entertained in this chapter: a social movement, a political campaign, a collaborative project, a resource allocation problem, a question of social justice, an industrial enterprise, a network of communications, a risky investment and even a sporting event. In each case, I have highlighted democratically oriented policies that take seriously the size and diversity of the activities and institutions devoted to the pursuit of knowledge today. All that is now needed is the political will and an experimental turn of mind to make the republican ideal a reality.

References

Albury, R. (1983) *The Politics of Objectivity*. Victoria: Deakin University Press.
Anderson, B. (1983) *Imagined Communities*. London: Verso.
Appiah, K. (1993) *In My Father's House*. Oxford: Oxford University Press.
Arndt, H.W. (1978) *The Rise and Fall of Economic Growth*. Chicago: University of Chicago Press.
Aune, J. (1993) Review of *Black Athena*, Volumes I and II, *Quarterly Journal of Speech*, 79: 119–22.
Barber, B. (1984) *Strong Democracy*. Berkeley, CA: University of California Press.
Barber, B. (1992) *An Aristocracy of Everyone*. New York: Ballantine Books.
Barry, B. (1965) *Political Argument*. London: Routledge and Kegan Paul.
Bazerman, C. (1988) *Shaping Written Knowledge*. Madison, WI: University of Wisconsin Press.
Beard, C. (1986 [1913]) *An Economic Interpretation of the Constitution of the United States*. New York: Free Press.
Beck, U. (1992) *The Risk Society*, 2nd edn. London: Sage.
Bell, D. (1973) *The Coming of the Post-Industrial Society*. New York: Harper & Row.
Ben-David, J. (1992) *Scientific Growth*. Berkeley, CA: University of California Press.
Berlin, I. (1958) *Two Concepts of Liberty*. Oxford: Clarendon Press.
Berman, P. (ed.) (1992) *Debating P.C.: The Controversy over Political Correctness on College Campuses*. New York: Dell.
Bernal, M. (1987) *Black Athena: The Afroasiatic Roots of Classical Civilization. Volume 1: The Fabrication of Greece 1785–1985*. New Brunswick: Rutgers University Press.
Biagioli, M. (1993) *Galileo, Courtier*. Chicago: University of Chicago Press.
Bohman, J. (1996) *Public Deliberation*. Cambridge, MA: MIT Press.
Bok, D. (1982) *Beyond the Ivory Tower: Social Responsibilities of the Modern University*. Cambridge, MA: Harvard University Press.
Bourdieu, P. (1975) The specificity of the scientific field and the social conditions of the progress of reason, *Social Science Information*, 14(6): 19–47.
Bourdieu, P. (1977) *Outline of a Theory of Practice*, 2nd edn. Cambridge: Cambridge University Press.
Bourdieu, P. (1984) *Distinction*. Cambridge, MA: Harvard University Press.

Boyer, E. (1990) *Scholarship Reconsidered: The Priorities of the Professoriate.* Princeton, NJ: Carnegie Foundation for the Advancement of Teaching.

Bryant, C. (1994) Economic utopianism and sociological realism: strategies for transformation in east-central Europe, in C. Bryant and E. Mokrzycki (eds) *The New Great Transformation?* London: Routledge.

Bush, V. (1945) *Science: The Endless Frontier.* Washington DC: Office of Scientific Research and Development.

Butler, J. (1989) *Gender Trouble.* London: Routledge

Cahn, S. (ed.) (1995) *The Affirmative Action Debate.* London: Routledge.

Campbell, D. (1988) *Methodology and Epistemology for Social Science.* Chicago: University of Chicago Press.

Carnegie Commission on Science, Technology and Government (1992) *Enabling the Future: Linking Science & Technology to Societal Goals.* New York: Carnegie Corporation.

Carpenter, J. and Hewstone, M. (1996) Shared learning for doctors and social workers: evaluation of a programme, *British Journal of Social Work*, 26: 239–57.

Carter, S. (1993) *The Culture of Unbelief.* New York: Doubleday.

Chancellor of the Duchy of Lancaster (1993) *Realising Our Potential: A Strategy for Science, Engineering and Technology.* London: HMSO.

Chandler, A. (1990) *Scale and Scope: The Dynamics of Industrial Capitalism.* Cambridge, MA: Harvard University Press.

Chubin, D. and Hackett, E. (1990) *Peerless Science.* Albany, NY: SUNY Press.

Clark, N. (1985) *The Political Economy of Science and Technology.* Oxford: Blackwell.

Close, F. (1991) *Too Hot to Handle: The Race for Cold Fusion.* Princeton, NJ: Princeton University Press.

Cockcroft, J. (1965) *The Organization of Research Establishments.* Cambridge: Cambridge University Press.

Cohen, I.B. (1980) *The Newtonian Revolution.* Cambridge, MA: Harvard University Press.

Cohen, I.B. (1995) *Science and the Founding Fathers.* New York: W.W. Norton.

Cohen, L.J. (1981) Can human irrationality be experimentally demonstrated? *Behavior and Brain Sciences*, 4: 317–31.

Cohen, M. and Nagel, E. (1934) *An Introduction to Logic and the Scientific Method.* London: Routledge and Kegan Paul.

Cole, S. (1992) *Making Science.* Cambridge, MA: Harvard University Press.

Coleman, J. (1990) *The Foundations of Social Theory.* Cambridge, MA: Harvard University Press.

Collins, H. (1990) *Artificial Experts.* Cambridge, MA: MIT Press.

Collins, R. (1979) *The Credential Society.* New York: Academic Press.

Collins, R. (1998) *The Sociology of Philosophies: A Global Theory of Intellectual Change.* Cambridge, MA: Harvard University Press.

Commoner, B. (1971) *The Closing Circle.* New York: Knopf.

Conant, J.B. (1970) *My Several Lives: Memoirs of a Social Inventor.* Cambridge, MA: Harvard University Press.

Cook, T. (1991) *The Great Alternatives of Social Thought.* Lanham, MD: Rowman & Littlefield.

Cordes, C. (1996) Critics say membership of federal science panels is too narrow, *Chronicle of Higher Education*, 8 March: A26.

Coulter, J. (1983) *Rethinking Cognitive Theory.* London: Macmillan.

Crosby, C. (1992) Dealing with differences, in J. Butler and J. Scott (eds) *Feminists Theorize the Political.* London: Routledge.

Curtius, E.R. (1989) Max Weber on science as a vocation, in P. Lassman and I. Velody (eds) *Max Weber's 'Science as a Vocation'.* London: Unwin Hyman.

Dahl, R. (1989) *Democracy and Its Critics*. New Haven, CT: Yale University Press.
Daston, L. (1987) *Classical Probability in the Enlightenment*. Princeton, NJ: Princeton University Press.
Deutsch, K., Markovits, A. and Platt, J. (eds) (1986) *Advances in the Social Sciences, 1900–1980*. Lanham, MD: University Press of America.
Diop, C.A. (1991) *Civilization or Barbarism?* Brooklyn, NY: Lawrence Hill Books.
Dolby, R.G.A. and Cherry, C. (1989) Symposium on the possibility of computers becoming persons, *Social Epistemology*, 3: 321–48.
Drahos, P. (1995) Information feudalism in the information society, *The Information Society*, 11: 209–22.
Dreyfus, H. (1992). *What Computers Still Can't Do*, 2nd edn. Cambridge, MA: MIT Press.
Dreyfus, H. and Dreyfus, S. (1987) *Mind over Machine: The Power of Human Intuition and Expertise in the Era of the Computer*. New York: Free Press.
Durant, J., Evans, G. and Thomas, G. (1989) The public understanding of science, *Nature*, 340: 11–14.
Elgin, C. (1988) The epistemic efficacy of stupidity, *Synthese*, 74: 297–311.
Elster, J. (1984) *Sour Grapes*. Cambridge: Cambridge University Press.
Elster, J. (1993) Constitutional bootstrapping in Philadelphia and Paris, *Cardozo Law Review*, 14: 549–75.
Elzinga, A. (1988) Bernalism, Comintern, and the science of science: critical science movements then and now, in J. Annerstedt and A. Jamison (eds) *From Research Policy to Social Intelligence*. London: Macmillan.
Etzkowitz, H. (1989) Entrepreneurial science in the academy, *Social Problems*, 36: 14–29.
Ezrahi, Y. (1990) *The Descent of Icarus*. Cambridge, MA: Harvard University Press.
Faust, D. (1984) *The Limits of Scientific Reasoning*. Minneapolis, MN: University of Minnesota Press.
Feyerabend, P. (1975) *Against Method*. London: Verso.
Feyerabend, P. (1979) *Science in a Free Society*. London: Verso.
Fischer, F. (1992) Participatory expertise: toward the democratization of policy science, in W. Dunn and R. Kelley (eds) *Advances in Policy Studies Since 1950*. New Brunswick: Transaction Publishers.
Fishkin, J. (1991) *Democracy and Deliberation*. New Haven, CT: Yale University Press.
Ford, K., Glymour, C. and Hayes, P. (eds) (1995) *Android Epistemology*. Cambridge, MA: MIT Press.
Frisby, D. (1992) *The Alienated Mind: Sociology of Knowledge in Germany, 1918–1933*. London: Routledge.
Fukuyama, F. (1992) *The End of History and the Last Man*. New York: Free Press.
Fuller, S. (1988) *Social Epistemology*. Bloomington, IN: Indiana University Press.
Fuller, S. (1992a) Epistemology radically naturalized: recovering the experimental, the normative, and the social, in R. Giere (ed.) *Cognitive Models of Science* (Minnesota studies in the philosophy of science, vol. 15). Minneapolis, MN: University of Minnesota Press.
Fuller, S. (1992b) Social epistemology and the research agenda of science studies, in A. Pickering (ed.) *Science as Practice and Culture*. Chicago: University of Chicago Press.
Fuller, S. (1993a) *Philosophy, Rhetoric, and the End of Knowledge: The Coming of Science & Technology Studies*. Madison, WI: University of Wisconsin Press.
Fuller, S. (1993b) The social psychology of scientific knowledge: another strong programme, in W. Shadish and S. Fuller (eds) *The Social Psychology of Science*. New York: Guilford Press.

Fuller, S. (1993c) *Philosophy of Science and Its Discontents*, 2nd edn. New York: Guilford Press.

Fuller, S. (1994a) The constitutively social character of expertise, *International Journal of Expert Systems*, 7: 51–64.

Fuller, S. (1994b) Towards a philosophy of science accounting: a critical rendering of instrumental rationality, *Science in Context*, 7: 591–621.

Fuller, S. (1994c) Why post-industrial society never came: what a false prophecy can teach us about the impact of technology on academia, *Academe*, 80(6): 22–8.

Fuller, S. (1995) On the motives of the new sociology of science, *History of the Human Sciences*, 8: 117–24.

Fuller, S. (1996) Recent work in social epistemology, *American Philosophical Quarterly*, 33: 149–66.

Fuller, S. (1997) *Science*. Buckingham: Open University Press.

Fuller, S. (1998) Society's shifting human-computer interface: a sociology of knowledge for the information age, *Information, Communication and Society*, 1: 182–98.

Fuller, S. (1999) Making the university fit for critical intellectuals: recovering from the ravages of the postmodern condition, *British Educational Research Journal*.

Fuller, S. (forthcoming) *Thomas Kuhn: A Philosophical History for Our Times*. Chicago: University of Chicago Press.

Fuller, S. and Gorman, D. (1987) Burning libraries, *Annals of Scholarship*, 4:3.

Fusfield, W. (1997) Communication without constellation? Habermas's argumentative turn in (and away from) critical theory, *Communication Theory*, 7: 301–20.

Galison, P. (1987) *How Experiments End*. Chicago: University of Chicago Press.

Genova, J. (1994) Turing's sexual guessing game, *Social Epistemology*, 8: 313–36.

Gergen, K. (1985) *Towards a Transformation of Social Knowledge*. Amsterdam: Elsevier.

Gergen, K. and Gergen, M. (1982) Explaining human conduct: form and function, in P. Secord (ed.) *Explaining Human Behavior*. Beverly Hills, CA: Sage.

Gerschenkron, A. (1962) *The Relative Advantage of Backwardness*. Cambridge, MA: Harvard University Press.

Geuss, R. (1999) *Morality, Culture and History: Essays on German Philosophy*. Cambridge: Cambridge University Press.

Gibbons, M., Limoges, C., Nowotng, H. *et al.* (1994) *The New Production of Knowledge*. London: Sage.

Giddens, A. (1990) *The Consequences of Modernity*. Cambridge: Polity Press.

Gilbert, N. and Mulkay, M. (1984) *Opening Pandora's Box*. Cambridge: Cambridge University Press.

Goldgar, A. (1995) *Impolite Learning: Conduct and Community in the Republic of Letters, 1680–1750*. New Haven, CT: Yale University Press.

Goldman, A. (1991) Epistemic paternalism, *Journal of Philosophy*, 88 (March): 113–31.

Goldman, A. (1999) *Knowledge in a Social World*. Oxford: Clarendon Press.

Goldman, A. and Shaked, M. (1991) An economic model of scientific activity, *Philosophical Studies*, 63: 31–55.

Golinski, J. (1992) *Science as Public Culture*. Cambridge: Cambridge University Press.

Gouldner, A. (1965) *Enter Plato*. London: Routledge and Kegan Paul.

Graff, G. (1992) *Beyond the Culture Wars*. New York: Norton.

Graff, H. (1987) *The Legacies of Literacy*. Bloomington, IN: Indiana University Press.

Hacking, I. (1975) *The Emergence of Probability*. Cambridge: Cambridge University Press.

Hague, D. (1991) *Beyond Universities: A New Republic of the Intellect*. London: Institute of Economic Affairs.

Hales, M. (1986) *Science or Society? The Politics of the Work of Scientists*, 2nd edn. London: Free Association Books.

Hanson, R. (1990) Could gambling save science? *Proceedings of the Eighth International Conference on Risk and Gambling*. London.

Hanson, R. (1995) Comparing peer review to information prizes: a possible economics experiment, *Social Epistemology*, 9: 49–55.

Haraway, D. (1990) *Simians, Cyborgs, Women*. London: Routledge.

Hardin, G. (1968) The tragedy of the commons, *Science*, 162: 1243–8.

Harding, S. (ed.) (1993) *The 'Racial' Economy of Science*. Bloomington, IN: Indiana University Press.

Hasian, M. (1996) *The Rhetoric of Eugenics in Anglo-American Thought*. Athens, GA: University of Georgia Press.

Haworth, A. (1998) *Free Speech*. London: Routledge.

Herrnstein, R. and Murray, C. (1994) *The Bell Curve: Intelligence and Class Structure in American Life*. New York: Free Press.

Hess, D. (1993) *Science in the New Age*. Madison, WI: University of Wisconsin Press.

Hewstone, M. (1989) *Causal Attribution*. Oxford: Blackwell.

Hirsch, F. (1976) *The Social Limits to Growth*. Cambridge, MA: Harvard University Press.

Hoch, P. (1987) Institutional versus intellectual migrations in the nucleation of new scientific specialties, *Studies in History and Philosophy of Science*, 18: 481–500.

Hohlfeld, R. (1983) Cancer research: a study in praxis-related theoretical developments in chemistry, biosciences and medicine, in W. Schaefer (ed.) *Finalization in Science*. Dordrecht: Reidel.

Holden, C. (1995) Careers '95: the future of the Ph.D, *Science*, 270 (6 October): 121–45.

Holton, G. (1978) *The Scientific Imagination*. Cambridge: Cambridge University Press.

Horgan, J. (1996) *The End of Science*. Reading, MA: Addison Wesley.

Hoskin, K. and Macve, R. (1986) Accounting and examination: a genealogy of disciplinary power, *Accounting, Organization and Society*, 11: 105–36.

Huber, P. (1991) *Galileo's Revenge*. New York: Basic Books.

Humboldt, W. (1970 [1810]) University reform in Germany: reports and documents, *Minerva*, 8: 242–50.

Jones, G. (1988) *Science, Politics and the Cold War*. London: Routledge and Kegan Paul.

Kerr, C. (1963) *The Uses of the University*. Cambridge, MA: Harvard University Press.

Kevles, D. (1977) The National Science Foundation and the debate over postwar research policy, 1942–1945, *Isis*, 68: 5–26.

Kevles, D. (1987) *The Physicists*, 2nd edn. Berkeley, CA: University of California Press.

Kinneavy, J. (1986) Kairos: a neglected concept in classical rhetoric, in J. Moss (ed.) *Rhetoric and Praxis*. Washington: Catholic University Press.

Kitcher, P. (1990) The division of cognitive labor, *Journal of Philosophy*, 87: 5–22.

Kleinman, D. (1995) *Politics on the Endless Frontier: Postwar Research Policy in the United States*. Durham, NC: Duke University Press.

Knight, D. (1986) *The Age of Science*. Oxford: Blackwell.

Knorr-Cetina, K. and Cicourel, A. (eds) (1981) *Advances in Social Theory*. London: Routledge and Kegan Paul.

Kohler, R. (1991) *Partners in Science: Foundations and Natural Scientists*. Chicago: University of Chicago Press.

Kuhn, T.S. (1970) *The Structure of Scientific Revolutions*, 2nd edn. Chicago: University of Chicago Press.

Kuznick, P. (1987) *Beyond the Laboratory: Scientists as Political Activists in 1930s America*. Chicago: University of Chicago Press.

La Follette, M. (1990) *Making Science Our Own: Public Images of Science 1910–1955*. Chicago: University of Chicago Press.

Lakatos, I. and Musgrave, A. (eds) (1970) *Criticism and the Growth of Knowledge*. Cambridge: Cambridge University Press.

Lambropoulos, V. (1993) *The Rise of Eurocentrism*. Princeton, NJ: Princeton University Press.

Langley, P., Simon, H., Bradshaw, G. and Zytkow, J. (1987) *Scientific Discovery*. Cambridge, MA: MIT Press.

Laslett, B., Kohlstedt, S., Longino, H. and Hammonds, E. (eds) (1996) *Gender and Scientific Authority*. Chicago: University of Chicago Press.

Latour, B. (1987) *Science in Action*. Milton Keynes: Open University Press.

Latour, B. (1989) *The Pasteurization of France*. Cambridge, MA: Harvard University Press.

Latour, B. and Woolgar, S. (1979) *Laboratory Life*. Beverly Hills, CA: Sage.

Laudan, L. (1981) A problem-solving approach to scientific progress, in I. Hacking (ed.) *Scientific Revolutions*. Oxford: Oxford University Press.

Laudan, L. (1984) *Science and Values*. Berkeley, CA: University of California Press.

Lederman, L. (1991) *Science: The End of the Frontier?* Washington DC: American Association for the Advancement of Science.

Le Goff, J. (1993) *Intellectuals in the Middle Ages*. Oxford: Blackwell.

Lenin, V.I. (1964 [1916]) *Imperialism, the Highest Stage of Capitalism* (vol. 22 of *Collected Works*). Moscow: Progress Publishers.

Levine, Z. (1994) *Biographical Information and Candidate Statements for the 1994 Election of Councillors to the American Physical Society*. Washington DC: American Physical Society.

Lindblom, C. (1991) *Inquiry and Change*. New Haven, CT: Yale University Press.

Luhmann, N. (1982) *The Differentiation of Society*. New York: Columbia University Press.

Lury, C. (1998) *Prosthetic Culture*. London: Routledge.

Lyotard, J.-F. (1983) *The Postmodern Condition*, 2nd edn. Minneapolis, MN: University of Minnesota Press.

McCloskey, D. (1987) *Economic Writing*. London: Macmillan.

MacKenzie, D. (1981) *Statistics in Britain: 1865–1930*. Edinburgh: Edinburgh University Press.

MacKenzie, D. (1990) *Inventing Accuracy*. Cambridge, MA: MIT Press.

Mannheim, K. (1940) *Man and Society in an Age of Reconstruction*. London: Routledge and Kegan Paul.

Martin, B. (1991) *Strip the Experts*. London: Freedom Press.

Marx, K. and Engels, F. (1975) *Collected Works* (50 vols). Moscow: Progress Publishers.

Merton, R. (1973) *The Sociology of Science*. Chicago: University of Chicago Press.

Mill, J.S. (1977 [1861]) *Considerations on Representative Government* (vol. 19 of *Collected Works*). Toronto: University of Toronto Press.

Mills, C. (1948) Distribution of American research funds, *Science*, 107: 127–30.

Mills, C.W. (1956) *The Power Élite*. Oxford: Oxford University Press.

Mirowski, P. (1989) *More Heat than Light*. Cambridge: Cambridge University Press.

Montgomery, S. (1995) *The Scientific Voice*. New York: Guilford Press.

Morus, I. (1992) Different experimental lives: Michael Faraday and William Sturgeon, *History of Science*, 20: 1–28.

Mukerji, C. (1990) *A Fragile Power*. Princeton, NJ: Princeton University Press.

Mulkay, M. (1990) *The Sociology of Science*. Bloomington, IN: Indiana University Press.

Murray, C. and Herrnstein, R. (1994) *The Bell Curve: Intelligence and Class Structure*. New York: Free Press.

Naess, A. (1974) *Ecology, Community and Lifestyle*. Oslo: Universitetsforlaget.

Nelkin, D. (1987) *Selling Science*. New York: W.H. Freeman.

New York Times (1993) Requiem for the Supercollider, editorial, 24 October.

Nickles, T. (1989) Heuristic appraisal: a proposal, *Social Epistemology*, 3: 175–88.

Nisbett, R. and Wilson, T. (1977) Telling more than we can know, *Psychological Review*, 84: 231–59.

Noble, D. (1984) *Forces of Production*. Oxford: Oxford University Press.

NSF (National Science Foundation) (1991) *Science & Engineering Indicators*, 10th edn. Washington DC: US National Science Board.

O'Connor, J.R. (1973) *The Fiscal Crisis of the State*. New York: St Martin's Press.

Office of Technology Asssessment (1991) *Federally Funded Research: Decisions for a Decade*. Washington DC: US Government Printing Office.

Olsen, M. (1992) The energy consumption turnaround and socioeconomic well-being in industrial societies in the 1980s, in L. Freeman (ed.) *Advances in Human Ecology*, vol. 1. Greenwich, CT: JAI Press.

Ong, W. (1958) *Ramus, Method, and the Decay of Dialogue*. Cambridge, MA: Harvard University Press.

Pavitt, K. (1996) Road to ruin, *New Scientist*, 3 August: 32–5.

Penslar, R. (ed.) (1995) *Research Ethics: Cases and Materials*. Bloomington, IN: Indiana University Press.

Pettitt, P. (1997) *Republicanism*. Oxford: Oxford University Press.

Pickering, A. (ed.) (1992) *Science as Practice and Culture*. Chicago: University of Chicago Press.

Pocock, J.G.A. (1975) *The Machiavellian Moment*. Princeton, NJ: Princeton University Press.

Pocock, J.G.A. (1985) *Virtue, Commerce and History*. Cambridge: Cambridge University Press.

Polanyi, K. (1944) *The Great Transformation*. Boston, MA: Beacon Press.

Polanyi, M. (1962) The republic of science, *Minerva*, 1: 54–73.

Popper, K. (1945) *The Open Society and Its Enemies*. New York: Harper & Row.

Popper, K. (1970) Normal science and its dangers, in I. Lakatos and A. Musgrave (eds) *Criticism and the Growth of Knowledge*. Cambridge: Cambridge University Press.

Porter, M. (1990) *The Competitive Advantage of Nations*. London: Macmillan.

Postman, N. (1986) *Amusing Ourselves to Death*. Harmondsworth: Penguin.

Power, M. (1997) *The Audit Society: Rituals of Verification*. Oxford: Clarendon Press.

Price, D. de Solla (1978) Toward a model of science indicators, in Y. Elkana, J. Lederberg, R. Merton, A. Thackray and H. Zuckerman (eds) *Toward a Metric of Science*. New York: Wiley-Interscience.

Price, D. de Solla (1986) *Little Science, Big Science . . . and Beyond*, 2nd edn. New York: Columbia University Press.

Proctor, R. (1988) *Racial Hygiene*. Cambridge, MA: Harvard University Press.

Proctor, R. (1991) *Value-Free Science? Purity and Power in Modern Knowledge*. Cambridge, MA: Harvard University Press.

Ravetz, J. (1971) *Scientific Knowledge and its Social Problems*. Oxford: Oxford University Press.

Rawls, J. (1971) *A Theory of Justice*. Cambridge, MA: Harvard University Press.

Reich, R. (1991) *The Work of Nations*. New York: Random House.

Reingold, N. (1994) Science and government in the United States since 1945, *History of Science*, 32: 361–86.

Rescher, N. (1978) *Peirce's Philosophy of Science*. South Bend, IN: Notre Dame Press.

Rescher, N. (1979) *Scientific Progress*. Oxford: Blackwell.

Rescher, N. (1984) *The Limits of Science*. Berkeley, CA: University of California Press.

Restivo, S. (1988) Modern science as a social problem, *Social Problems*, 35: 206–28.

Ringer, F. (1979) *Education and Society in Modern Europe*. Bloomington, IN: Indiana University Press.

Rorty, R. (1988) Is natural science a natural kind? in E. McMullin (ed.) *Construction and Constraint*. South Bend: Notre Dame Press.

Rose, H. (1994) *Love, Power and Knowledge: Towards a Feminist Transformation of the Sciences*. Cambridge: Polity Press.

Rosenberg, N., Landau, R. and Mowery, D. (eds) (1992) *Technology and the Wealth of Nations*. Palo Alto: Stanford University Press.

Ross, L. (1977) The intuitive psychologist and his shortcomings, in L. Berkowitz (ed.) *Advances in Experimental Social Psychology*. New York: Academic Press.

Said, E. (1978) *Orientalism*. New York: Random House.

Sardar, Z. (1989) *Explorations in Islamic Science*. London: Mansell.

Schaefer, W. (ed.) (1983) *Finalization in Science*. Dordrecht: Reidel.

Schiappa, E. (1992) *Rhetorike*: what's in a name? Toward a revised history of early Greek rhetorical theory, *Quarterly Journal of Speech*, 78: 1–15.

Schlick, M. (1974 [1925]) *The General Theory of Knowledge*. Berlin: Springer-Verlag.

Schott, T. (1991) The world scientific community: globality and globalization, *Minerva*, 29: 440–62.

Schumpeter, J. (1950) *Capitalism, Socialism and Democracy*, 2nd edn. New York: Harper and Row.

Science Policy Research Unit (1996) *The Relationship Between Publicly Funded Basic Research and Economic Performance*. London: HM Treasury.

Sedgwick, E.K. (1990) *The Epistemology of the Closet*. Berkeley, CA: University of California Press.

Shapin, S. (1988) The house of experiment in seventeenth-century England, *Isis*, 79: 373–404.

Shils, E. (ed.) (1968) *Criteria for Scientific Development: Public Policy and National Goals*. Cambridge MA: MIT Press.

Shils, E. (1992a) Do we still need academic freedom? *The American Scholar*, 62: 187–209.

Shils, E. (1992b) The idea of the university: obstacles and opportunities in contemporary societies, *Minerva*, 30: 301–13.

Simon, H. (1945) *Administrative Behavior*. New York: Macmillan.

Skinner, Q. (1997) *Liberty before Liberalism*. Cambridge: Cambridge University Press.

Slezak, P. (1989) Scientific discovery by computer as empirical refutation of the Strong Programme, *Social Studies of Science*, 19: 563–600.

Smith, A. (1970 [1776]) *The Wealth of Nations*. Harmondsworth: Penguin.

Sohn-Rethel, A. (1978) *Intellectual and Manual Labor*. Atlantic Highlands, NJ: Humanities Press.

Sorokin, P. (1928) *Contemporary Sociological Theories in the First Quarter of the Twentieth Century*. New York: Harper & Row.

Stehr, N. (1994) *Knowledge Societies*. London: Sage.

Stephan, P. and Levin, S. (1992) *Striking the Mother Lode in Science: The Importance of Age, Place, and Time*. Oxford: Oxford University Press.

Stern, C. (1998) The right to be wrong, *The Responsive Community*, 8(2): 24–32.

Stewart, J., Kendall, E. and Coote, A. (1994) *Citizens' Juries*. London: Institute for Public Policy Research.

Stewart, L. (1992) *The Rise of Public Science*. Cambridge: Cambridge University Press.

Stich, S. (1996) *Deconstructing the Mind*. Oxford: Oxford University Press.

Stich, S. and Nisbett, R. (1984) Expertise, justification, and the psychology of inductive inference, in T. Haskell (ed.) *The Authority of Experts*. Bloomington, IN: Indiana University Press.

Stinchcombe, A. (1990) *Information and Organizations*. Berkeley, CA: University of California Press.

Tainter, J. (1988) *The Collapse of Complex Societies*. Cambridge: Cambridge University Press.

Thagard, P. (1988) *The Computational Philosophy of Science*. Cambridge, MA: MIT Press.

Thomson, A. (1998) Contract lecturer campaign hot up, *Times Higher Education Supplement*, 20 November.

Times Higher Education Supplement (1996) Editorial, 19 April.

Tompkins, J. (1980) The reader in history: the changing shape of literary response, in J. Tompkins (ed.) *Reader-Response Criticism: From Formalism to Post-Structuralism*. Baltimore, MD: Johns Hopkins University Press.

Toulmin, S. (1964) The complexity of scientific choice, *Minerva*, 2: 343–59.

Toulmin, S. (1990) *Cosmopolis: The Hidden Agenda of Modernity*. New York: Free Press.

Traweek, S. (1988) *Beamtimes and Lifetimes*. Cambridge, MA: Harvard University Press.

Turner, S. and Chubin, D. (1976) Another appraisal of Ortega, the Coles, and science policy: the ecclesiastes hypothesis, *Social Science Information*, 15: 657–62.

Turner, S. and Turner, J. (1990) *The Impossible Science*. Newbury Park, CA: Sage.

Unger, R. (1986) *The Critical Legal Studies Movement*. Cambridge, MA: Harvard University Press.

Unger, R. (1996) *What Should Legal Analysis Become?* London: Verso.

US Congress (1945) *Senate Subcommittee of the Committee on Military Affairs, 'Hearings on Science Legislation'*, 79th Congress, 1st session (November), pp. 225–7. Washington DC: US Government Accounting Office.

US Congress (1947) *House Committee on Interstate and Foreign Commerce, 'Hearings on the National Science Foundation'*, 80th Congress, 1st session (March), pp. 73–6. Washington DC: US Government Accounting Office.

Veysey, L. (1965) *The Emergence of the American University*. Chicago: University of Chicago Press.

Wallerstein, I. (1991) *Unthinking Social Science: The Limits of 19th-Century Paradigms*. Cambridge: Polity Press.

Weber, M. (1958) Science as a vocation, in H. Gerth and C. Wright Mills (eds) *From Max Weber*. Oxford: Oxford University Press.

Wedgwood, J. (1939) *The Economics of Inheritance*, 2nd edn. Harmondsworth: Penguin.

Weinberg, A. (1963) Criteria for scientific choice, *Minerva*, 1: 159–71.

Weinberg, S. (1992) *Dreams of a Final Theory*. New York: Pantheon Books.

Wells, W. (1993) *Working with Congress: A Practical Guide for Scientists and Engineers*. Washington DC: American Association for the Advancement of Science.

Woolgar, S. (1988) *Science: The Very Idea*. London: Tavistock.

Wuthnow, R. (1989) *Communities of Discourse: The Reformation, the Enlightenment, and Nineteenth-Century Socialism*. Cambridge, MA: Harvard University Press.

Yankelovich, D. (1991) *Coming to Public Judgment*. Syracuse: Syracuse University Press.

Index

166 The governance of science

WORK, CONSUMERISM AND THE NEW POOR

Zygmunt Bauman

- Can poverty be fought and conquered by orthodox means?
- Should we seek new solutions like 'decoupling' the right to livelihood from the selling of labour and extending the socially recognized concept of work?
- How urgent is it to confront these social questions and find practical answers?

It is one thing to be poor in a society of producers and universal employment; it is quite a different thing to be poor in a society of consumers, in which life projects are built around consumer choice rather than work, professional skills or jobs. If 'being poor' once derived its meaning from the condition of being unemployed, today it draws its meaning primarily from the plight of a flawed consumer. This is one difference which truly makes a difference – in the way living in poverty is experienced and in the chances and prospects to redeem its misery.

This absorbing book attempts to trace this change, which has been taking place over the duration of modern history, and to make an inventory of its social consequences. On the way, it tries also to consider to what extent the well remembered and tested means of fighting back advancing poverty and mitigating its hardships are fit (or unfit) to grasp and tackle the problems of poverty in its present form. Students of sociology, politics and social policy will find this to be an invaluable text on the changing significance and implications of an enduring social problem.

Contents
Introduction – Part one – The meaning of work: producing the work ethic – From the work ethic to the aesthetic of consumption – Part two – The rise and fall – The work ethic and the new poor – Part three – Prospects for the new poor – Notes – Index.

128pp   0 335 20155 5 (Paperback)   0 335 20156 3 (Hardback)

SOCIAL EXCLUSION

David Byrne

- What does the term 'social exclusion' mean and who are the 'socially excluded'?
- Why has there been such a significant increase in 'social exclusion'?
- How can we attempt to tackle this and the problems associated with it?

'Social exclusion' is the buzz phrase for the complex range of social problems which derive from the substantial increase in social inequality in Western societies. This timely and engaging volume examines these problems in societies where manufacturing industry is no longer the main basis for employment and the universal welfare states established after the Second World War are under attack. It reviews theories of social exclusion, including the Christian democratic and social democratic assertions of solidarity with which the term originated, Marxist accounts of the recreation of the reserve army of labour, and neo-liberal assertions of the sovereignty of the market in which the blame for exclusion is assigned to the excluded themselves.

Drawing on a wide variety of empirical evidence, the author concludes that the origins of social exclusion lie with the creation of a new post-industrial order founded on the exploitation of low paid workers within western capitalism, and that social policies have actually helped to create an unequal social order as opposed to simply reacting to economic forces. This controversial but accessible text will be essential reading for undergraduate courses on social exclusion within sociology, politics, economics, geography and social policy, as well as students on professional courses and practitioners in social work, community work, urban planning and management, health and housing.

Contents

Introduction – Part one – The possessive individualists: blaming the poor – Order and solidarity: collectivist approaches – Exploitation matters: Marxist approaches to exclusion – Part two – Dynamic society – dynamic lives – The dynamics of income inequality – Divided spaces: social divisions in the post-industrial city – Conclusion: what is and what is to be done about it – Notes – Bibliography – Index.

176pp   0 335 19974 7 (Paperback)   0 335 19975 5 (Hardback)

WHAT IS THIS THING CALLED SCIENCE? (THIRD EDITION)

A. F. Chalmers

This indispensable new edition brings Chalmers' popular text up to date with contemporary trends and continues its status as the best introductory text-book on the philosophy of science.

Over the last 20 years this account of modern scientific attempts to dethrone empiricist thought has become both a bestseller and a standard university text with translations into fifteen languages.

This revised and extended edition offers a concise and illuminating treatment of major developments in the field over the last two decades, with the same accessible style which ensured the popularity of previous editions. Of particular importance is the examination of Feyerabend and the new experimentalism, as well as new chapters on the nature of scientific laws and recent trends in the realism versus anti-realism debate.

> Crisp, lucid and studded with telling examples. As a handy guide to recent advances and excursions (in the philosophy of science) I find this book vigorous, gallant and useful.
>
> *New Scientist*

Contents

288pp   0 335 20109 1 (Paperback)

SCIENCE

Steve Fuller

Congratulations to Steve Fuller! After this book, the public's understanding of science (and the scientists' too) will never be the same
again. He combines philosophical acuity, sociological insight and historical depth, and then tells his story in a sparkling prose. Like any
other ageing institution, science must learn to become self-aware if it is
to adapt and survive; and so Steve Fuller is actually science's best friend.
Jerome Ravetz (author of *Scientific Knowledge
and Its Social Problems*)

What qualifies such seemingly disparate disciplines as paleontology, high-
energy physics, industrial chemistry and genetic engineering as 'sciences',
and hence worthy of sustained public interest and support? In this innovative
and controversial introduction to the social character of scientific knowledge,
Steve Fuller argues that if these disciplines share anything at all, it is more
likely to be the way they strategically misinterpret their own history than any
privileged access to the nature of reality. The book features a report written
in the persona of a Martian anthropologist who systematically compares
religious and scientific institutions on earth, only to find that science does not
necessarily live up to its own ideals of rationality. In addition, Fuller highlights science's multicultural nature through a discussion of episodes in which
the West's own understanding of science has been decisively affected by its
encounters with Islam and Japan. An important theme of the book is that
science's most attractive feature – its openness to criticism – is threatened by
the role it increasingly plays in the maintenance of social and economic order.

Contents

*Preface – The public understanding of science: our latest moral panic – The sociological
peculiarity of the natural sciences – 'Science', 'scientific', 'scientist': some exercises in
conceptual analysis – Science as a superstition: a lost Martian chronicle – The secret
of science's success: convenient forgetfulness – Western science from the outside in: the
view from Islam and Japan – Science as the standard of civilization: does it have a
future? – Notes – Suggested reading – References – Index.*

176pp   0 335 19847 3 (Paperback)   0 335 19848 1 (Hardback)

THE SOCIAL SHAPING OF TECHNOLOGY (SECOND EDITION)

Donald MacKenzie and Judy Wajcman

Reviews of the First Edition:

> This book is a welcome addition to the sociology of technology, a field whose importance is increasingly recognised.
>
> *Sociology*

> This collection of essays sets a remarkably high standard in breadth of coverage, in scholarship, and in readability and can be recommended to the general reader and to the specialist alike.
>
> *Science and Society*

> This remarkably readable and well-edited anthology focuses, in a wide variety of concrete examples, not on the impacts of technologies on societies but in the reverse: how different social contexts shape the emergence of particular technologies.
>
> *Technology and Culture*

- How does social context affect the development of technology?
- What is the relationship between technology and gender?
- Is production technology shaped by efficiency or by social control?

Technological change is often seen as something that follows its own logic – something we may welcome, or about which we may protest, but which we are unable to alter fundamentally. This reader challenges that assumption and its distinguished contributors demonstrate that technology is affected at a fundamental level by the social context in which it develops. General arguments are introduced about the relation of technology to society and different types of technology are examined: the technology of production; domestic and reproductive technology; and military technology.

The first edition of this reader, published in 1985, had a considerable influence on thinking about the relationship between technology and society. This second edition has been thoroughly revised and expanded to take into account new research and the emergence of new theoretical perspectives.

Contents

Part one – Introductory essay and general issues – Part two – The technology of production – Part three – Reproductive technology – Part four – Military technology – Bibliography – Index.

480pp   0 335 19913 5 (Paperback)   0 335 19914 3 (Hardback)

$\boxed{\text{Context of discovery + justification}}$ + $\boxed{\text{context of}}$

Early 20th century:

What is foundation of science?

Q: We see new scientificic theories, so what are grounds to adopting theories

contrast w/

How it came about, why it happened when it happened, etc

Part 3 Fuller discussion

Has science become the "Catholic Church" of the modern age

Has science supplanted religion?

Prof: Why does Fuller think that government funding of
Q   research will not promote the republican ideal?

Prof: Will not allowing gov. funding of science create
Q   a situation congruent w/ the republican ideal?

3-11-04

Prof: We don't want elected officials making decisions; big science has organized itself in such a way it is impossible for 3rd parties on outside to regulate science. Fuller sees this as a problem. Last chap. addresses (or tries to) this issue.

Artificial barriers put in place by science to reinforce barriers between various specialties. ~~It is~~ World is no more complex than ever — specializations are largely artificial.